CONSUMED

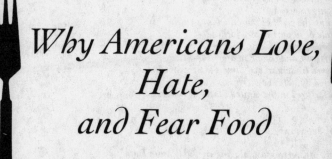

*Why Americans Love,
Hate,
and Fear Food*

MICHELLE STACEY

A TOUCHSTONE BOOK
Published by Simon & Schuster
New York London Toronto Sydney Tokyo Singapore

TOUCHSTONE
Rockefeller Center
1230 Avenue of the Americas
New York, New York 10020

First Touchstone Edition 1995
TOUCHSTONE and colophon are
registered trademarks of Simon & Schuster Inc.
Designed by Edith Fowler
Manufactured in the United States of America

10 9 8 7 6 5 4 3 2 1
10 9 8 7 6 5 4 3 2 1 (Pbk)

Library of Congress Cataloging-in-Publication Data
Stacey, Michelle
   Consumed: why Americans love, hate, and fear
   food/Michelle Stacey.
      p.   cm.
    Includes index.
   1. Food habits—United States. 2. Food
   habits—United States—Psychological aspects.
   3. Nutrition—United States—History.
I. Title.
GT2853.U5S73   1994
394.1'4'.0973—dc20   93-34940
                                                 CIP

ISBN: 0-671-76754-2
      0-671-50101-1 (Pbk)

To DAVE, ANNA, and HENRY

CONTENTS

A PINCH OF ANXIETY, A DASH OF SIN

Fin de Siècle Eating in America

•

Jacques Pépin, renowned chef and author of more than a dozen cookbooks, dean of special programs at the French Culinary Institute in New York, star of the TV show "Today's Gourmet," has been watching Americans eat ever since he moved here from France more than thirty years ago. Over time, in the way that often comes more easily to visitors than to natives, he began to observe a pattern. "When I came to this country," he said to me one day in late 1992, "people would have a steak that was a pound and a half hanging off the side of the plate, and they would have three martinis before dinner—this was the right way to do things. Then the steak went down to ten ounces and they started trimming it, then it went down to a rack of lamb with a glass of cabernet sauvignon, then from this to chicken with a glass of chardonnay, and now we're down to a piece of fish with a glass of Evian water." Which is fine, he said, except for one thing: the attitude that has accompanied the shift. He summed up that attitude succinctly: "People are berserk about their food."

His favorite example involved a classic of old-fashioned culinary indulgence: pound cake. "If I tell people I'm going to do a pound cake—which by definition is made of a pound of butter, a pound of sugar, a pound of egg, and a pound of flour; that's the reason it's a pound cake—they will get crazy. We are now terrorized of butter, and if people see a tablespoon of cream in something they can't stand it. But if I do a pound cake and put a cup of grated carrots in it and call it a carrot cake, then everybody will plunge on it and eat it because they are saving their lives."

As a cook and as a Frenchman, this amused and frustrated Pépin, but it also saddened him. "When you transcend the level at which food is not enjoyment anymore, then you've lost a great deal," he said. "After the physical function of food, which is to nourish the body, came civilization and enjoyment and the art of the table. There are many other things that go along with the food itself—the time that you spend at the table, the family gathering, dress code, etiquette of the table, and other things that encompass a whole life. It's not only food. But people here have lost a great deal of that. They want to go into a corner and just swallow something in two and a half seconds and think they're saving their life."

Some time after I spoke with Pépin I went for a walk through my local supermarket, in Westchester County just north of New York City, this time not to shop in my usual blindered rush, but just to look. In the meat section, little signs and banners hailed Coleman Natural Beef ("25% less fat!"), and packages of pork proclaimed "lean, tasty pork" in red letters, in an effort at image adjustment. Those messages were somewhat undercut by the adjacent frozen meat department, which featured unreconstructed Steak-umm microwave sandwiches ("Cheesesteak to go," which microwaves in four minutes) and Weaver chicken nuggets ("Tender Juicy Chicken Chunked, Shaped and Breaded"). In the condiments aisle, Hellman's "No Cholesterol" offered to save eaters the 5 milligrams of cholesterol they would otherwise ingest with Hellman's "Real" Mayonnaise, a negligible amount in the context of a recommended daily intake of about 300 milligrams. Next to Hellman's "No Cholesterol" sat Kraft's "Free" (no fat at all). In fact, "free," as shorthand for fat free, was ubiquitous—salad dressings were free, cream cheese was free, cookies were free. Promise Extra Light margarine was so low in fat that it was "not recommended for baking or frying." Snackwell's Devil's Food Cookie Cakes were fat free with no cholesterol ("Eat Well, Snack Well"). Mr. Phipps Tater Crisps Sour Cream 'N Onion flavor were "Baked, Not Fried! Less Fat Than Potato Chips!" Pastas were announced as "a sodium and cholesterol free food." Campbell's Healthy Request pasta sauce featured a list on the label: "Low in Fat. No Cholesterol. 330 Mg. of Sodium. 50 Calories. Mm-mm Good!" It was a rare product that couldn't find something reassuring to say for itself: no salt added; 100% natural; 14 essential vitamins and minerals; contains fiber-rich oat bran; no cholesterol; no saturated fats; no tropical oils; low in sugar; 97% fat free; light, lite, and free.

Against this background of bizarre juxtapositions (cholesterol-free breakfast links—"artificial sausage flavor textured vegetable protein"—abutting Sara Lee Strawberry Cream Cheesecake) and the buzz of incessantly repeated health claims, the cereals aisle appeared as the epicenter: a blast of nutritional white noise punctuated by the momentary silences of pure junk food. This was where the big ones—Nabisco, Post, Kellogg's, General Mills— made their most eloquent (and most competitive) appeals. While the front of the packages packed in all the usual come-ons (100% daily allowance of 12 vitamins and minerals; very low fat; whole-grain goodness with high fiber), it was the sides and the back that were the true battleground. Lists, graphs, diagrams of wheat and oat kernels, quotes from nutritionists and their research studies— this was science for breakfast. "With many nutrition experts recommending a diet higher in fiber with less fat and less cholesterol, Post Bran Flakes is a truly sensible choice." Cheerios admonished: "You can read your morning paper at breakfast time to get the latest news. Or you can study your cereal box. Because right here is the big news of the USDA's new Food Guide Pyramid. . . . The Pyramid makes it easy to choose from the food groups and get a balanced diet." Kellogg's Product 19 went the furthest, devoting both the side and back panels to the food pyramid, a diagram of a healthy breakfast, and a lengthy comparison of Product 19 to lima beans (for vitamin C), sweet potatoes (for vitamin E), potatoes (vitamin B_6), low-fat yogurt (riboflavin), and brussels sprouts (folic acid). The earnestness of these appeals was thrown into greater relief by the brazen importuning of neighboring brands, whose names proclaimed their single purpose: Cap'n Crunch's Peanut Butter Crunch, Cocoa Pebbles, Count Chocula ("artificial chocolate flavor frosted cereal with chocolate flavor marshmallows"), Trix ("fruity sweetened corn puffs"), Frosted Flakes, Cinnamon Mini Buns, Cocoa Krispies, Fruit Loops, Smacks. The notion that breakfast food should save your life is constantly challenged by the American predilection for mass-produced sweets.

I began to wonder how an outsider to American supermarket culture, a young Jacques Pépin newly arrived from France, might see all of this. The internal logic and deep ambivalence of a package of Frosted Mini-Wheats carrying health claims—"no salt, fat free, a cholesterol free food," and a side panel discussion of "facts on wheat bran fiber" (diagram included)—suddenly seemed a quintessentially American fact of life. Its very familiarity can mask the fact that Pépin is right: American notions of food *are* berserk. Americans have begun to treat their food as something other than what it is. But the genesis of these strange ideas about eating goes back much further than the thirty years of Pépin's observation. To begin to understand what has happened to food in America today, one can remain in the cereal aisle but look back more than a hundred years, to the prescient story of John Harvey Kellogg—the man whose name now adorns boxes of, among many others, Corn Flakes, Nutri-Grain, Cracklin' Oat Bran, Raisin Bran, and Frosted Flakes ("Fat free as always").

In 1876 Kellogg, a young doctor and Seventh Day Adventist, decided that Americans were not choosing their food wisely. This conviction had been creeping up on him for some time, prompted by a few seminal experiences of his early life. After surviving several serious childhood illnesses, he became fascinated with the teachings of health reformer Sylvester Graham, who in the 1830s and 1840s preached against gluttony as "the greatest of all causes of evil" and advocated a spare vegetarian diet.[1] At the age of fourteen, Kellogg converted to vegetarianism.[2] He put his dietary beliefs into tangible form at the age of twenty-four, in 1876, by taking over the Western Health Reform Institute in Battle Creek, Michigan, rechristening it the Battle Creek Sanitorium, and announcing that it would be a "University of Health" where "people learn to stay well."[3] That same year, Kellogg wrote: "Men and women are subject to few diseases whose origins may not be traced to the kitchen. Closely following diseased physical natures come mental and moral inefficiency originating in the same prolific cause."[4]

Kellogg worked to outsmart this "prolific cause" in every way possible, and in the process became a stunningly successful entrepreneur in the business of improving health through food and lifestyle. His Sanitorium (dubbed "the San" by its acolytes) became the Canyon Ranch Spa of its day, attracting such luminaries as John D. Rockefeller, J. C. Penney, and Mrs. Walgreen with its Spartan regimen.[5] He published a booklet entitled "Rules for 'Right Living,' " which stayed in print for decades and which set forth in Kellogg's characteristic scolding style the many mistakes culinary sinners were likely to make. "In consequence of our abuses and neglects," he wrote, "the human race is becoming dwarfed and weazened, neurotic, daft, dyspepsic, and degenerate . . . the perversions of our modern civilization . . . are responsible for the multitudinous maladies and degeneracies which yearly multiply in number and gravity." Some of his dietary rules included: Prefer natural foods; Avoid too much protein; Avoid meats, fish, flesh, and fowl because they are unnatural foods and hence not adapted to man's use as are natural foodstuffs; Use eggs sparingly, and only when known to be perfectly fresh; Give preference to vegetable fats, excepting butter; Restrict the use of cane sugar; Eat bran or other bulkage freely to encourage colon activity; Do not drink tea, coffee, cocoa, or maté.[6] In sum, a regimen not unfamiliar to those in the business today of preserving or perfecting health through a discriminating choice of foods.

In 1877 Kellogg extended his message into another commercial arena, creating a cold breakfast cereal of mixed grains called Granola. By 1893 he had refined his manufacturing process and produced a flaked cereal he first named Granose Flakes—later Corn Flakes—thereby initiating a revolution in American breakfast habits the repercussions of which have persisted to this day. In the nascent days of packaged foods and brand marketing, Kellogg, with the help of his younger brother Will, positioned Corn Flakes as a health food that would replace meat at breakfast. Kellogg was one of the first food-product manufacturers to understand the effectiveness of marketing tools that have become twentieth-century clichés—catchy names, slogans, symbols—and his Corn Flakes became wildly popular.[7] By the 1890s Kellogg's was no longer a singular voice; in the cereal market he was hotly pursued by C. W. Post, a former patient at the Sanitorium, who had brought out Post's Grape Nuts, and in his proselytizing he was joined by many other health reformers who educated the middle class in the notion that food and health were closely linked and exhorted them to correct their "popular errors in living."[8]

The Kellogg most of us are familiar with today is considerably less personal—it is the corporate Kellogg of Special K, Rice Krispies, Frosted Flakes, a monolith among packaged-food giants. For most of the twentieth century this Kellogg was not perceived as a health-food purveyor; the American passion for vegetarianism and what had been known as "scientific eating" had cooled and Kellogg's products were marketed instead for their taste, their convenience, their "snap, crackle, pop." But, in an odd full-circle effect, the Kellogg Company regained the mantle of health-food promotion in 1984 when it broke a hitherto unchallenged law of food marketing and presented its All-Bran cereal as a potential weapon against cancer, including on its label a message about fat and fiber under the aegis of the National Cancer Institute. That action, as it happened, opened the floodgates to a barrage of food health-claims from every quarter and practically every manufacturer. In 1989 Kellogg followed up with a cereal specifically designed to prevent heart disease, named Heartwise and packaged in a box plastered with health messages.

The two incarnations of Kellogg—the man and the company he founded—both function as a paradigm of sorts for an actual historical shift; they are an example in miniature of a way of thinking about food that is engrossing this country today much as it did a century ago. It is a way of thinking that draws much of its power from elements of daily life—the pervasiveness of marketing and advertising, the American faith in scientific knowledge, and the most basic feelings about food as friend, enemy, and even moral force—but its bottom line is this: Food's importance lies in its relationship to health. This makes eating, now as in the 1890s, an activity often laced with some anxiety, uncertainty, ambivalence, and moral significance. It is not too surprising that the Quaker Company's recent, somewhat pious tag line on advertisements for oatmeal as a healthy breakfast—"It's the right thing to do"—recalls Kellogg's long-ago best-seller "Rules for 'Right Living.'"

The cook and bon vivant Julia Child, as disturbed by this as is her friend Jacques Pépin, has taken to calling this way of thinking "fear of food," perhaps in self-defense, and that is part but not all of its description. If this is a time of perceiving some foods as the enemy—not just fattening but cancer- and heart attack–inducing, cholesterol laden, too salty and too sugary, and somehow morally corrupting—it is also a time when other foods can attain a magic, saviorlike status. Oat bran can save us from heart disease, carrots and broccoli from cancer, fat-free ersatz ice creams from obesity. The shared doctrine here is one of symbolism: Food is not merely tasty, filling, and sustaining of life but a force that can either steal life away or prolong it indefinitely. Food is no longer simply food but preventive medicine, a scientific abstraction, a moral test, and, sometimes, a literally mortal enemy. This love/hate relationship invests food with more freight than it can carry and at the same time strips away one of its most basic functions: the giving of pleasure.

When this thinking is put into words—as it is perhaps most

often by the media and the marketing and advertising community—it lends itself, almost inevitably, to some level of obsessiveness, contradiction, and exaggeration. This is best revealed by example. Take, for instance, the search for the next oat bran. When the instant stardom of that nutrient showed how hysterically the public could embrace the concept of magically curative foods, marketers and newswriters alike dreamed of future triumphs. In the space of two years, between 1989 and 1991, four different foods or nutrients were trotted out: the grain psyllium, incorporated into cereals and hailed by *Time* magazine as "the newest candidate for nutritional knighthood" before it was found to induce allergic reactions in some people; the nutrient beta-carotene, found in many dark-green, orange, and yellow fruits and vegetables but also sold in supplement form (advertised by the Hoffmann–La Roche pharmaceutical company under the headline "New Research Findings: Beta Carotene and Heart Disease"), and about which the *New York Times* postulated, "Beta carotene may be the next nutrient in the public spotlight"; rice bran, made fit for human consumption only as recently as 1989 (by stabilizing an enzyme that normally turns it rancid) and introduced in new breakfast cereals a year and a half later ("There was a lot of hope that it would be the next oat bran," said a spokesperson from Quaker Oats); and garlic, described by one newspaper writer as "a successor to oat bran" with "magical properties."[9]

Take, also, the "60 Minutes" incident. On November 17, 1991, that show aired a segment called "The French Paradox," which suggested that the inclusion in the French diet of such items as red wine and foie gras might help keep heart attack rates there lower than in the United States. In the four weeks following the broadcast, sales of red wine in supermarkets increased 44 percent, and foie gras importers and manufacturers in the United States reported a surge in sales.[10]

The vilification of fats deserves a category all its own. If magic food along the lines of beta-carotene or rice bran were to have an evil food counterpart, that role would surely be filled by fats of almost all description (with the occasional exception of olive and canola oil). The scariness of fats has become a persistent drumbeat—in news stories, in official pronouncements from government agencies, and, less directly, in the rise of "fat free" as the most powerful selling point available. The drumbeat is having an effect: In the eight years from 1984 to 1992, the percentage of shoppers who said they were more concerned about fat than anything else about their food rose from 8 percent to 48 percent.[11] In 1992, 1,257 new low-fat or nonfat products were introduced into supermarkets[12], making it the first year ever that more new products boasted of being low-fat than of being low-calorie (and that's not counting the products that never had any fat to begin with but altered their packaging to proclaim their fat-free status; cereals and pastas have been the most expert at this). A writer in *Vogue* magazine described her attempts to dress a salad while on a practically fat-free diet: "A little raspberry vinegar is fine on its own; honestly, you don't miss the oil. (Lemon juice mixed with Dijon mustard is another big-taste, zero-fat dressing.) As with salads, so with everything else: beware the glue that holds things together."[13]

Food writers have responded enthusiastically to the low-fat call. Marian Burros of the *New York Times* has practically made low-fat cooking a personal obsession, and her zeal is unmatched. In a May 1992 newspaper article titled "The Dream of Low-Fat Baking," she begins with these words: "For those of us who love sweets too much for our own good, the discovery of no-fat baking ranks right up there with the discovery of penicillin." She goes on to admit that "let's be clear: desserts baked without fat will never taste as good as desserts baked with fat. . . . The zucchini bread has a little rubbery spring in each bite. But it's amazing how quickly you can get used to such baking when you crave something sweet but don't want 20 grams of fat along with it."[14] In another article, Burros exulted that "this menu represents a breakthrough in low-fat cooking"; the breakthrough consisted of mixing cornstarch with nonfat yogurt and light ricotta cheese as a substitute for cream in pasta sauce—not exactly a match in terms of taste, but Burros was convinced that the result was "a rich pasta sauce."

Other Burros articles have been headlined "Weaning Americans from the Meat Habit," "Fat's in the Fire: A Guide for the Wary," and "You May Not Realize How Much Fat You Really Eat." No compromise in flavor is too great when it comes to cutting fat: in writing about 93-percent-lean hamburger meat, Burros advises that it "does much better in combination dishes like meat sauce, even though it lacks the full meaty taste. The addition of other flavors masks the unpleasant aftertaste."[15]

This is the kind of thing that drives Julia Child wild. "I think we're in kind of a state of hysteria over nutrition and poisons and cholesterol and heart troubles and salts, and we're not enjoying our food and having fun the way we should," she says. "Why is everyone so afraid? We should try to restore the joy of food." There is not much joy in a piece of meat with an aftertaste so unpalatable that you must search for spices to override it. While Child feels that the matter of eating well is not terribly complicated ("Healthy eating is just knowing the facts—that you're supposed to have a little bit of everything; on a twenty-five percent fat diet, you can *enjoy* a tablespoon or two of butter"), the overwhelming paradigm for eating now is of a tremendously complex puzzle, a test that we are all failing.

"We are a people ignorant of good nutrition," chides *New York Times* health columnist Jane Brody in her 576-page *Jane Brody's Nutrition Book*. "Many of the choices people make in an effort to improve their nutritional well-being are based on sweeping generalities, half-baked data, ignorance, prejudice, and superstition."[16] Magazines publish arithmetical equations for figuring up the exact number of grams of fat one should consume per day based on one's age and weight (or desired weight), in encouragement of meals-by-number.[17] When the National Research Council sat down in 1989 to work up recommendations for what Americans should eat, its answer was 1,300 pages long, a document entitled *Diet and Health: Implications for Reducing Chronic Disease Risk*.[18] And even government recommendations do not represent a consensus in the increasingly impenetrable logic of correct eating; one registered dietician asked in a newspaper article, "Are official diet guidelines the best?" and suggested that truly healthy eaters should go beyond them: less fat, less cholesterol, more fresh fruits and vegetables.[19]

As we venture further into the thickets of nutritional minutiae, the meaning of our culinary vocabulary itself is blurring. The Food and Drug Administration began working in 1991 on new rules for food packaging that would alter the definitions of words like "light," "low-fat," "fresh," and "healthy." "In effect, the FDA is writing a food-labeling dictionary," explained one legal consultant to the project. "It means that consumers will be given a wealth of information, but it also means that consumers must now be educated to know what the information means."[20] We must all, in short, be not just eaters but experts.

There is nothing wrong with understanding our food and what it does for us, especially in light of the rather remarkable research that has emerged in the last ten years alone about the relationship between diet and health. But somehow, and for some telling reasons, that reasonable goal has been swallowed up in a kind of unfocused and underinformed irrationality. One clear precipitator is a peculiarly American impulse that might be called the all-or-nothing approach. Explains Mona Doyle, president of the marketing firm Consumer Network, Inc., in Philadelphia: "American consumers, when they're cutting down on a product, they want to cut it *out*. Look at soft drinks with fruit juice, for example, that have twenty-five or ten calories. They didn't work. The consumer went for an artificial sweetener and only one calorie." Such logic demands that if low-fat is good, nonfat must be better. A nutrition professor described this phenomenon to the *New York Times*: "Americans can't do anything halfway. If you tell people to limit sugar intake, suddenly sugar is the villain. If you recommend increasing fruits and vegetables, the average American will say, 'Aha! Wouldn't it be even better if I ate *only* fruits and vegetables?'[21] A telephone survey by the American Dietetic Association in 1991 showed that, indeed, many respondents believed that they must eliminate fat from their diets.[22]

Such a regimen is, of course, not only unpalatable but in a

practical sense nearly impossible. But the belief that such a radical and self-denying change is necessary leads to a curious mixture of guilt, rebellion, fantasy, and desperation—not good feelings to have about one's food. In a tangible sense, such beliefs have led to the creation of an entirely new genre of food product: the "no-sin" pleasure-givers. Now we have entire cakes and cartons of ice cream that contain no fat, hot dogs with only 1 gram of fat (instead of 20), the McDonald's McLean burger (with seaweed standing in for some of the fat), and nonfat cheeses filled with vegetable gums. In 1990 a new cookie debuted that seems designed to enable the eater to devour the entire bag without guilt. Called Lisa's Merangos, the cookies each have 11 calories and come ten to a bag; for about the same amount of calories as a banana you can eat the whole bag and take in less than 1 gram of fat and absolutely no cholesterol, preservatives, butter, oil, or flour.

A tremendous amount of energy has been put into creating such innovations, and many of these products have been embraced with the delight of a people unsurprised to find that the reaches of science have once again found a way for them to live comfortably. "Cooks and shoppers have dreamed for years about desserts that, like doctors, are pledged to do no harm," proclaimed one article in *Newsweek*. "Pulses raced when Entenmann's introduced its fat-free cakes and cookies in 1989 . . . "[23] Technology is much beloved in this country, not least because it helps take away any sense of compromise. When we can't go out to a movie we can call one into our televisions on pay-per-view; we don't have to wait forty-five minutes for a frozen dinner to be ready because the microwave can do it in five; and we can perfect our diets without even being aware of it by buying perfectly adjusted products. Of course, three large slices of fat-free cake may not be as truly satisfying as a small slice of the real thing, eaten slowly and appreciatively and not in front of the television, but quality is not really the point in this equation.

The point is, in part, preserving what Julia Child calls "a childlike approach to things." The fruits of our scientific labors allow us to indulge a child's view of the world and of our behavior in it—a world of simplistic black-and-white values (fat is bad, oat bran is good), and a world, too, where we can have everything we want with no consequences, where we can eat all the luscious things we crave without getting fat or sick. The products of technology allow us to be out of control—"pigging out"—and in control at the same time, because those pig-outs carry no dietary sins. To talk about simple moderation—good, satisfying food in normal amounts—is to talk like an adult, a parent, and that's never as fun.

The idea of pigging out, of bingeing, is a strange but definite undercurrent of the techno-food business. Marian Burros, in describing recipes with little or no fat, seems to acknowledge as much: "Everything has plenty of calories. It's enough that they contain almost no fat. If, for example, you sat down and ate half of the zucchini cake, you would consume 3 grams of fat. And well over 2,000 calories. I know that sounds preposterous, but for those of us who have binged, nothing is impossible."[24] Lisa's Merangos cookies clearly seem designed to be devoured in one sitting, to be eaten by the handful rather than by the cookie. Researchers studying eating and dieting habits hypothesize that bingeing almost never occurs without dieting first; that is, the urge to binge—to overeat in an extreme, out-of-control fashion—is not a naturally occurring phenomenon but is a response to earlier self-denial and overcontrol.[25]

This impulse for self-denial, like the closely related all-or-nothing impulse (as if the choice must be between a Big Mac or dry toast, bingeing or starving) and the drive to make technology reconcile the two with a McLean burger, has in its genesis something uniquely American. In fact, it is tempting to see much of this particular, one might say disordered, way of thinking about food as a national disorder, a patently American invention. There are certainly some psychological roadmaps to be found in some of this country's shaping ideas.

It's impossible, for instance, to dismiss the continuing, subliminal impact of the very first European ideas that came to this continent: those of the Puritans. This was not a group of people who felt that bodily pleasure and the satisfaction of appetites were priorities. Historian Samuel Eliot Morison described their creed like this: "Religion should permeate every phase of living. Man belonged to God alone: his only purpose in life was to enhance God's glory and do God's will; and every variety of human activity, every sort of human conduct, presumably unpleasing to God, must be discouraged if not suppressed." When those ideas were applied to daily life, wrote Morison, they resulted in a system that kept tight reins on the physical: "Puritanism was an enemy to that genial glorification of the natural man, with all his instincts and appetites, that characterized the Renaissance, and the great Elizabethans. . . . [Puritanism] taught that natural man was wholly vile, corrupt, and prone to evil."[26]

A thread of guilty pleasure is woven through the fabric of American history, expressed in the culinary arena in frequent flirtations with temperance, periods of food reform, and even our often-noted habit of rushing through meals. Eighteenth- and nineteenth-century visitors to the United States frequently remarked on the American habit of shoveling food in at a precipitous rate, and even today the typical American dinner, cooked quickly and eaten quickly, bears little resemblance to a European meal, which might stretch over several hours. It seems easier here to think of eating as something one must do for sustenance and health, and more difficult to devote oneself openly and wholeheartedly to an enterprise that has as its goal simply physical pleasure and fulfillment. When we do eat for pleasure alone, guilt often follows. Fewer and fewer of us can eat a piece of flourless chocolate cake or a crème brûlée (in company) without apologizing for it. The word "sin" has a powerful resonance in this country, and these days it is often applied to food.

Another peculiarly American assumption seems embedded in the notion that somehow, by consciously manipulating our way of living, we can gain control over our mortality—that we can put off our own deaths, with the ultimate, unspoken hope that we might outsmart death entirely. There is a certain hubris that accompanies this hope; perhaps only a people who ventured into the wilderness time and again, and eventually conquered it, could en-

tertain such a notion with a straight face. This idea is a close part-
ner to the American faith in science and technology as forces that
will eventually change all the rules in our favor. We have been in
love with an idealized view of the scientific future for a long time,
from 1950s dreams of robot-servants to today's visions of anti-ag-
ing vitamins that prevent all the diseases of decrepitude. And even
earlier: writing about American health reformers like Sylvester
Graham in the first half of the nineteenth century, social historian
Roberta Pollack Seid points out that "Enlightenment notions
about natural science had slowly spread the heady idea that human beings could control their health, that they needn't just re-
sign themselves to disease and early death. . . . The presumptions
of dietary and health reformers and of certain scientists and physicians—that humans could control their health and the state of
their bodies and that God intended both to be unblemished—reflected the rise of a profoundly new worldview."[27]

This worldview—that we could control our fates through the
science of health, and more specifically of eating—went on to
reach two peaks. One was at the close of the nineteenth century;
the other is at the close of this century. The most immediately obvious connection between them is in the matter of timing: the
proximity of the century's end may not be coincidental. Historian
Hillel Schwartz has written about the fin de siècle phenomenon,
and described recurring "anxieties about pollution and decay at
century's end . . . desires for purification and rejuvenation at century's turn."[28] There is something apocalyptic about the nineties—
certainly about the turn of the millennium that we are approaching—something that calls up thoughts of mortality, of end-
ings, of historic and even religious shifts that are so large as to be
out of our control. The bright side of that anxiety, as Schwartz
points out, is the promise of a new beginning, a final chance to get
one's act together.

All of these ideas can contribute to an urge to control one's
fate in whatever manner available. If our current preoccupation
with eating scientifically and correctly, our paranoia about dangerous or evil foods, our inundation with technological and heavily

advertised solutions to our life-threatening food habits, our investment of food with moral power—if all of these are echoed in a time a hundred years past, that offers a hint of something deeper; not just a passing flirtation with a particular aggregation of ideas but a more enduring affinity for those ideas that may express something fundamental in the American outlook. The first step in understanding our current obsessions, then, may be to examine this earlier era in America's culinary life in some detail, seeking in its heightened concerns and everyday discoveries some clues to the roots of our new, and strikingly similar, anxieties. This territory is traversed in the next chapter.

Our contemporary confusion and ambivalence about food is a layered and complex thing, which is, perhaps, only to be expected. Food, and eating, is so fundamental to our lives that our feelings about it impinge on virtually every aspect of our social structure. To see this large picture clearly it seems necessary to see first a series of smaller pictures—snapshots of the American struggle with the meaning of food. In this book each of these snapshots comprises a chapter that delves into an aspect of our food paranoia, exploring the societal and cultural settings for our feelings about food and looking at the people who are framing those feelings. By bringing the focus down from the general to the particular—not just particular ideas but particular people who articulate those ideas—we begin to see these concepts about food in action rather than in the abstract. Food itself is anything but abstract, and to understand its identity in 1990s America we need to see Americans living with it: what and how they eat, how they talk about their food, how they feel about their food.

When we hear the voices of those most actively and publicly involved in our food—in rethinking it, selling it, cooking it, refiguring it in the lab—we begin to understand what drives the larger forces of American eating. The man who invented the first FDA-approved fat substitute introduces us to the idea of technologically engineered foods designed to fool us into eating well; the head of scientific research at Quaker Oats takes us through the rise and fall of a quintessentially American health-food fad, a story that says much about the power of marketing to manipulate our feelings about food. A chef reveals a kitchen's-eye view of America's conflicted eating patterns, and a lobbyist for futuristic foods that would function as preventive medicines describes the legal and psychological roadblocks in the way of that goal. The story these people ultimately tell is of a culture trying to reconcile a near-impossible desire for food to be both naughty and righteous, a technologically engineered experience of pleasure and a guarantee of prolonged, indeed almost endless, life. When we listen to what they say—and see what and how and why they eat—their experiences, taken together, seem to represent a particularly American repast: a serving of anxiety, another of opportunism, a teaspoon of regret, and a sizable dollop of (guilty) sin.

Chapter One

•

SEEDS OF SELF-DENIAL

The Transformation of Food in the 1890s

•

It may come as something of a surprise to those embedded in today's culture of technologically altered foodstuffs and double-blind studies of cholesterol and heart disease to learn that many aspects of our current response to food were foreshadowed one hundred years ago, in an age when electricity was new and polyunsaturated fats virtually unknown. The end of the nine-teenth century was a time of leaps in knowledge about food and leaps in anxiety as well, an era of fads and scientific yearnings and the beginning of a food-marketing industry that would soon swell to gigantic proportions. The shared obsessions that link the 1890s to today are telling, and serve not only as intriguing social history but also as a vivid illustration that our current worries are more than a blip on the radar of social change. We've traveled this road before, perhaps in a less sophisticated manner but in a similar frame of mind; clearly, much of our emotional relation-ship to food has deep roots in the American past.

•

The Tyranny of the Calorie

If the 1890s had a nutrition guru, it was in the person of an earnest, reform-minded, rather scolding chemist at Wesleyan University named Wilbur Olin Atwater. Atwater was Marian Burros, Jane Brody, and John Harvey Kellogg rolled into one: He exhorted Americans on the evils of their diet, educated them in the basics of nutrition (then a new science), and discoursed on the moral effects of various diets. Although his name has faded now, he was long widely known as the man who introduced the calorie and its components to the American eater, and along with it a potent philosophy for how those calories should be apportioned.

Until about midcentury, people had no means by which to analyze their food, no knowledge that the body could make different use of bread than of meat or vegetables. Nutritional values of various foods were thought to be basically equal, and nutritional advice centered on amounts rather than types of food. The science of nutrition as we know it now began in the 1840s in Germany with the scientist Justus von Liebig, who was the first to find a way to break down foods into proteins, fats, carbohydrates, and minerals.[1] The calorie—a measure of the energy obtained from foods in the form of heat generated—had been discovered in the eighteenth century by a French chemist, Antoine-Laurent Lavoisier, but was little known well into the next century.

Atwater single-handedly introduced these concepts to the American public, first in a series of articles in The Century magazine in 1887 and 1888, and later in the first government-sponsored lists of the nutritive values of various foods, published by the United States Department of Agriculture in 1895. (Interestingly, we have recently been again in a time of redefinition of the nutritive value of foods through the auspices of the USDA, in the emergence of the Eating Right Pyramid to replace the Four Food Groups, a process that was racked by controversy.) Atwater's food lists were largely the result of his own research; he was the first director of the new federal Office of Experiment Stations for the study of human nutrition, and in 1893 wangled a special appropriation from Congress for his work. In one of his publications for the USDA he described the unwieldy tools of his investigations— a respiration apparatus and respiration calorimeter invented in Munich: "They consist of metal-walled chambers large enough for the subject (sometimes a man, sometimes a dog, sheep, or other animal) to live in comfortably for several days, and are furnished with devices for pumping air through and measuring and analyzing it as it enters and leaves the chamber. With such an apparatus it is possible not only to measure all the food and excreta, but also the materials given off from the lungs in the breath, and to make accurate determinations of the matter entering and leaving the body."[2]

But Atwater wasn't simply an objective man of science and the first American to investigate how food works in the body; he was also a man with a mission, and many of his words of admonishment echo those of latter-day nutrition standard-bearers. "Most of us understand very little about what our food contains," he wrote, "how it nourishes us, whether we are economical or wasteful in buying and preparing it for use, and whether or not the food we eat is rightly fitted to the demands of our bodies. The result of our ignorance is great waste in the purchase and use of food, loss of money, and injury to health. . . . We consume relatively too much of the fuel ingredients of food, such as the fats of meat and butter, the starch which makes up the larger part of the nutritive material of flour and potatoes, and sugar and sweetmeats. Conversely, we have relatively too little of the protein or flesh-forming substances, like the lean of meat and fish and the gluten of wheat. . . . Thirdly, many people, not only the well-to-do, but those in moderate circumstances, use needless quantities of food. . . . How much harm is done to health by our one-sided and excessive diet, no one can say."[3] (One of the few differences between this commentary and one you might encounter today is that now we *do* say how much harm is done; Oliver Alabaster, M.D., director of the Institute for Disease Prevention at George Washington University, wrote recently that "there is compelling evidence that more than 50 percent of heart disease and stroke, and about 35 percent of cancers, are caused by bad eating habits.")[4]

Atwood's answer to the crimes of food ingestion he observed was a new one and greatly influenced by the tenor of the times: treat the body like a machine, and food solely as its fuel. Pleasure had most emphatically nothing to do with it. In his 1895 USDA publication "Food and Diet," he wrote: "In our actual practice of eating we are apt to be influenced too much by taste, that is, by the dictates of the palate; we are prone to let natural instinct be overruled by acquired appetite; and we neglect the teachings of experience. We need to observe our diet and its effects more carefully, and regulate appetite by reason. In doing this we may be greatly aided by the knowledge of what our food contains and how it serves its purpose in nutrition. . . . Part of the principle is found in the fact that the human body is a machine. . . . "[5] Food is not simply food—tasty, filling, and of course nourishing—but a collection of elements, recorded and counted. A mother shopping for dinner, he wrote, is buying not just meat and milk but "certain nutritive substances in the food—flesh formers and fuel ingredients. . . . "[6] Almost exactly one hundred years later, in January of 1991, a dietician at the Doral Saturnia Health Spa told her spa guests, "Look at food as fuel for building a healthy, strong body. Basically, firm food like vegetables and grains will make firm tissue. Fatty food like butter, cheese and meat will make fatty tissue."[7]

Atwater's attitudes clearly had not only a powerful but a lasting effect. Hillel Schwartz, in his history of dieting, *Never Satisfied*, describes the way Atwater "thoroughly stripped food of its body. . . . [He] entirely reconstrue[d] the meanings of foods without reference to taste, ethnic tradition, or social context. . . . Atwater was so successful at this balancing act that he reset the nutritional standards for the nation."[8] But what's particularly remarkable about Atwater is not only the reach of his philosophy—which we experience today every time we look at a calorie chart or consult a food label for a protein count—but the way in which he embodied in his time nearly every ambient idea about food, so many of which are echoed today.

His view of food as fuel, for instance, was a direct but more scientifically sophisticated descendant of the health-reform movement that had stirred earlier in the century with Sylvester Graham and was being so cleverly tapped into by Kellogg and others. Graham's preferred diet included heavy, unleavened bran bread (later sweetened and commercialized as Graham crackers), vegetables, and water; no liquor, coffee, spices, or meat. In the 1830s, Graham proclaimed: "Excessive alimentation is the greatest dietetic error in the United States—and probably in the whole civilized world." He also outlined these rules for eating: "Treat your stomach like a well governed child; carefully find out what is best for it, as the digestive organ of your body, and then teach it to conform to your regimen."[9] Control and moral education, not gustatory enjoyment, was the goal.

By 1850 an American Vegetarian Society was founded, beginning as an animal-rights group based on morality, then incorporating a scientific basis from health reformers like Graham. Meat was blamed for many sins—bad digestion, corpulency, early aging, decreased intellectual power. Vegetarians claimed variously that those who used animal foods were "those who wish to become corpulent," "those who wish to have their fluids continually in a half-putrid state," "idiots," and "those who wish to become stupid, like idiots." One vegetarian dismissed his challengers by saying, "It often happens that what is plain and clear to the mental perception of a vegetarian, is obscure, if not wholly incomprehensible to the mind of the flesh-eater."[10]

The tone of moral superiority so evident in these statements was another legacy bequeathed to Atwater by early reformers. Atwater decided that diet and morality were inextricably linked. In the introduction to his 1895 list of food values for the USDA he wrote: "We are coming to realize that not merely our health, our strength, and our incomes, but our higher intellectual life, and even our morals, depend upon the care which we take of our bodies, and that among the things essential to health and wealth, to right thinking and right living, one, and that not the least important, is our diet."[11] In a sternly prescriptive article titled "What

We Should Eat," published in *The Century* in 1888, he went even further. After outlining a properly balanced "mixed" diet, he suggested: "I venture to ask, in all seriousness, whether there may not be, between the intellectual, social, and moral force of [a] people and the dietary usages of which those here instanced are a part, an important connection, one that reaches down deep into the philosophy of human living?"[12]

In Atwater's system, morality could essentially take the place of enjoyment and taste in the experience of eating; if food were regarded as largely scientific, a fuel for a machine, its spiritual value could be redefined not as the giving of pleasure but the giving of moral fiber. We are not quite as obvious about it today—the Quaker Oats "right thing to do" being the exception—but the morality of eating, and the judgments we make based on that, swirl around us now at every meal. A piece of steak becomes a concession to gluttony, one of the seven sins, and grilled fish a sign of uprightness. The terms "good" and "bad" come to refer not to taste but to an abstract moral equation of healthy foods versus "sinful" ones. "I've been very good today," writes a woman in *Vogue* magazine about her very low-fat diet (undertaken not for weight loss but for health reasons). "Breakfast was raisin bran and skim milk."[13]

Atwater was joined in his concern about food and morality by a group of reformers, largely women, who focused their efforts on the kitchen rather than the laboratory. At the moment that he was discoursing on the scientific basis for eating, these women were leading a closely allied movement for scientific cooking, or, as it came to be known, "domestic science" (later called home economics). Here, too, spiritual considerations ranked high. "The prosperity of a nation depends upon the health and the morals of its citizens, and the health and the morals of a people depend mainly upon the food they eat, and the homes they live in," wrote Ellen H. Richards, one of the founders of the domestic science movement and an instructor in sanitary chemistry at the Massachusetts Institute of Technology, in her 1885 book *Food Materials and Their Adulterations*. "Strong men and women cannot be 'raised' on insufficient food. Good-tempered, temperate, highly moral men cannot be expected from a race which eats badly cooked food, irritating to the digestive organs and unsatisfying to the appetite. Wholesome and palatable food is the first step in good morals, and is conducive to ability in business, skill in trade, and healthy tone in literature."[14]

The belief that, as one historian puts it, "good health encouraged a Christian soul and ultimately a moral and strong nation" led one cookbook author of the time to comment that "the system of morals therefore becomes identified with that of cookery."[15] The domestic science movement held this moral connection as one of its bedrock beliefs, but its other goal was to apply the kind of precision and scientific knowledge Atwater was disseminating to what had been until the late nineteenth century a more instinctual arena: the household. Just as Atwater's model was of the body as a machine, the women leading the domestic science charge held up the household as a machine as well. The women stoking this machine must therefore be defined not so much as chefs creating tasty dishes, but rather as chemists and engineers who apply a knowledge of nutrition and hygiene to their family cooking.

"The machinery of daily life should respond to the slightest touch of the house engineer," wrote Richards, "the one who knows all about it. The running of a household is a no less responsible task than the running of a steamboat or an engine. The time has come when the same kind of care must be given to the food of the family as the stockraiser gives to that of his animals. The modern stock farm has given us most of the scientific knowledge we possess on the question of foods. . . . Shall the human animal be considered of less consequence? . . . A knowledge of the elements of chemistry and physics must be applied to the daily living."[16]

The denizens of domestic science attacked this problem on several fronts: they constructed elaborate charts and lists of nutrients and daily diets; they investigated food adulteration (widely practiced at the time) and spoilage (a knowledge of bacteriology was just beginning); they went about standardizing measurements that had previously been as impressionistic as "butter the size of an egg" or "a teacupful of milk"; and they combined foods based on their nutrients and "digestibility" rather than their aesthetic appeal. Atwater's work was an indispensable adjunct to their efforts. "At the height of their reputation," writes Laura Shapiro, author of *Perfection Salad,* a history of cooking at the turn of the century, "teachers of scientific cookery liked nothing better than to take up Atwater's food composition tables and bring them to life in the kitchen. Protein, fat, and carbohydrate became categories to be wielded in the assembling of a rational meal. . . . The manipulation of nutritional components that went on in scientific kitchens was never simply cookery in the minds of its practitioners; it was what an MIT chemist called 'external digestion.' . . . Scientific cookery was cookery in the service of digestion, cookery at its most pragmatic."[17]

Scientific cookery was demanding of the cook in a way that has, perhaps less overtly, insinuated its way back into today's kitchen. "A well-grounded knowledge of the chemistry and physiology of foods is the foundation upon which all good work in cooking must be laid," wrote "Miss M.A. Boland, instructor in cooking in the Johns Hopkins Training School for Nurses" in an 1893 issue of the *Popular Science Monthly.*[18] While today's nutrition writers take a less stern tone, the underlying message is just as challenging.

"The anti-fat patrol has some home cooks ready to retire their spatulas," writes Molly O'Neill in the *New York Times,* in an article entitled "Riddle for Healthful Cooks: How to Leave Out the Fat?" "Defatting is hard to do. For cooks, the explosion of industrially made low-fat foods, technological products that cannot be duplicated in the home, has reinforced feelings of powerlessness." But O'Neill goes on to give tip after tip for cooking with virtually no fat; she quotes a cook saying, "Most people I know have one fat-busting trick they cling to like a life line." These educated cooks, O'Neill goes on, "can push their carts proudly past aisles of expensive 'low fat' processed food. They no longer need a factory to be dietetically correct."[19]

Marian Burros is even more earnest. In a piece about cutting back on meat and dairy because "such diets may be a contributing cause to the chronic diseases of the industrialized world," she briskly presents a minicourse in kitchen nutrition: "A diet with few meat and dairy products does require more careful choices than a diet in which they are central. Dairy is an excellent source of calcium; meat, of iron and some B vitamins. When they are used in small amounts, the diet has to be more carefully structured to make certain those nutrients are not lacking. . . . Iron in vegetables is not as well absorbed as iron in meat, fish and poultry. But the absorption is enhanced if iron-containing vegetables are combined in the same meal with vegetables and fruits that contain vitamin C, like citrus fruits. . . . Vitamin C improves calcium absorption, but eating too much protein or fat interferes with it. . . . "[20]

Recipes published in newspapers and magazines, even those not prepared for restricted diets, now routinely include nutritional analyses with listings of calories, fat, cholesterol, sodium, protein, and carbohydrates. One cook, a botanist and researcher for the U.S. Department of Agriculture named James Duke, goes so far as to label his recipes Cataract Tea, Candied Carotene, Antioxidant Soup, and Anti-Cancer Slaw; he calls them "culinary medicine." Even Pierre Franey, author of the *60 Minute Gourmet* cookbooks and for years an unregenerate cook of the old French school, prefaced a recent recipe for pork tenderloin with a discussion of the fat contents of beef and pork tenderloin compared with that of skinless chicken breast.[21] Today's cooks can hardly escape the message: They are expected to be chemists and nutritionists in the kitchen, aware of all nutrients and arranging them in the most advantageous groupings. This is the sort of outlook that might lead to a firm belief in yogurt and ricotta, mixed with cornstarch, as a dead ringer for cream sauce.

The Evil That Diet Does

In 1832 a satirist, responding to Sylvester Graham's call for dietary reforms, suggested the creation of a Society for the Suppression of Intemperance. In an uncanny presage of today's symbolism of food as hidden killer, he wrote: "Disease lurks behind the fat sirloin, and there is Death in the tureen of turtle-soup. Whenever I go to a dinner party, it seems to me that I see in my mind's eye, the incarnate forms of Gout, Apoplexy, and Fever, bringing in the dishes and coaxing their victims, just to take one slice more."[22] The metaphorical linkage of food with disease described here lost some currency after Graham's death in 1852, but by the time such ideas revived later in the century—popularized by Kellogg, Atwater, and others—they were powerful enough to prompt what historian Harvey Levenstein calls "a veritable Golden Age of food faddism."

Levenstein, in his book *Revolution at the Table*, describes the groups that made up this Golden Age: vegetarians, divided into fruitarians, nutarians, lacto-ovarians, and other subgroups; raw foodists who would eat nothing cooked; proponents of schemes to do away with "poisonous" bacteria that lived in the colon. In previous eras such beliefs had been folkloric; by the end of the nineteenth century they were invested with an aura of scientific sophistication.[23] Atwater and the scientific cooks, along with the doctors who published articles inveighing against the nation's gastronomic mistakes, were not operating in a vacuum. The public was happy to try on their ideas one after another, and the obsessiveness with which they did so is indicated, at least in part, by the satire that resulted.

In 1889, fifty-seven years after the satirical passage quoted above, an anonymous book appeared entitled *Dinnerology: Our Experiments in Diet from Crankery to Common Sense—A Tale for the Times*. *Dinnerology* recounts the very tongue-in-cheek trials of an upper-middle-class couple who resolve to reform their diets. They have been married ten years and find themselves gaining weight, feeling distinctly dyspeptic (a Victorian catchall term for all kinds of indigestion and aches and pains), and willing to try every new health tonic that comes along. The husband pontificates on the choice that awaits them, giving in the process a précis of the circulating ideas of the day: "We may do one of two things, we may either trust to the kitchen customs of the day, as the outcome of the rough and ready experience of our ancestors, or we may reason that scientific investigation (a long-winded word for fact-getting) may have something eye-opening and valuable in this as well as in other directions, which may revolutionize our system of feeding as it has done our system of lighting and distance-talking. . . . I only insist on the wisdom of using the lamp of knowledge to throw its penetrating light upon the dishes on our table. It brings out their little secrets, their good or bad designs upon us, their powers of revenge, their ability to console and succor and bless. Let me know my friends from my enemies, say I.

"Now we have got to learn our ABC of foods and their properties. Everything we eat and drink has a certain amount of waste in it, often a mischievous amount. In the solids there is more liquid than we fancy, so much flesh-forming material, so much force-furnishing material, and a residue of solid waste. Get to know what proportions of these materials there are in your bread, mush, steak, fish, and pie crust and then you are for the first time in your life qualified to outwit the doctor in his own domain by preventing nine-tenths of the ailments which nine-tenths of the medicos never cure." He goes on to present an appropriately skewed account of Atwater's food-value charts. "Good gracious, George!" his wife exclaims at one point. "Did you expect to stuff all that jargon into my head? Haven't we agreed that we will *enjoy* our food? How on earth could anybody enjoy life if they had to keep counting and comparing those hideous things with every mouthful we eat!"

They go on to stagger through several dietary regimens, beginning with becoming vegetarian (although they overcompensate so much with other foods—sweets, puddings, nuts, cheese—that the whole family gains weight); discussing cutting out alcohol but deciding against it (George doesn't want to give it up); and applying Atwater-style economies to work their daily food expenditure down to ten cents a head. Along the way they have run-ins with doctors who advise various "dietaries," affording the writer some sly potshots at the prevailing medical wisdom. They finally make their peace with their food and feel great pride that they have accomplished food economy and applied the popular food scholarship. They list their new, ascetic menu:

BREAKFAST—mush, wheat, oatmeal, hominy with milk, cup of coffee, and cracker.

DINNER—lentil or pea soup, beef extract flavoring, vegetable condiments (or macaroni and cheese, or beans and butter or bacon fat), a few raisins, a fig or banana, or a nip of cheese and cracker.

TEA—cup of tea, coffee, cocoa, with milk and sugar, homemade bread with butter or jam, or stewed fruit.

SUPPER—bread and cheese and glass of beer; or mush and stewed fruit, macaroni and milk, cocoa, bread, and butter; or egg, bread and butter, milk pudding.[24]

Taking into consideration differences in tastes of the times (mush and hominy not being big items these days), this regimen, with its breads, beans, grains, and fruits, is not unlike some vegetarian regimens today, although milk and cheese have decidedly fallen out of favor with the health-conscious (too much fat and unnecessary protein).

Dinnerology attests to the widespread popularity of the new nutrition and its notions of proper diet as another scientific milestone in America's progress. The food and health manuals of the day are just as hyperbolic, if more straightforward. Consider this introduction to the 1888 book *Eating for Strength; or, Food and Diet in their Relation to Health and Work*, by M. L. Holbrook, M.D.: "In no period of the world's history has there ever been so deep an interest in the subject of foods as at the present. At no time since Adam and Eve left the Garden of Eden has agriculture and horticulture been so perfect, and the human race supplied with so many choice and nourishing articles of diet. And, also, at no time have so many been engaged in laborious researches on the nature of that which we eat and its relations to health and work. It would almost seem as if the time had nearly arrived when mankind would eat to live, would feed themselves so as to nourish their bodies most perfectly and render themselves capable of the most labor, and least liable to disease. . . . There is no doubt but man may double his capacity for work and for enjoyment by improving his dietetic habits."[25]

In our current era of scientific eating we are no less earnest. Take, for example, a Jane Brody column titled "In Pursuit of the Best Possible Odds of Preventing or Minimizing the Perils of Major Diseases," which includes a chart labeled "Preventing Disease: A Menu of Health-Saving Tactics" (among those are, of course, a high-fiber diet and a diet high in vegetables and fruits). This modern earnestness has called down its own satire or protest, though in rather modest amounts. In May 1991, *Newsweek* commented on healthy-eating paranoia with an article titled "Feeding Frenzy," which lamented that "assaulted by a blitz of nutrition advice in recent years . . . many Americans have thrown up their hands. . . . Recently Americans woke up to some particularly discouraging headlines: the latest dietary bugaboo is food itself. Or so it seemed." But the magazine couldn't resist joining in the very thinking it was mocking by sprinkling in liberal amounts of nutritional advice: "Strawberries: Eat your fill; the news about fruit is all good and getting better every day"; "Fish is still an excellent choice, but keep the portions small and pass the rice. That's what the Japanese do." Even the moral tone was present: "If you like pasta with tomato sauce, you're already thinking right."[26] Another protest was lodged later in 1991 on the *New York Times* editorial page, on the day before Thanksgiving, by a writer who claimed that the idea of dieting on Thanksgiving is "symptomatic of a time when nutritional terrorists see every pat of butter as poison and a full-blown turkey dinner as a big step toward the cardiac ward." The editorial goes on: "Ever anxious over grams of cholesterol, fat, sodium and sugar, we are encouraged to push ourselves away from a table that once manifested our extraordinary abundance and culinary heritage."[27]

That heritage is now part of the problem. It is not too strong to call our culinary traditions the enemy, a force to be resisted and rejected rather than a celebration of plenty that can be occasionally indulged (perhaps more wisely than we currently do) without irreparable harm. One newspaper article entitled "Weaning Americans from the Meat Habit" reiterates that Americans have been eating too much fat for a long time, and claims, rather condescendingly, "Weaning Americans from a dinner plate in which meat plays the starring role is like asking a three-year-old to give up a security blanket."[28] A letter to the editor in the *New York Times* asserts that "the typical American diet has created an epidemic of degenerative diseases that cause widespread premature death and morbidity,"[29] although most experts will agree that there are many unanswered questions about the relationship between diet and health—questions about the role of exercise, genetics, gender, and other factors. "The typical diet in this country," writes a dietician, "provides only about eleven grams of fiber a day, but far more calories, sugar and fat than is necessary."[30] Various books and magazines play to the guilt and anxiety that such proclamations foster, promising to help us kick the habit of American eating and learn to recognize good food from bad (much as George in *Dinnerology* sought out the "little secrets" and the "good and bad designs" of his food in 1889). An ad for a nutrition newsletter in 1991 begins: "You get plenty of advice from food companies about what foods to buy when you shop. But it's rare that you get expert advice about what to *avoid*. If you care about your health, I'd like to help you avoid the worst foods—those with the hidden fats and salt that promote heart disease or cancer."[31]

The level of help that Americans feel they need is indicated by the food-labeling hoopla that began in the late 1980s and reached a crescendo in the early 1990s. After years of tight regulation the FDA had loosened its vigilance over the kinds of health claims food companies could make on their product labels (beginning with Kellogg's All Bran in 1984), and by the late eighties the health-claim business was out of control. Almost everything was "lite" or "natural" or "97% fat free," and it was clear that something had to be done; in many cases the public was being completely misled about the nutritional properties of foods. Exactly what should be done remained unclear, and the FDA has been wrestling with the massive problem of how to define terms that keep shifting meanings, and how to make a fair presentation of the relative healthfulness of various foods—particularly in light of the fast-moving changes in our understanding of nutritional benefits. Do we allow claims that a low-fat diet helps prevent cancer? What about beta carotene and heart disease? Should broccoli sport a label saying that it contains sulforaphane, a chemical found to resist the growth of cancerous tumors?

The confusion over what role the government should play in protecting us from evil foods and teaching us about disease-fighting foods recalls in some aspects the 1890s concern over government protection from what was the food bugaboo of the day: commercial adulteration and spoilage. Ellen Richards, in devoting an entire book to the problem (*Food Materials and Their Adulterations*, written in 1885), commented, "So much has been said on the subject of adulteration in the past few years, that the peace of mind of a conscientious woman is quite gone, and she appeals to the lawmakers to protect her family."[32] Richards goes on to devote chapters to the nefarious ways that common food articles could be adulterated: pepper, with wheat flour, ground rice, or cornmeal; mustard, with starches, wheat, rice, or corn flour; coffee, with seeds or roots. Adulteration was indeed widespread, and there were few legal protections to prevent the practice. Concern about adulteration gathered steam throughout the 1890s and grew to a fever pitch with the 1906 publication of Upton Sinclair's *The Jungle*, which exposed the unclean practices in stockhouses and helped lead to the creation of the Pure Food and Drug Act the same year.[33]

In the minds of the scientific cooks, adulteration was joined by another looming danger: spoilage, or "putrefaction." The principles of bacteriology were still new—Ellen Richards pointed out that much about "germ theory" had been learned in the twenty years before she wrote her book—and the domestic scientists took the new information to heart. A significant portion of M. A. Boland's 1893 *Popular Science* article, "Scientific Cooking: A Plea for Education in Household Affairs," was devoted to a discussion of bacteriology and the insistence that every cook understand its workings. "Micro-organisms are everywhere," Boland warned. "They exist in the earth and the sea; in plants and animals; on the surface of our bodies and in the digestive canal; in cooked and un-cooked food; in refuse, particularly animal waste; on our clothing, books, furniture, and in the dust of the atmosphere. Wherever they find suitable food, warmth, and moisture they increase with wonderful rapidity, and, if undisturbed would in time completely transform the object upon which they fall." The problem here, she pointed out, is that certain foods may thus become transformed and contain "poisonous matter in small quantities, which produces in human beings, when those foods are eaten, grave digestive disturbances. Should the eating of such food be continued for a length of time, or the amount of poisonous matter be large, serious results of illness, or even death, may follow."[34]

The Victorian image of food as the silent harborer of invisible agents of illness, or impurities introduced by amoral marketers, recalls recent phobias: over Alar and other possibly hazardous chemicals, unclean seafood, misleadingly labeled packaged foods. Any hint of contamination or commercial obfuscation is likely to cause a stampede, accompanied by calls for more regulation. This paranoia seems intimately connected to the realities of our industrialized age: the producers of our food are far away and unknown to us, and food often comes to us in a form quite far removed from its original state—dried, flash frozen, preserved, reconstituted. So it's particularly intriguing to consider that these fears had their first heyday at the end of the nineteenth century—not coincidentally, a time of tremendously rapid change in the technology of producing and selling food.

At the Mercy of the Market

In the middle of the nineteenth century, Americans obtained their food in much the same way they had for centuries: from small, independent store-owners who bought goods from middlemen—wholesalers who in turn bought from farmers and regional manufacturing companies. Most foods were sold in bulk, without brand names. A retailer carried one kind of flour, sugar, butter; he bought manufactured items like crackers and cookies from regional factories and placed them in cracker barrels, to be scooped out and sold by weight. Customers trusted their retailer to choose their goods for them. When they went grocery shopping there were no food-packed aisles to browse in; they went directly to the front counter to request their needs.

During the latter half of the century this neat system virtually exploded. In the space of those few decades nearly everything about the way Americans received their food changed, as the result of a remarkable surge in the technology of food transportation and production. New railroad systems transported food much more quickly and efficiently, factories became exponentially more productive, and those changes led in turn to the emergence of large national food companies, national brands, and perhaps most transforming of all, food marketing and advertising as it had never been used before.

Take, for example, the Heinz canning company. H. J. Heinz of Pittsburgh opened his company in 1869 with a single product: pickled horseradish. In that year, canning technology was at the beginning of a steep climb in popularity; although the process itself was invented in 1809 by a Frenchman, it had remained for decades a laborious and sometimes imprecise process. Then, in 1849, a machine was invented that made the tops and bottoms of cans (the most difficult parts), so that while in 1840 two skilled tinsmiths produced 120 cans per day, by the 1850s two unskilled workers could make 1,500 cans per day. In 1860 5 million cans of food were produced; by 1870, 30 million. In the 1870s a new method of packing under steam pressure was refined that made even larger scale production possible. Heinz capitalized on the burgeoning canning (and jarring) technology: By the 1890s, he had the "57 Varieties" that became the slogan for his company, and by 1900 he was the largest general food processor in the country.[35] But his success was accompanied by an inherent problem: other canners were profiting by the new technology, too, and by the more efficient transportation system that allowed companies to be truly national in scope and led to greater abundance and hence falling prices. The only way for Heinz to distinguish his products, which were identical in price and quality to their competitors and available in the same stores, was to advertise—to create a reason to choose Heinz products over others. Heinz was not the only company to realize this: at the largest American ad agency of the time, N. W. Ayer, food advertising accounted for less than 1 percent of the agency's business in 1877; by 1901 food accounted for 15 percent, the largest of any category, and remained the largest until the 1930s, when it was overtaken by cars. Heinz's solution was massive. The company pioneered many marketing concepts, including tours of its plants and the new system of "vertical integration": buying its own farmland, factories, freight cars, bottling plants, so that the entire production process was under its control. The advertising itself was enormous: at the turn of the century the corner of Fifth Avenue and Twenty-third Street in New York was dominated by a six-story electrified sign in the shape of a Heinz pickle.[36]

There were other reasons that the boom in industrialized foods created a greater need for advertising. One was that the consumer, of necessity, became more removed from the food and more anxious about it. Instead of receiving food directly from bins and recommended by the grocer, customers bought foods disguised in packages. Technology had changed the physical shape of food purchasing. The first paper bag–making machine was patented in 1852; in the 1870s new methods were created for printing on metals and tins; by the early 1880s folding cardboard cartons for crackers and cereals could be made by machine. Customers could not smell or even see the products they were buying, and they were naturally suspicious: Why should this unseen food produced in a giant factory by unknown workers and recommended by no one be better than homemade, or better than food chosen by the local grocer and purchased from local small manufacturers? How could it even be trusted?

The manufacturers' answer was brilliant: They turned the argument on its head. Not only could factory-produced foods be *more* sanitary, they said, because they were "untouched by human hands" and then packed in protective packages, but the customer could rest easy that, with its name on the package, the company would have more incentive to take responsibility for its products and guarantee its own accountability. These messages were conveyed in advertising and emblazoned on packages themselves. Words like "fresh," "pure," and "wholesome" were favorites. Advertisers also took advantage of the currency of scientific cookery to promote their products as modern, scientific, and efficient. They were so successful at this that by late in the century many people preferred condensed evaporated milk over fresh milk, for coffee and tea but also in children's foods, because it was "hermetically sealed."[37]

A prime dealer in these new ideas about producing and selling food was the National Biscuit Company, which is credited with single-handedly doing away with the corner grocer's traditional cracker barrel. The company brought out Uneeda brand biscuits in 1899 with enormous fanfare and provided a blueprint for modern food marketing: a catchy name (obvious and almost silly-sounding in the way of so much early advertising); a focused psychological campaign (Uneeda biscuits were superior not only in taste but because they featured "In-Er-Seal" packages that protected the contents from moisture and the kinds of contamination that were inevitable with a common cracker barrel); saturation advertising (newspapers, magazines, billboards); and innovative distribution (a company sales force that bypassed middlemen and went directly to stores, and an aggressive use of railroads to move the product to all regions of the country). Uneeda ended up with 70 percent of the American cracker business.[38]

By the end of the nineteenth century there was for the first time a national market—a national market quickly becoming skilled at receiving commercial messages, and primed to be influenced by those messages. Writes historian Harvey Levenstein: "Only the emergence of large corporate entities profiting from mass markets for their mass produced foods allowed the mounting

of large campaigns designed to change food habits through per-
suasion. . . . The great changes in business organization would
play a major role in dictating what Americans would consume."[39]
A hundred years later, we are so conditioned to being told what to
consume and why—it's tastier *and* healthier and has a memorable
name and only 3 grams of saturated fat—that imagining being
without such information is almost impossible.

Social historian T. J. Jackson Lears has devised a fascinating
theory, couched in psychological terms, for why the modern consumer culture sprang up so powerfully at the end of the nineteenth century, and why that culture was so oriented toward
self-improvement, or what he calls the "therapeutic ethos." His
reasoning casts some interesting light on our latter-day therapeutic ethos, the one that has resulted in, among other things, the
nearly out-of-control food labeling situation that seems to have so
baffled the FDA. Lears posits that the rise of a consumer, ad-dri-
ven culture was only possible after a national shift in moral cli-
mate "from a Protestant ethos of salvation through self-denial
toward a therapeutic ethos stressing self-realization in this
world—an ethos characterized by an almost obsessive concern
with psychic and physical health defined in sweeping terms." This
new ethos was partly the result of the erosion of the social frame-
works of community or religion. By the end of the nineteenth
century, writes Lears, "the quest for health was becoming an entirely secular and self-referential project. . . . The coming of the
therapeutic ethos was a modern historical development, shaped by
the turmoil of the turn of the century."

These forces made fertile ground for a consumer culture anxious to make itself, somehow, better, but Lears sees a further psychological impetus in what he calls "feelings of unreality." These
feelings, he hypothesizes, stemmed from several sources, including urbanization and technological development, and the rise of an
interdependent market economy. Urban life and the anonymity of
the city had what Lears calls a "corrosive impact on personal identity," and the new luxuries and comforts that surrounded the middle class—plumbing, heating, canned and packaged goods—cut

them off from daily hardships that seemed somehow more real and close to the nature of things. These conveniences, says Lears, "made life seem curiously insubstantial." That sense of unreality was intensified by a larger, more complex, more remote economy, in which jobs were more specialized and less autonomous, dependent often on changes and shifts that occurred far away and over which the worker had no control. Success seemed to depend less on the genuine, the inner character or the skills of the worker, and more on externals like personal "magnetism" or pleasing others or the swings of a huge, mysterious economy. Lears describes a workforce saddled with feelings of inner emptiness in which "selfhood lost coherence"; the old rules had changed, and it was hard to know how to play by the new ones. "The decline of autonomous selfhood lay at the heart of the modern sense of unreality," writes Lears. "The feeling of unreality helped to generate longings for bodily vigor, emotional intensity, and a revitalized sense of selfhood."

The flight from that sense of unreality, according to Lears, ran anxious Victorians right into an age in which advertisers and marketers gained ascendance. Their promises, he says, relied on these assumptions: the nostalgic notion that farmers, children, and others "close to nature" enjoyed a vigorous health that others had lost; "a belief that expert advice could enable one to recover that vigor without fundamental social change"; and "a tacit conviction that self-realization was the largest aim of human existence." "The therapeutic ethos," writes Lears, "implied not only that one ought to pursue health single-mindedly but also that one ought to be continuously exuding personal magnetism and the promise of ever more radiant, wholesome living." Enter advertising. Lears goes on, "National advertisers helped to popularize a pseudo-religion of health and an anxious self-absorption among the American population."

The strategies these advertisers devised, adjusted just a little for changes in style and products, were remarkably "modern": that is, they exist in almost the same form today, because we are in the hold of the same therapeutic ethos. There was, for example,

the "Reason Why" approach that "addressed nonrational yearnings by suggesting the ways [a] product would transform the
buyer's life," ostensibly using reason and rationality; consider
television car ads in which a voice-over earnestly intones lists of
features like anti-lock brakes and airbags while the visuals suggest
that this car will bring its owner excitement, adventure, and, of
course, a beautiful woman. Nineteenth-century advertisers also
came up with the "natural" pitch that rings remarkably true today. Writes Lears: "A characteristic therapeutic strategy linked domestic responsibilities with nostalgia for a pristine, 'natural' state.
'Mothers, do you not know that children crave natural food until
you pervert their taste by the use of unnatural food?' " read a
1903 Shredded Wheat ad. "The advertiser defined the 'natural' as
the good, implied that modern life was full of artificial irritations,
and promised salvation through his product—which was ironically
all the more natural in this case since it was *made in the most hy-
gienic and scientific food laboratory in the world.*"[40]

There was a time earlier in this century when "natural" was
not a particularly powerful sell, but today it is near the top of the
pantheon of magic commercial words that advertisers use to convey not just a quality of food but a universe of meaning. We too,
like turn-of-the-century consumers, fear our loss of connection to
the "real" and the natural, while earlier epochs have instead celebrated the progress that that loss symbolized (think of the 1950s'
love affair with the futuristic and the scientific, the glorification of
the coming "twenty-first century"). We may love what technology does for us, but we distrust it, too. Now that the twenty-first
century is upon us it looks a little scary, as the unknown always
does, because it is out of our control. If one can't control the economy or the psychological demands of technology, however, one
can still control oneself. Food marketers are perfectly willing to
show us the way to that control—through an exorcism of the
"bad" (fats, calories, overindulgence) and the invention of the
"good" (magic foods that promise life).

• • •

Too Much of Many Good Things

The anxieties described by Lears prompted a somewhat different response from Atwater and the domestic scientists. They attempted to exert control over the scary elements of the rapid technological transformation of daily life by pinpointing a concrete culprit—overabundance—and postulating ways to tame it. The idea of overabundance followed directly from the revolution in food production and distribution; it was that revolution that produced, for the first time, an embarrassment of culinary riches. Factories churned out food products, grocery stores ballooned into emporiums stacked with thousands of goods packaged with colorful and beseeching labels, and the American consumer was tempted at every step.

Atwater and others who were prescribing "dietaries" put their own moralistic spin on the matter of this abundance—rather than something to be lauded as a sign of progress, they said, it was to blame for the myriad unhealthy eating patterns they observed. Americans were simply doing too well; life was too easy, and we were being led astray by our natural but base yearnings for pleasure and availability. Ellen Richards wrote in 1885: "Now, the food products of the whole world are accessible to the people of the United States, through the use of improved methods of transportation—the refrigerator car and steamship compartment—and through improved methods of preservation, by cold storage, and by the canning process. This very abundance brings its own danger; for the appetite is no longer a sufficient guide to the selection of food, as it was in the case of the early people who were not tempted by so great a variety. Many diseases of modern civilization are doubtless due to errors of diet, which might easily be avoided."[41]

The metaphors of overabundance and overnutrition were everywhere at the end of the nineteenth century. Atwater took those ideas as the bedrock of his work. "Many of us eat far too much of meats, of fats, and of sweetmeats," he wrote in 1888. "Not only are the quantities of nutrients in the dietaries of our working people very large, in some cases enormously so, but those of people whose occupation involves little muscular work supply protein and fats and energy far in excess of what the best evidence indicates as the actual demand, even for active exercise. . . . This all means great waste of money and, as the hygienists tell us, still greater injury to health." If Americans could only shake the matter of taste, Atwater suggested, they would be far better off: "Appetite would be a better guide," he added, "if it were not for the demands of the palate."[42] It was continually irksome to Atwater that the palate had such a strong hold, because it destroyed people's ability to resist the temptations of abundance. "Food is plenty," he wrote a few years later. "Holding to a tradition which had its origin where food was less abundant, that the natural instinct is the measure of what we should eat, we follow the dictates of the palate. Living in the midst of abundance, our diet has not been regulated by the restraints which obtain with the great majority of the people of the Old World, where food is dear and incomes are small."[43]

The question of overabundance was so central to Atwater's philosophy that it formed the basis for a grand plan for wiping out poverty by whittling down American eating habits. "What is to be done for the future maintenance of the position of our laboring people at home and in their competition with others in the markets of the world?" he wrote. "Part of the answer, at any rate, must be sought in a reform in the purchase and use of food. Instead of our present wastefulness, there must be future saving. With increase of population and closer competition with the rest of the world, the abundance which tempts us to our lavishness must grow gradually less, and closer economy will be needed for living on our present plane of nutrition."[44]

Other doctors and writers joined Atwater in attempting to stem the perceived American penchant for overindulgence. One doctor, writing in an 1897 article entitled "Popular Errors in Living and Their Influence Over the Public Health," presented an equation that has wide currency today: the idea that the bounty that surrounds us, rather than being a source of strength or dietary diversity or legitimate pleasure, will tempt us unto death. "Another error to be noted," he wrote, "consists in the excessive quantity of food consumed. . . . The quantity of food that many people *naturally* eat is very large as compared with their actual physiological requirements; add to this the many tempting forms in which food is presented to the palate by our modern culinary arts, the sharpening of the appetite by the ante-prandial cocktail, the stimulus afforded the appetite by a bottle of good wine, and the result is often the consumption of an amount of food that simply overwhelms the assimilative organs. . . . It should, therefore, excite no special surprise that so large a proportion of our well-to-do people die from Bright's disease, heart failure, and allied diseases at fifty or fifty-five, who should, and under properly regulated lives and habits would, have attained the natural ages of seventy or over. . . . The truth is that the well-to-do man of to-day lives in a faster age than that of his father and grandfather; he meets with greater opportunities and possibilities, and therefore greater stimulus to all his energies; he more easily acquires pecuniary resources, and in larger amounts, and therefore he possesses greater luxuries of domestic life. With these come greater temptations to excess."[45]

Another manifestation of the campaign against overnutrition was the shift in ideas about protein intake. This shift was first popularized by a health faddist named Horace Fletcher, who proposed that the key to most health problems was a failure to chew one's food adequately. Fletcher proposed chewing each mouthful one hundred times, a time-consuming system that resulted in, among other things, much lower food intakes. His ideas—so popular that they were translated into the verb "to fletcherize"—had a great impact on the physiologist Russell H. Chittenden, the first director of Yale University's Sheffield School of Science and later author of *The Nutrition of Man*. Chittenden invited Fletcher into his lab for extensive tests, and observed that he was able to maintain his weight on much less food and protein than had been thought necessary—much less, even, than advised by Atwater. Chittenden went on to investigate further, and eventually recommended that everyone reduce protein intake by two-thirds, commenting that "the taking of an excess of food is just as harmful as insufficient nourishment, involving as it does not only wasteful expenditure, but what is of even greater moment, an expenditure of energy in the part of the body which may in the long run prove disastrous."[46] Chittenden was joined by other doctors and researchers, among them John Harvey Kellogg and Professor Henry C. Sherman, author of *The Chemistry of Food and Nutrition*, in his campaign against excess protein.

Diet-fad historian Hillel Schwartz sees in this prevailing fear of overabundance the roots of what he calls "the American crusade against fatness,"[47] and while he gives some credit for this to Atwater and the doctors, he feels the domestic scientists played a key role in translating that fear from the general to the personal. "As a system of household science," he writes in *Never Satisfied*, "as a means for precise internal regulation, domestic economy instilled a truly new fear of abundance which extended from the larder to the human body itself. While housewives had long been accustomed to the world as a rich, messy space of spontaneous eruptions, plentiful attachments and supervening bodies, home economists urged a clean, lean, purposeful flow."[48] The key to taming the problems of overabundance was control—both self-control and the control exerted by rules, by scientific lists of food values and appropriate "dietaries," by the ascendance of correctness over taste, defeating the willful tyranny of the palate.

Today, it also seems universally agreed that we take in too much of everything (except vegetables and fruits, of which we take in too little). America's afflictions are now often called the "diseases of affluence"—cancers, heart disease, strokes, diabetes. "Nearly everyone agrees that there are virtually no deficiencies in the American diet," proclaims an FDA spokesman. "The problems today are from overnutrition."[49] Says another nutrition researcher: "We eat too much protein. We've clearly gone over the deep end and it's got to be moved back to a diet that's more fit to the way we evolved."[50] "The reality is that most Americans actually get too much protein," concurs a writer for a healthy-eating guide. "We need surprisingly little compared to what we actually get. Protein is abundant in the food supply. And too much of a good thing can be dangerous."[51] The *New York Times* proclaimed the overabundance fear a trend in a 1990 article entitled "The New Nutrition: Protein on the Side," in which a restaurant consultant was quoted as saying, "The best-educated, most affluent people in America want to pay top-dollar to eat a third-world diet."[52]

Protein, of course, runs as a second to the top fear of too much fat in our affluent diet. "The problem most Americans face is not undernutrition," claims a magazine article entitled "Foods and Immunity." "Our diets err on the side of too much, not too little, and the biggest problem is the enormous fat content of the foods we eat."[53] A few years ago a coalition of thirty-eight federal health agencies got together to announce that all Americans over the age of two should reduce the amount of fat they eat (a conclusion opposed by some doctors and researchers who were not convinced that such a diet was best for everyone).[54] A magazine writer whose weight has swung from low to high describes what is known in the laboratory as a cafeteria diet—a diet that features many different foods, which tends to encourage overeating—and laments: "The modern world is one grand multiethnic cafeteria. The modern world is designed to make you overeat and then ostracize you when you do."[55] Linda Weintraub, director of the Edith C. Blum Art Institute at Bard College, comments that "in a culture where food is abundant, the lean body is glorified for its discipline."[56]

There is in all of this an element of head-hanging, a smidgen of guilt: Despite our persistent national problems with poverty and homelessness, we are essentially a nation of abundance—hamburgers, convenience foods, high-fat dairy products. When third-world countries get richer, their diets become more like the American diet and their death rates go up; they begin to suffer from the diseases of affluence and abundance. Those early-death rates appear to be almost a punishment for enjoying ourselves too much. The answer that emerges from many of these sources, time and again, is to exert control. We must regulate our fat and protein intakes and, consciously turning our tastes back to the "third-world" diet that the rest of the world is trying to leave behind, rediscover the joys of deprivation.

Saved by a Bell Pepper

There is one other, perhaps more appealing, answer to the overabundance dilemma, a solution proposed particularly persuasively by those in the food industry but also by hopeful researchers and nutritionists: the idea that by consuming certain perfect and health-giving foods we can negate the effects of over-nutrition. The best example of this is the oat bran phenomenon of the late 1980s. The same impulse that drove a nation to consume oat bran–enhanced muffins and pretzels and potato chips has threatened to make phenomenons as well out of psyllium and beta-carotene, and also drives the current new wave of fascination with vitamin supplements. The idea of magic foods is attractive for obvious reasons. If they were truly magic they would allow us to eat whatever we want and yet still outwit the looming dangers of food: killer fats and cholesterol, excessive protein and sugar, all of the things that make foods taste good but that we repeatedly murmur we know we should cut down on.

The appeal of this notion leads to curious occurrences: a broccoli fad, for instance. (Broccoli has been increasingly cited as a weapon against disease, particularly cancer, most recently because it contains a chemical called sulforaphane, which appears to prevent tumor formation. One grocery store manager said his sales of broccoli increased 50 percent in the first two weeks after the news media reported on the sulforaphane studies, and over the last decade broccoli sales have gone up 33 percent.[57]) That same appeal led 74 percent of Pepsi drinkers surveyed by an advertising agency in the late 1980s to say they would switch to Coke if it had oat bran in it, and leads husbandry experts to try to rewrite the recipe for one of nature's most self-contained foods, the egg, in hopes of lowering its cholesterol content and thus making it less sinful.[58] Marketers dream of the day when they can freely tout all kinds of life-saving qualities on food packages, going far beyond today's "low-fat" blandishments: frozen carrots, high in beta-carotene, that could prevent cancer or heart disease; bread made with flaxseed, which contains omega-3 fatty acids and could also fight heart disease or cancer; hot dogs with commercial gums replacing most of the fat, which one could argue might help fight those same diseases by promoting a lower overall fat intake.

The Victorians also deified certain foods in the hope of redeeming their culinary sins. The current articles touting sulforaphane and beta-carotene have their echo in magazines and books published at the end of the last century, though of course the particulars differ—and the evidence for the perfect foods of the 1890s often rested on data as preliminary and sketchy as the various studies that we eagerly accept as gospel today. "The physiological effects of the grape are significant," wrote Dr. M. L. Holbrook, professor of hygiene at the New York Medical College and Hospital for Women, in his 1888 manual *Eating for Strength; or, Food and Diet in Their Relation to Health and Work.* "Eaten with other suitable food, and especially with bread in quantities of from one to two pounds daily, they increase nutrition, promote secretion and excretion, improve the action of the liver, kidneys and bowels, and add to the health. . . . The dextrine of the grape promotes the secretion of pepsine, and this favors digestion. . . . The phosphoric acid, of which there is considerable, acts most favorable on all the bodily functions, and especially on the brain. . . . Grapes have been found excellent in cases of diarrhea, a result possibly due to the tannin, but it cannot be entirely owing to this substance." Holbrook goes on to prescribe a Grape Cure that consists of eating between three and eight pounds of grapes daily, and quotes other doctors who claim that grapes can be effective in treating diseases of the digestive organs, bronchial catarrh, scrofula, lung complaints, asthma, enlargement of the spleen, fever, urinary infections, Bright's disease of the kidneys, and tuberculosis.[59]

M. A. Boland, in her 1893 *Popular Science* article, even suggested that the right diet might prevent insanity. She described the then-popular practice of "stuffing," in which sufferers of melancholia, ailments of the nerves, or even hallucinations and "acute mania," were put to bed and fed quantities of "as much nutritious and wholesome food as they can be made to eat." "What woman," Miss Boland went on to ask, "with the belief that it was within the bounds of the probable for her to save a member of her family from even the possibility of any form of insanity, would not devote months, even years, to the study of those principles and conditions of life by which robust health may be maintained? It should not be understood that I would imply that bad food is the cause of insanity, but it can be said that we have sufficient proof to lead us to believe that many cases of insanity might have been prevented had the individuals been properly nourished."[60]

Perhaps one reason for the resonance of the healing-foods ethic in both eras—the common wish to heal as if by magic so that one does not, in the end, have to heal by deprivation—is that both times featured a deep fissure between appearance and reality, between what one says and what one does. Spokesmen and ordinary people alike in both epochs have given much lip service to the ideas of self-control and self-denial in the name of health, and yet both the 1890s and the 1990s are also characterized by scenes of great culinary indulgence. Stories are legion, for example, of the laden tables and multiple-course dinners of even the most middle-class of Victorians—not to mention the gargantuan feasts thrown for the wealthy. Here is the menu for a dinner for thirty people at Delmonico's restaurant in New York, in 1880, given in honor of General Winfield Scott Hancock, soon to be the Democratic party's nominee in that year's presidential election: raw oysters; choice of two soups; hors d'oeuvre; fish course; *relevés*—saddle of lamb and filet of beef; *entrées*—chicken wings with green peas and lamb chops garnished with beans and mushroom-stuffed artichokes; Terrapin *en casserole à la Maryland*; sorbet to clear the palate; "roast" course—canvasback ducks and quail. Desserts: *timbale Madison*; array of ice cream, whipped creams, jellied dishes, banana mousse, fruit, and *petit fours* (this menu reflects also

America's recent discovery of French haute cuisine).[61]

While today's eaters are not as comfortable with open displays of huge amounts of food, our records of consumption indicate a furtive indulgence of fairly generous proportions. For all our talk of cutting back and cutting out, our efforts have not taken us very far. Since the late 1970s we have consumed much less palm and coconut oil (heavily saturated fats), and somewhat less whole milk, beef, and butter. On the other hand, in the same time frame we've consumed about 40 percent more cheese, cream, and sour cream and dips, and more than 50 percent more salty snacks.[62] Our eating patterns are full of such contradictions. While many people cite the rise in the consumption of chicken, which is somewhat less fatty than beef, as evidence that Americans are becoming more nutritionally sophisticated, 52 percent of the chicken consumed in restaurants in 1991 was fried—not a method of preparation that is likely to lower one's overall fat intake (and that percentage was up four points from 1988).[63] Consumption of premium ice creams (which have much more fat than regular brands), pizza, and the perennial favorite, sugar, are continually on the rise. Burger King sells two million Whopper hamburgers per day. In the summer of 1992 the *New York Times* reported on a restaurant trend toward gargantuan portions; "It may seem paradoxical in this belt-tightening, cholesterol-counting, treadmill-thumping age," wrote food critic Bryan Miller, "but there is a growing movement among many restaurants to serve food portions that could choke a python."[64]

Every survey on food consumption notes this paradox: what people say and what they eat are two different things. One business writer commented in early 1991: "To the frustration of many a market researcher, the consumer is a health-conscious Dr. Jekyll when answering surveys, but a junk-food-loving Mr. Hyde when fork comes to mouth."[65] In 1992 the *New York Times* reported that a recent survey conducted for Weight Watchers Frozen Foods had found that "among consumers who said they were most concerned about dietary cholesterol and fat, consumption of such high-fat foods as regular cheese, hot dogs, gravy, ham, pork, eggs, beef and mayonnaise was not affected. In addition, 84 percent of those most concerned about cholesterol and fat selected regular cheese as their top dairy product."[66] This having-it-both-ways makes marketing a dicey business, because there is little logic in the conflicted desire of American consumers to both eat whatever they want and eat what will make them live forever. So Kentucky Fried Chicken scores a success selling Lite 'n Crispy skinless fried chicken that, because it is still coated with batter and deep-fried, is only infinitesimally lighter than old-fashioned fried chicken, but Pizza Hut completely flops with a light pizza.[67] A columnist for the trade magazine *Food and Beverage Marketing* devoted a column to the phenomenon: "If everyone's trying to cut down on sugar and artificial color, how do we account for such cereals as Dinky Donuts and Breakfast with Barbie? . . . Rich taste in a cigarette, beer, or liquor is good, but mention it in the context of food and it's considered unhealthy. If we all seem to be on a diet and we all spend time in the health club, how do we account for the success of Ben and Jerry's, Häagen Dazs, and cheesecakes? How can the same people who gorge themselves on gourmet ice cream drink diet sodas?"[68]

But he's missing the point: A prime reason for having diet soda in existence at all is to compensate for other indulgences— it's an equation, a numerical trade-off, and perhaps a little game we play with ourselves. Thanks to Atwater we know that a 1-calorie soda leaves a hole that a 500-calorie piece of pie could fill. Perhaps if we weren't quite so determined, in our Dr. Jekyll persona, to turn food into medicine, to rein in our sins and impose control over many quite natural impulses (such as the occasional longing for a piece of cheesecake), we wouldn't need to be quite so ravenous in our Mr. Hyde incarnation. Maybe all that time in the health club, and all those 250-calorie packages of Healthy Choice nutritious frozen entrées or slabs of rubbery fat-free cheese, inevitably lead to secret Häagen Dazs pig-outs. Julia Child is convinced that that is the case. "The main reason we have so many fat people, in my opinion," she says, "is they're eating terrible food for their meals—frozen TV dinners and things like that—and they're not satisfied, so then they snack. And they're never really satisfied, so they keep snacking. If they ate a properly cooked, good, satisfying, delicious meal, they wouldn't want to snack."

Of course, with all the highly touted nutritional information that floods the media almost daily, it's getting harder to know what a proper meal is anymore. (Hence a statistic like this: a survey by the National Consumers League found that 52 percent of people check the fat content on food labels, but only 1 percent make sure the serving size on the label is what they actually eat.[69]) But such confusion is only part of the problem. Americans may not particularly *want*, at the bottom of all this open concern about the healthfulness of their food, to eat a proper meal. With magic foods we can cling instead to the idea of a nutritional swap: a nonfat meal, or a psyllium meal, or a beta-carotene meal, that leaves the way open to later sinning of a higher order. Similarly, the Victorian anxiety about their widespread "dyspepsia," along with their scientific cooking and counting of nutrients, coexisted with and perhaps tried to compensate for a style of eating that often verged on the gluttonous.

Such powerful contradictions, in both eras, suggest at heart a continuing struggle over control—over one's runaway desires, one's life, one's death. If that inner battle is as fierce now as it was in the days of Atwater's strict pronouncements, perhaps it is because the goal is, in some way, false; such complete control cannot be claimed. So we seek it in smaller ways: in the 1890s, a food chart in the kitchen and sanitary cans of evaporated milk in the cupboard; in the 1990s, no-cholesterol mayonnaise and a fast-food hamburger constructed partly out of seaweed. In neither time has this seemed quite enough.

Chapter Two

•

FOODS FROM THE LAB
Building the Illusion of Fat

•

There may be no other product more emblematic of our complicated inner struggle over "good" and "bad" foods than fat substitutes. These synthetic doppelgangers are being cooked up in corporate labs across the country both to assuage our guilt over indulgence and to provide a way of continuing that indulgence indefinitely. In this model, technology supersedes nature. No sooner was the issue raised by scientific discoveries showing that fat can be bad for you and that we consume too much of it than a scientific solution was offered: Change the nature of the fat itself, and consumers can eat a carton of not-really-ice-cream without fear.

Almost every major food company has perceived the blinding commercial potential for such a magic product, making this one of the most competitive arenas in the food-technology business. But as scientists hover over secretly constructed processing machines taste-testing new batches of nonfat treats, there is another machine that may yet trip up their efforts to cash in on our longings: the still-mysterious human body.

•

Norm Singer, the inventor of the first FDA-approved fat substitute, is a disciplined man when it comes to diet. He counts calories, has weaned himself from whole milk all the way down to skim, rarely touches sugar, and treats himself to a tuna salad plate for lunch at the local burger joint. Although he calls himself a "chocoholic" (or perhaps because he so labels himself), his chocolate consumption is minimal and his chocolate rewards carefully meted out: "I eat the equivalent of a one-dollar chocolate bar over a period of two months," he says. "But I savor every little bite." Faced with the offer of a french fry or two over lunch, he declines unhesitatingly: "No, no. If I had one I'd eat the whole plateful."

As a man who is not only intimately acquainted with the sensual pleasure of food but openly appreciative of it, Singer is scornful of those who downplay its importance. The phrase "hedonic gratification," applied to eating, crops up frequently in his conversation, as do less academic expressions of gustatory satisfaction—"delicious!" "delightful!" "wonderful!" These two attitudes toward food would seem utterly contradictory were it not for the nature of Singer's work, which is to combine both—control and abandon, self-denial and self-indulgence—in products that purvey what he calls a "sensory illusion." That is the illusion of fat—creamy, smooth, lingering in the mouth, and, lately, much reviled as the most malign of food ingredients.

Fat may or may not be malign, but it has proven to be difficult to mimic. To create Simplesse, the fat substitute he developed at the NutraSweet Company, Singer had to break apart the experience of eating fat—to analyze the joy and desire of it right down to the molecular level. He described this years-long process to me in his office at the Research and Development branch of NutraSweet, a low, sprawling, modern building located in the neatly squared-off Chicago suburb of Mount Prospect. A serious man whose expression is only occasionally lightened by a flash of wry humor, Singer sports a mustache and small goatee, both beginning to gray, and modified aviator-frame glasses. Although he says he has "fought the battle of the bulge" all his life, the only evidence of that is a slight heaviness around the middle. His office is modest, lined with shelves of scientific journals and books on subjects like "gums for food products," but beyond it lies his true workspace: a labyrinth of laboratories and technical areas devoted to tinkering with and producing Simplesse. These house the futuristic tools of modern food technology: microscopes equipped with computers that digitize and count particles of proteins and fat globules; an atomic microscope that needs no lenses and no lights, reading the shape and dimensions of a sample "like a blind man feeling the surface," according to Singer; a machine that tests the firmness of foods down to the minutest level, detecting precise differences in, say, the firmness of egg white versus the firmness of milk whey; machines with robotic arms that instantaneously analyze foods for proteins, fats, carbohydrates; a mainframe computer that takes up an entire floor, keeps track of everything from fermentation in the labs to the results of blind taste tests, and is tightly protected from corporate spies by an elaborate security system. All of this impressive technology is directed at a goal of equally ambitious proportions, as Singer presents it: to tinker with some of the most basic rules of nature in order to enable people to live, in effect, more naturally—that is, in tune with their natural longings for physical pleasure and comfort, longings many people, even Singer himself, have been at pains to suppress.

The sophisticated machinery that he uses in this quest actually comes in only at the final stage—the quantified and controlled result of the very personal experience that begins at the mouth, when the tongue presses a dollop of ice cream (or a dollop of nonfat "frozen dessert," such as the NutraSweet Company's Simple Pleasures, which is made with Simplesse) against the hard palate in search of the very particular sensation of creaminess. Singer has entered into the experience of creaminess on more levels than the average eater, even the gourmand, would consider necessary. There is, certainly, the physical level: mouth-feel, textures, flavor, sense of substantialness or fullness, firmness, aftertaste, lubricity. Singer seems constantly in search of the example that demonstrates most precisely the perception of fat, of creaminess. One of his favorites has to do with cashews. He elaborated on the cashew test in his office, leaning back in his chair and sipping his tea. "One of the experiments I invite new employees to do, to think about creaminess and all its dimensions," said Singer, "is to eat a quarter-pound of cashews. Cashew starts out crunchy, and turns quickly into a heavy paste which then turns into a heavy cream which then turns into a light cream, as you chew on it, and when it's about at a light cream you swallow. And it's magic, because it's the only nut that really does that. That creaminess, from a dry, crunchy beginning, it's a very pleasing kind of experience."

That is only one of many experiments that Singer is constantly suggesting, as a way of illustrating this or that point. Put a drop of vanilla into cream, he said, and a drop into nonfat milk— the former will smell richly of vanilla, the latter will smell vaguely artificial and chemical. (That's why making a good nonfat vanilla frozen dessert was extremely difficult. "Vanilla is a unique flavor," said Singer. "Getting from strawberry to a good vanilla was like going uphill, uphill against water coming down.") Or, after blocking your sense of smell, taste a cube of apple and a cube of potato and see if you can tell the difference. (They're almost indistinguishable, although "if you were a very astute taster, you would say, 'They're both crunchy and moist and so on, but this crunchy moist substance I have here also gives me a powdery mouth-feel afterwards, whereas this other one doesn't.' " This shows both the importance of aroma in determining taste, and the grainy, powdery texture that results from the large particles that make up starches like potato.) Or, notice the next time you eat a chocolate bar that the last feeling you have as you swallow is one of powderiness. (That's because the particles of sugar, milk protein, cocoa protein, and so on are, unlike the particles in dairy cream, large enough to be sensed by your tongue.) Or, take a Dairy Queen soft-serve home, seal it, and put it in the freezer for two or three days; what you will find is "nothing at all like the Dairy Queen you had. It will be coarse, icy, thinner-feeling. A pretty junky experience." (That's because the tiny ice crystals and air bubbles, which give the soft-serve its texture, have hardened and coalesced.)

Singer's job, in part, is to constantly quantify, describe, deconstruct taste, to peel the experience of food down to its inner mechanisms. Thus, perhaps, his predilection for the concrete example, the do-it-yourself taste experiment. But he also approaches the puzzle of fat—its essence, and the perception of that essence—on a level beyond the physical, on what might be called the mental, almost the philosophical, level. Creating a fat substitute, he said, "is a problem in classical gestalt psychology. If you can provide enough of the pieces of the impression so that the consumer can unthinkingly complete the pattern, then it's the same experience. If you leave too many points out, then the consumer, the experiencer, is left with a puzzle. What happened here? What's going on? It's a perceptual dissonance."

Singer seems to enjoy toying with the question of what precisely determines our experience of taste and texture, and in doing so he is not wedded to the obvious. When considering a substitute for deep-fat frying he pointed out, "There are other ways of getting the effect of crunchy outside and moistness inside. That's what we want—we don't necessarily want food out of this rancid oil, what we want is the joy of the crunchy surface and the moist interior, and the specific flavors that are created at those temperatures. Delightful! But there are other ways of achieving that."

Singer takes his philosophy of fake fats one step beyond gestalt, beyond the experience of fat and creaminess, to a justification for the experience itself. "Food is not just a source of nourishment," he said. "It is also a very important source of a special kind of hedonic gratification—a special kind. Food needs to be pleasing in order to help us achieve that state of comfort with the world that we are designed to approach. Now we're no longer concerned about the classic problems of food—which are, one, getting any, and two, being killed by that which you got, either in the process of getting it or because you kept it too long under the wrong conditions and it became toxic. Those were the problems for millions of years. Now we have different kinds of problems. And there are people who would say, well, we just have to become more ascetic and live without these things. That's baloney. In order to improve people's health—which I think is more important than improving their moral fiber—you should make it easier for them to do the right thing. It's difficult for people who are young and healthy to visualize how limiting life can be when you start cutting out, start eliminating, some of the—it's the reason we named our product this—the simple pleasures of life. When you get rid of those, your life gets harsher, sterner, colder. There are very few things in our lives that we can do for ourselves that produce the kinds of pleasant feelings that good food can."

That belief in technology as a flexible and ever-expanding solution to what Singer sees as the twentieth-century problem of food—craving that which is not healthy to eat—is a faith shared by many other food manufacturers. In fact, the illusion of creaminess that Singer has been working to conjure is a highly prized commodity these days, as the words "low-fat" and "nonfat" become potent marketing tools. "Nonfat" alone is clearly not sufficient; plenty of foods have very little fat—beans, rice, vegetables, fruits. Those foods are not, to use the word Singer often employs about Simplesse, magic. What is magic is nonfat but fatlike, nonfat but you'd never know it. When Singer created Simple Pleasures, he tried to model its taste experience after Häagen Dazs, a premium brand of ice cream that has twice as much fat as ordinary ice cream.

The perfect fat substitute, the one that exactly reproduces the sensations of fat and is applicable to many different products, is the grail in this particular search. Many of the largest food companies have joined the quest—Procter & Gamble, Pepsico, Frito-Lay, Nabisco, Kraft, Quaker. And although Simplesse was the first to gain FDA acceptance (others have used more common ingredients that did not require direct FDA approval), no one, not even Singer, its creator, claims that it is yet a perfect match for fat. Reproducing the experience of fat has in fact turned out to be an extremely daunting project, and in the eyes of most financial analysts the fat-substitute market has yet to live up to its potential.

Embedded in Singer's eloquence on the innovative technology of Simplesse's fat mimicry is a certain measure of defensiveness, for many in the food business have used Simplesse as an example of how not to handle a fat substitute, citing faulty business judgment and promises of quality that the product has not fulfilled. Singer puts the best face on Simplesse's bad press by pointing out that the fat substitute is now being used in other products, including cheese, and insisting that Simple Pleasures in some flavors actually tastes *better* than Häagen Dazs. But Simplesse has certainly failed to duplicate the NutraSweet Company's raging success with aspartame (the artificial sweetener brand-named NutraSweet), which swept the food industry in the 1980s.[1]

Simplesse's troubles may be emblematic of the problems inherent in trying to imitate fat, which most researchers agree is a more complex experience than the experience of sweetness. And despite Singer's elaborate dissection of the physical workings of our apprehension of creaminess, there remain unanswered questions about how fat operates in the human body. It may be, some researchers have suggested, that it is easier to fool the mind than the body; that however much we may want to keep our diets lean and still eat something that resembles ice cream, our bodies—the focus of all this solicitude and expensive technology—are not so easily satisfied.

Norm Singer seems most comfortable speaking of particulars, especially the physical particulars of the way things work. His description of how a food that is fat free might taste and feel as if it were plump with butterfat thus begins with a quick tour through the basic molecular structure of cream, the substance that Simplesse aims to reproduce. That structure, he explained, is central to understanding the "magic" of Simplesse. "Dairy cream is made of little globules of butterfat floating in milk," he began. "Every globule has a jacket, a thin membrane, of protein. It's the protein that keeps the globules dispersed in the milk; without that membrane the globules would band together the way oil drops normally do when you mix them with water. Now, that means that our first physical contact with cream is actually a contact with protein rather than with the butterfat itself. So, say you could go into those fat globules and make the fat disappear—Scottie, beam out the fat—and beam in more protein, leaving the membrane the same. The first impression would be the same—you'd be sensing the protein jacket. That, essentially, is Simplesse. We've created particles that are similar in size to fat globules, we introduce them into a food so that they're about as dense a population as the fat globules would have been. And lo and behold, we get a food which is very much like what it would be if it had fat in it. In appearance, in spoonability, in mouth-feel."

That is the broad brush-stroke of Simplesse, the founding principle. Perfecting the illusion demanded a further manipulation of nature, and in this the tongue plays a leading role. "The way humans experience creaminess," explained Singer, "is that the food in question is pressed by the tongue against the hard palate and/or the back of the upper teeth. When that happens, considerable pressure is exerted, and you end up with a very thin layer squeezed out. It appears that one reason for this is to sense any particulateness—perhaps because, in an evolutionary, survival sense, particulateness or powderiness signals unripeness, before the starches have been converted to sugars. The absence of powderiness is a very pleasing experience; we call it smoothness.

"What the tongue senses when it presses cream against the palate is a collection of fat globules that are each about ten microns in diameter, and that compress under the force of the tongue. Now, if you were to have ten-micron-size bits of a gelled protein like Simplesse instead of the fat globules, those gelled bits are firmer than fat globules and the substance would feel kind of sandy to the tongue. We found that in order to evade detection, in order to feel smooth, a gelled protein has to be smaller than ten microns; it has to be about three microns. But if on the other hand you get particles that are too small—less than a tenth of a micron—there's a lack of what I suggest should be called substance. Picture the difference between drinking a mouthful of whole-fat milk and then a mouthful of nonfat milk; the nonfat milk is kind of watery and empty. It's made up of particles that are less than a tenth of a micron, and the result is it doesn't give that feeling of substantialness. So we found a window: Below about a tenth of a micron, there's no substance, it's like water. Above two to three microns, it's powdery or chalky or gritty. But between those two values you have both substance and the absence of the sense of particles. And that's what makes Simplesse effective—that's the magic. When those two things are superimposed on the mind, the conclusion that's reached is, Oh, that's creamy."

Despite the logic that is implied by these calculations, the genesis of what is now Simplesse lay in a scientific side-trip, a digression in search of an utterly different result. It was the late 1970s, and dietary fat was not of great general interest. Singer was working for the Canadian company John Labatt, Ltd., maker of beer and, at that time, owner of many other food-manufacturing subsidiaries as well. As one of many research tasks, Singer was given a problem to solve: Find a use (preferably a profitable use) for the huge lake of whey, a byproduct of cheese making, outside the Labatt's subsidiary cheese company in the picturesque town of Winchester, Ontario. Singer obliged by finding a way to separate out lactose syrup from the whey to serve as a carbohydrate source for the yeast that produced Labatt's beer.

But that left the whey protein, a product for which no one could think of any use at all. Singer suggested further research, just in case he and his colleagues could find something more profitable than throwing it in the garbage. After several experimental dead ends, they began looking at the gelling ability of whey protein, as a possible substitute for egg white. "After all," said Singer, "egg white was at the time going for about three dollars a pound, and whey protein was at the time worth about fifty cents a pound; it seemed like this was a way of making some money."

What his team came up with was a gel, but it was nothing like egg white. "Where gelled egg white breaks like glass, a nice, smooth, vitreous break, this stuff broke more like a Styrofoam coffee cup," said Singer. "I picked up a piece of the broken gel and popped it in my mouth. In the food industry, you've got to taste things; you've got to taste and feel and smell. And—son of a gun, what's this? I was expecting egg white and what I got was more like cream cheese. That was a real surprise." Singer ran the sample down to the microscope lab. "I'd seen lots of food structures," he said, "but I'd never seen one like this." What he saw were two types of particles: smaller particles that rolled around like ball bearings, and larger particles that seemed to be made up of the smaller ones welded together. When Singer squeezed the cover slip, the structures flexed but didn't break up. "So I figured maybe the small ball-bearing things give kind of a creamy texture and the large curdy pieces give a curdy texture, and together cream and curd is cream cheese," said Singer. The first thing he did, after force-feeding it to his boss (who thought it was cream cheese, al-beit bad cream cheese), was send a description of it to the com-pany's patent attorney.

That was the beginning of what Singer called micro-curd. He spent a percentage of his time over the next several years improv-ing the formula—making new machinery, changing the cooking temperature, altering the ingredients, and eventually, using it as an ingredient in new test-food products. In the midst of this work, in the early 1980s, Labatt restructured and eventually closed down its corporate research department. When Singer accepted a job at NutraSweet in 1983 he convinced the company to buy from La-batt's the micro-curd patent he had developed. The reason for making a frozen dessert as the first micro-curd product (Singer's original idea had been mayonnaise and salad dressings) was sim-ple: it would be the most profitable. When it comes to dollar-value, the fat in ice cream is much more valuable than the fat in mayon-naise, pound for pound. Presumably, if consumers will pay top dollar for sinfully delicious ice cream, they will pay at least as much for the ice cream without the sin.

Singer's recipe for Simplesse (as it came to be called after Nu-traSweet's marketing department got its hands on it) has evolved over the years, but it rests upon a fairly simple principle. The whey protein is subjected to both cooking and cutting (known as "shear"), similar to the high-speed cutting that occurs in a blender. What is happening is simultaneous homogenization, in which the fat globules of milk (in this case, the protein globules of the whey) are broken down into much tinier globules that stay suspended in liquid; and pasteurization, in which heat is used to kill disease organisms. As a result of these dual processes, the protein globules aggregate to the size that fits Singer's window of sensory creaminess, somewhere between one-tenth of a micron and two to three microns. What comes out of the machine looks, says Singer, "like a double cream, heavy cream." The machine itself is what he calls "a proprietary device"; in other words, something he invented that still occasions a fair amount of secrecy.

Every food manufacturer worries about protecting his secret recipe from competitors, but in the highly technological area of food substitutes the problem of security amounts almost to an obsession. "You practice a sort of professional paranoia," says Singer. "You assume that anyone you talk to is married to someone who's in charge of research at a competitor's place; you keep that model in mind. Because one time out of fifty or a hundred it could be something close to the truth." Singer's secrecy even threatened what he calls a "lifelong friendship" with someone else in the business; when his friend found out that Singer had been working on the Simplesse project for ten years without ever telling him about it, says Singer, "he felt very hurt. It took him about a year to get over it. But you have to do that."

The Simplesse people went so far as to create, through biotechnology, an antibody that would identify proteins with the specific structure of the proteins that make up Simplesse. If Simplesse technicians suspect a theft of their formula, they simply slip a sample of the offending matter under a microscope, apply the antibody (in a process called immunogold staining), and if it reacts with the sample, they get in touch with the legal department. "We have found a number of companies who are, they claim unwittingly, making Simplesse-like material in their food," says Singer. "In one case, it happened that they were suddenly able to do that after they were in a research agreement with us for six months. Now they're paying us a royalty. Immunogold staining is one of the tools in our arsenal, and the job becomes one of mounting a defense against the invasion of those who have no right to be there."

That Singer uses the metaphors of war here is no accident. In a field that has mushroomed in the last few years, the fighting—for customers and for reputation—is fierce. David Braff, president of the food-marketing firm Braff and Company in New York, offers this analogy: "In the Middle Ages, the alchemists' obsession was how to make gold out of lead; the person that actually, really, totally duplicates fat may have that possibility." The nonfat frozen-dessert market, currently perhaps the most visible segment, is only a small corner of a potential fat-substitute business that encompasses almost every food category—baked goods, processed meats, salad dressings, dairy items (yogurts, cheeses, butterlike spreads), and sauces. Dan Rizzo, former director of new products for A. E. Staley, who was with the company when it introduced a cornstarch-based fat substitute named Stellar, describes the incentive for food manufacturers in graphic dollar terms: "Everybody is trying to come up with the right fat replacer because we consume about 16 billion pounds of fat a year, 5 to 6 billion pounds of which is in processed foods. So if the low-fat or nonfat segment would replace, say, 20 percent of that fat in processed foods, that means there would be about a billion pounds of fat replaced per year. For hypothetical purposes, if all of that fat were replaced by the Stellar product, they'd be selling about 250 million pounds of Stellar a year, since one pound of Stellar replaces four pounds of fat. That's a significant size of market."

Rizzo has created a shorthand way of looking at the fat-substitute field, breaking it into three tiers. The first is what he calls "synthetic fat, a chemical synthesis of some ingredients that will actually look and act exactly like fat. It could be used in frying, salad oils, processed foods. That is the ideal fat replacer, but it will definitely require FDA approval." The next tier is the one inhabited by Staley's Stellar product: ingredients that are designed to replace fat within foods, usually by using existing food substances that have been manipulated in some way, and therefore not usually needing FDA approval. Within the food industry, these substances are known by the acronym GRAS—"generally recognized as safe." Stellar, for instance, is made by heating a mixture of cornstarch and water and adjusting the acid content in a way that breaks down certain parts of the starch molecule into a network of starch particles that mimic the particle formulation of cream. Simplesse could also be put into this category; the FDA has approved its use under GRAS guidelines.

What Rizzo calls the third tier of fat substitutes is the one Norm Singer derisively calls "old wine in new bottles." Rizzo is a little more polite, saying they are "existing technologies that have fat-sparing properties because of the incentive to replace fat." In other words, manufacturers take an ingredient that has been used for decades to make a food smoother or more solid or to perform one of many other functions, ingredients like starches or gums or emulsifiers or pectin, and find a way to use more of them in a food product, thus edging out a little more fat. These ingredients are indeed striving to breeze along on the coattails of the nonfat movement, and the further development of more technically sophisticated fat substitutes will probably make them obsolete.

In an effort to present Simplesse as dominating the current field of fat substitutes, Singer is wont to say that his product, which made its debut in February of 1990, was indisputably the first. "The low-fat movement really didn't take hold until February of eighty-eight," he says sweepingly. "It's a matter of documentable fact. We announced here at NutraSweet that we were working on Simplesse in late January of eighty-eight, and we have since had a number of folks tell us that the day after our announcement their research director in this, that, or the other company gave them marching orders." For some of the third-tier substitutes, that may be true. But at least one completely original fat substitute—olestra, made by Procter & Gamble—was in development as early as the 1970s, although it is still awaiting FDA approval. (Animal tests have shown various problems with olestra, including gastrointestinal distress.)[2] Singer considers olestra to be in a different category from Simplesse, because it can be used in high-temperature frying and baking, whereas Simplesse until recently was usable only in cold or frozen products. (A new generation of Simplesse can be cooked—for instance, a cheese made with

Simplesse can be melted on pizza—but it still cannot be used for deep-fat frying, as olestra can. Stellar can be baked after it has been incorporated into a product, but not for long or at high temperatures.)

Something else happened in 1988, as well, that might help account for the explosion of interest in low-fat products: the Surgeon General officially recommended that Americans reduce their fat consumption to 30 percent of calories (from an average of 40 percent) to help prevent heart disease and other chronic health problems. Awareness of dietary fat as a health concern jumped appreciably, translating rather quickly into a potential marketing focus. For instance, breakfast cereals that have always been fat free began advertising that fact on their packages—and, as it happens, manufacturers of those types of products are the only ones to truly profit, as yet, by the public enthusiasm for nonfat foods. "The people who are making the biggest bucks are the ones who were fat free to begin with, like Kellogg's with their Special K," remarks John McMillin, an analyst who follows the food industry for Prudential Securities. "The fact is, fat free sells. But everybody's in a spending phase right now with fat substitutes, nobody's in an earning phase. Everybody's trying to invent a better mousetrap. But we're in the first inning of the game, so to say who's winning or losing is not really a relevant question yet."

Simplesse's problem, says David Braff (whose firm has helped introduce other low-fat products, including Staley's Stellar fat substitute), was partly that it claimed to be a home run. "The product didn't perform well," Braff claims. "The public did not embrace the product—it didn't taste like Häagen Dazs, and that's how it was ballyhooed. It was somewhat gritty, it had taste problems." What's more, he adds, after raising expectations unrealistically high for the quality of Simplesse as a fat substitute, the NutraSweet Company then thwarted itself by bringing out Simple Pleasures, a product that would compete with other products that might otherwise have bought Simplesse as an ingredient to be used in their own frozen desserts. "Their idea of competing with their own potential customers was a flawed strategy," says Braff.

"Simplesse is a well-known product, because it was touted very highly, but it is not a particularly successful product."

Norm Singer bristles at questions of quality, and goes into elaborate descriptions of blind taste panels (which, he says, have scored Simple Pleasures coffee flavor higher than Häagen Dazs coffee) and the "psychological loading" that goes on if the tasting is not blind and the taster is expecting an inferior product. "There's been a lot written that confuses the hell out of me," he says, describing an article in a Washington, D.C., paper in which local gastronomes were fed various frozen desserts and asked for their comments. "They fed them right out of the containers," Singer says. "And one guy tasted Simple Pleasures and said, 'That's the worst thing I ever . . . !' Well, that's ridiculous. Nobody out of the thousands of people who've tasted under controlled circumstances, where they didn't know what they were eating, has ever responded that way."

The issue of taste is, in one sense, central; the American consumer has shown a growing predilection for richer, sweeter, "super-premium" products. But taste is also only the most conscious, accessible part of the fat-substitute experience. Once a bite of fat-laden or Simplesse-laden ice cream gets past the palate it is subject to a new universe of rules that researchers are just beginning to understand. No matter which of the many current competitors to reproduce fat manages to make the smoothest, subtlest, most butterlike confection, or manages to adapt its use to the most products, there is a deeper level of success that must be reckoned with—a level dictated completely and ruthlessly by the unthinking human body.

"Nothing is as good as fat," declares David Braff. "Fat is smooth, fat is tasty, fat performs well in cooking, it's marvelous stuff." The warring fat-substitute makers have set themselves a large challenge. There is a reason Norm Singer keeps circling back to the word "magic" in describing Simplesse; there is something magic about fat itself. For a lecture he gives, Singer has made a chart titled "Functions of Fat in Food," and it contains six head-ings—Heat Exchange Medium, Shortening, Rheological Control, Mouth-Feel, Flavor, Appearance—each with subheadings like Viscosity, Tenderness, Solvency, Opacity.

Fat is not only multitalented, it is still in many ways mysterious. Since the mid-1980s, when "low-fat" was first emerging as a high concept, researchers have been attempting to dissect fat, and humans' relationship to it, in a way that they had for many years been dissecting our relationship to sugar. (There is a very simple and practical reason for this: until recently sugars and starches received much of the blame for the persistent and ever-increasing American problem with obesity; now, fats are perceived as the more likely culprit, in addition to their newly perceived role in promoting cancer and heart disease.) Although much of this research is as yet more suggestive than it is conclusive, in delving into the mechanisms of fat it holds some clues to the central riddle of fat substitutes, as well—that is, whether substitutes can work the magic of fat in the human body without carrying its penalties.

First, there are the duties fat actually performs on a physical, sensory level. One function of fat is to "bind water," according to Adam Drewnowski, director of the Human Nutrition Program at the University of Michigan in Ann Arbor. This is how fat makes baked goods so soft and moist; it holds and stabilizes the water within the drier medium of the cake, a function that is difficult to reproduce with substitutes. Conversely, this is why ice creams tend to be successful candidates for fat substitution, says Drewnowski. "The products already contain a lot of water, so fat replacements can work very nicely. But when you put fat substitutes in solid foods, like bakery products, you have very variable success. Take the Entenmann's fat-free cakes, which use starches and gums to bind the water. They begin nicely; they're all right if they're freshly baked, but they dry out very quickly. Once you open a box you'd better eat the whole thing at once, because they have a very low shelf life."

Drewnowski points out another, more familiar function of fat in foods: it makes everything taste better. "Fats create richness of flavor by delivering flavor molecules to the palate, to the taste receptors," he says. Points out Mark Friedman, associate director of the Monell Chemical Senses Center in Philadelphia and a specialist in the study of appetite, "One of the reasons it's hard to reduce the amount of fat in your diet is that the food simply doesn't taste as good as it used to."

But there is another role that fat plays in the human body, on a deeper level than simple sensory pleasure, and it may hold another clue to why humans find fat so attractive: fat delivers calories in much higher density than do carbohydrates or proteins. That function appears to be prized by the body, however much it is decried by the mind. This is one area where substantial research has been done, and although many questions remain, one finding emerges again and again: animals prefer foods that deliver calories. The evolutionary reason for this is self-explanatory: calorie density makes for more efficient fuel, and more calories means more potential leftovers to go into fat storage for the lean months.

Anthony Sclafani, a professor of psychology at Brooklyn College and director of the college's Feeding Behavior and Nutrition Laboratory, has been looking at why animals seem to like fat, and in particular has tried, within that preference, to separate the sensory characteristics of fat from its nutritional qualities. What he has found is a two-pronged process: both an unlearned (perhaps innate) positive response to fat and a learned one. Sclafani found that baby rats, with no food experience beyond their mother's milk, showed a preference for an oil-and-water mixture over plain water. "We tested each animal only once, so we know their response was not conditioned by any nutritional effects, and we got the same response whether we used corn oil or a non-nutritive mineral oil," says Sclafani. "That suggests, although it's not definitive proof, that the rats may have an unlearned preference for the sensory qualities of fat."

That preference is enhanced by learning, according to Sclafani's research. In another experiment, Sclafani let rats drink Kool-Aid flavored water while putting corn oil into their stomachs, "so they're not tasting the corn oil but they're getting the nutritional benefit of the oil. The animals learned to prefer various

Kool-Aid flavors associated with the oil. So our working model is that there may be an unlearned or very early acquired preference for some of the sensory characteristics of fat, but also a conditioned preference, based on the nutritional effects of fat. These two, we think, combine in the adult animal so that our preference for fat is magnified by associating the flavor with the nutritional effects." A double whammy, in other words. Putting it in human terms, Mark Friedman comments: "Just as we can learn aversions to foods that make us ill, it looks like we learn preferences for foods that are satisfying, that provide the right metabolic payoff in terms of calories. We might attribute our liking of these foods to the flavor, when the liking could be due to the metabolic effect."

Adam Drewnowski postulates another potentially significant physiological inducement to eat fats, especially fats in conjunction with sugar: what is known as the "endogenous opioids" theory. Opioids, popularly known as endorphins, are morphinelike, pleasure-giving substances manufactured by the brain that appear to be released in response to various stimuli—including, according to some studies, certain foods. Drewnowski cites experiments in which rats' brains released opioids in response to eating chocolate, and others in which rats injected with morphine ate selectively more fat (that is, they did not eat more of all foods available to them, just more fat). One experiment that was safe to conduct using humans, in which subjects were injected with an opiate blocker used to wean addicts from opiates, showed that human preference for chocolate went down when opioid activity was blocked. Similarly, rats injected with opiate blockers still ate the same amount of laboratory chow, but ate less of the sugar-and-fat-filled cookies that were available to them. "It looks like sugar-fat mixtures, especially chocolate, somehow influence or are involved in the opiate peptide system," says Drewnowski. But other researchers are not yet convinced that there is literally an addictive quality to our liking for fats. Mark Friedman calls endogenous opioids "a sexy idea," but says, "I think at this point in time it's a leap of faith to go from people liking Häagen Dazs to the idea that it releases opioids."

Friedman has, however, found some evidence for yet another

mechanism that may contribute to a taste for fats, a sort of circular phenomenon in which the more fat we eat the more we want to eat. "Our work would suggest that the amount of fat in the diet might set the preference for fats," he explains. "With a high-fat, high-carbohydrate diet, what seems to happen is that more of the fat gets stored, when it really should be being burned. The appetite mechanism then misses those fats, because the appetite mechanism is paying attention to fuels that are actually burned. The appetite mechanism perceives this as a deficit, so you crave more fats."

Some of these theories have marshalled more evidence than others, but altogether they point to some powerful physiological inducements to eat fats. Whether these physical systems and preferences can be circumvented, or perhaps satisfied, by other, similar substances that don't carry the same nutritional baggage as fat, is, as Sclafani puts it, "the sixty-four-thousand-dollar question." Drewnowski adds, discouragingly, "It's a big, big question, and at the moment we have no idea. If you reach for Simplesse or another frozen dessert, the question is whether it gives you the same satisfaction at the central brain level that you would get from a Häagen Dazs full-fat ice cream with sugar, in terms of releasing peptides and calming you down and so on. The question is, are the cravings satisfied?"

But we do have some clues to whether the body can be fooled, and the answers so far would not be encouraging to the fat-substitute purveyors. Sclafani's rats, again, offer a few hints. When first given a choice between corn oil or mineral oil, the rats don't show a strong preference, but, says Sclafani, "when you give them experience, rats will rapidly learn to prefer the corn oil, presumably based on learning that it's got nutritional value and the mineral oil does not." Sclafani has also given rats an experimental drug that inhibits or slows down fat digestion, to see if fat is still as attractive to rats when it doesn't deliver as hefty or immediate a dose of calories to the body. The rats became less interested in fat when they were on the drug that inhibited its nutritional action. "Again, rats are very good at learning that you've done something to the fat and it's now less preferable to them," he says. Sclafani has even gone so far as to give rats a choice between Entenmann's fat-free cakes and the full-fat versions; they prefer the full-fat.

On both the rat and the human level, there is also the issue of compensation: does the body sense a temporary fat-intake deficit when substitutes are used, and urge greater consumption later to make up the difference? Mark Friedman cites blind studies that show exactly that behavior in humans. "There have been studies done recently—two in adults and one in children—where the amount of fat in one meal was replaced with fat substitutes, without the subjects knowing of it, and both the adults and the children compensated for the calories that were lost. So, at least in casual use of low-fat foods—say reducing the fat in one meal a day—it looks like you can't fool the body. On the other hand, in experiments where people have no choice, where the only food available is low-fat, then they will reduce their overall calorie intake and lose weight, at least for a period of time."

But that, as Friedman points out, is not the "real world." In the real world, people have many high-fat choices available to them at all times, and they also have the one element that can never be translated into animal studies: what researchers call the cognitive aspect, which is perhaps the most complex issue in the fat-substitute business. Will fat substitutes do their job—lowering our overall consumption of fat and calories—when they're up against the wily contortions of the human mind?

Friedman has seen some research that indicates they won't. "One study found that if you tell people a particular meal is low in fat, they increase their food intake outside of that meal and wind up eating more." This is the kind of information that can practically be proven empirically on one's own, in the type of do-it-yourself experiment Norm Singer is fond of describing; this one might involve a pint of Ben and Jerry's (in the neighborhood of 16 percent) and a pint of nonfat Simple Pleasures. Knowingly lowering one's fat intake with substitutes also opens the door to dealmaking, along the order of: I had Simple Pleasures instead of Ben and Jerry's, so I can have cream cheese on my bagel.

Amidst these discouraging indications, there is one potential role for fat substitutes that researchers have pondered as a kind of blue-sky fantasy: perhaps they can be used to actually reset people's taste for fats, weaning us from what we crave by taking away the caloric bonus fats have traditionally offered. Friedman speculates, "The fact that you tend to like things that have this caloric impact, well, the converse would be that you won't like things as much that don't have it. So it's possible that you may come to dislike, or to like less, the foods that are low in fat or calories *because* they're low in fat or calories. You would be basically uncoupling the taste from the calories, and asking people to unlearn that connection." But this uncoupling could only work if it were uniform; that is, if all fats were substitutes, so that none of them carried that caloric benefit that makes them so attractive to the human metabolism. If only some of the fats were low-calorie ersatz fats, says Friedman, "There's no way people could unlearn that connection when they're eating a lot of other foods where those contingencies—fat equals calories—still hold."

There is actually, in the present-day real world, a way to reduce one's craving for fats, and that is to simply eat much less of them. But this solution, which has been supported by clinical research, may be actively sabotaged by the use of fat substitutes. "We've done studies that show that if you go on a low-fat diet you tend to prefer foods that are lower in fat," says Friedman. "That reaction shows up in two to three weeks. On the other hand, it's possible that if you maintain the sensory feel of fats in the diet, that may not happen. If we allowed the subjects to use a low-fat substitute for salad dressings, butter spreads, things like that, rather than just going without, they didn't seem to show the shift in preferences toward less fat as much as the others."

On the whole, current research into the complexities of fats appears to paint fat substitutes, at least as presently constituted, as rather superficial items—not a magic formula to repair the wayward American diet as much as a novelty that might momentarily relieve our guilt. However, that is merely a scientific conclusion, and in the contemplation of fat, science sometimes must bow to philosophy. Maybe it's not as surprising as it seems that Drewnowski, Friedman, and Sclafani all extend their qualified approval to the development of fat substitutes—not because there is so much that is good about them but because there may not be too much that is bad. And all three preface their approval by reiterating how little we know about the workings of these substances.

"When you're asking people to reduce the fat in their diet, that's hard to do, and one of the reasons it's hard is that food doesn't taste as good as it used to," says Friedman. "So to the extent that we can come up with foods that taste good but offer the reductions or changes in nutrient composition that people want, if that helps them adhere to their diets, that's fine. I think one can have a philosophical problem with fat substitutes, and I understand that, but if they can be made safely and used voluntarily by an informed public, I don't see anything wrong with that—and they might have a quality-of-life or, better yet, a health benefit."

Adam Drewnowski is less equivocal: he feels we can't change the national diet without help from technology. "Sugar and fat consumption has been absolutely linked to the gross national product of a given nation," he says. "Basically, if you have a rich society, animal protein is going to replace vegetable protein. If we want to change that, we need to have very sophisticated strategies in place to do it. So far, we've had a just-say-no approach—just stop eating fats and eat grains and vegetables and fruits—which I think is absolutely doomed to failure. It won't work. So, for example, to supply people with options, essentially by altering the food supply, diluting the fat content of the food supply, is probably good. It's one approach. My work suggests that there are a number of systems involved here, and we should look at all of them; so far we've just been looking at this kind of behavioral model, like wearing seat belts."

Anthony Sclafani, too, despite his rats' ability to sniff out imposter fats, thinks fat substitutes are "a reasonable approach to try. If you're not trying to eliminate fat entirely, just trying to reduce the proportion of fat calories to other calories, we might have more success with these substitutes than just using a diet." But he is blunt in expressing how little we know, and how essentially un-scientific our approach to understanding the ramifications of ersatz fats has been. "What we're doing," he says, "is a nationwide ex-periment, except it's an uncontrolled experiment—these things are just being introduced into the market, people are buying them, but there's little experimental data on how they're using them. So the experiment is, essentially, being done in the marketplace." Which is where, in American fashion, many of our most potent ideas find their expression.

"People can reset their parameters for pleasure," says Norm Singer. "But the resetting is done within certain limits, within a window. When you are in the business of trying to produce a sub-stitute, a replacement for an old traditional standby, you learn how narrow that window is; but over time, that window can change. For example, look at whole milk and low-fat milk—over twenty years, consumption patterns have really switched toward the low-fat. People reset their standards, and then the full-fat vari-ety starts to taste kind of too-rich. In the realm of fat replacement, I suspect that over a decade or so we will see somewhat the same thing, where people will find that they like the flavor of Simple Pleasures better than a full-fat ice cream because the full-fat is just too heavy." Singer's theory echoes Friedman's hypothesis about uncoupling the taste of fat from the calories, but with an added fillip: In a way, it takes the fat-substitute manufacturers off the hook. If people reset their parameters for the enjoyment of the sensory experience of fat, then fat substitutes don't have to be a perfect match for the real thing.

Not that anyone in the fat-substitute business has given up that goal; the growing competition in the field seems to have strengthened the faith of the combatants, and even of some of the bystanders to the business. "I'm a believer," says Prudential ana-lyst John McMillin. "I'm a believer that it's just a matter of time, that they'll get it right. The food business has become more of a technology business, and I do believe these products, over time, will work." A. E. Staley's Dan Rizzo is even more specific: "We know that fat replacers are not perfect; there isn't yet a magic bullet. But I think the industry will get there sometime after ninety-five. Those of us working with existing ingredients will be pushing the edge of the envelope, using technology to make incremental improvements in the product to get closer and closer to the ideal. And somebody is going to come up with the right combination of molecular changes, on the synthetic-fat side, to get it through the FDA, and we'll have a synthetic fat for frying and those kinds of uses."

Singer too envisions the technology creeping forward, progressively bringing the substitutes closer to the magical qualities of fat. "We are still early in the whole progression," he says. "We're working on a couple of adjunct technologies which will further extend or complete the patterns of illusion, so that the foods become more and more pleasing and so that Simplesse can be used in more and more foods." One of those adjunct technologies, announced in early 1992, is a method for removing 95 percent of the fat and 95 percent of the cholesterol from egg yolks. "We plan to sell this to people making mayonnaises and ice creams and so on," says Singer. "And it works very well with Simplesse, it enhances the Simplesse effect, because often when you have fat in traditional foods you also have a lot of egg yolk. Egg yolk is the natural emulsifier. Ice creams, pastries, sauces—hollandaise, béarnaise. We've come to expect that eggy flavor along with the creamy impression."

The money that goes into refining these "patterns of illusion" is, of course, considerable: NutraSweet spent more than $100 million, for instance, on developing Simplesse.[3] But the payoff could be staggering. While Norm Singer's motivation is, as any businessperson's would be, dictated by such a huge potential prize, he is also genuinely excited about retaining our earthly pleasures—nothing wrong with pizza, for instance, that a little Simplesse-based cheese couldn't fix. "With pizza, we have a food that is hedonically fine, it's lifestyle fine, it's not outrageously expensive," says Singer. "Only problem is, it's got too much fat and cholesterol. Well, get rid of that and it's something that can be enjoyed more often, and without the sense of guilt. There are lots of puddles of grease in our diet. I don't mind the drops of grease, but the puddles we can get rid of."

There is, of course, another way to reduce the puddles to drops, but it is not one that makes any sense to manufacturers: One could simply consume drops—but deliciously untampered-with drops—rather than puddles. "Americans are not willing to give up the things they really like," says marketing consultant David Braff. "The truth is that if you want to eat healthy you eat smaller; you eat good stuff, just less of it. That's the truth, but that's very hard to impose." That way of eating also has no power-ful voices behind it, for the most basic and American of reasons: No one will make substantial amounts of money from advocating limiting oneself to just the daintiest wedge of full-fat Havarti cheese, the smallest scoop of true vanilla ice cream with the indis-putably correct mouth-feel. The message conveyed by fat substi-tutes is so much simpler, unhampered as it is by trade-offs or limits: No fat, no guilt, no compromises. "People have been ap-pealing for a new American diet," says Singer. "Well, Simplesse is a way of getting there, without putting on a hair shirt."

Chapter Three

•

INSIDE THE HYPE MACHINE

The Life and Death of Oat Bran

•

The story of oat bran is the story of food marketing at the height of its powers: Consumer interest is piqued by several scientific studies and a popular self-help book; marketers scramble to adjust recipes, packaging, advertising; newspapers and magazines remark on the new culinary sensation; and something that is a small, limited element of a healthy diet becomes a superstar, a cure-all, and a guarantee of sales. But if oat bran was a larger-than-life example of marketing savvy, it also became an exemplar of overkill, a victim of its own success. The forces that drove both oat bran's success and its ultimate failure are the forces that drive our search for perfect foods: the desire for simple, painless answers; the trust in scientific studies; the susceptibility to the blandishments of advertising. In the late 1980s those forces were at work at many corporate food giants, but at none quite so high-profile as the Quaker Oats Company—a century-old monolith that, in all logic, should have reaped the benefits of the oat bran phenomenon, but instead suffered the punishments meted out by a hype machine out of control.

•

Steven Ink, senior manager of nutrition research for the Quaker Oats Company, can remember the precise moment that the oat bran bubble burst. If there was much about the growth of the oat bran phenomenon that was history-making—no one had seen anything quite like it in the intensity of its marketing appeal—there turned out to be something equally remarkable about its demise: It essentially collapsed and died in one day. That day was January 15, 1990, a day when Ink was in New York City to help run a press conference called Quaker and Answers. Quaker was working to enhance the natural advantage that came from being the most visible representative of the oats business, trying to present itself as the most responsible and authoritative purveyor of the new star among health foods and, not incidentally, trying to increase sales. Sales, oddly, had been somewhat of a problem for Quaker; the company was not reaping as much profit from the oat bran boom as some other cereal giants were, a fact that caused considerable concern among Quaker's management.

The press conference had started out well. Luther McKinney, Quaker's senior vice president for regulatory and corporate affairs, outlined Quaker's efforts urging the Food and Drug Administration to tighten rules on food-health claims, a position that could only make Quaker look good. (The Federal Trade Commission had, just six months before, dismissed charges by the Center for Science in the Public Interest that Quaker was misleading consumers with its ad copy mentioning oat bran's effect on blood cholesterol.) Then Katherine Smith, vice president for consumer affairs, rose to describe a recent Quaker consumer survey that showed that people were beginning to understand the relationship between oat bran and blood cholesterol levels. She also conducted an entertaining electronic exercise in which audience members could punch in their own answers to questions about oat bran, which would be instantly tallied and compared both to consumers' responses and to the correct answers.

Ink himself spoke next, describing new research with other fibers beyond oat bran—barley, psyllium, the oat bran challengers—to give a sense of Quaker's earnest interest in nutritional research even when it involved competing products. Finally, De-Witt Goodman, director of the Atherosclerosis Research Center at Columbia University and also cochair of the National Cholesterol Education Adult Treatment Panel Report, described a new nation-wide screening effort for blood cholesterol levels, lending a note of sober establishment concern.

Then, just when things were feeling under control, came The Question, from the *New York Times*'s health columnist Jane Brody. She addressed it to Ink. She had heard that that week's *New England Journal of Medicine* was going to publish a study coming out of Harvard that cast some doubt on the connection between oat bran and lowered levels of cholesterol, a study that showed basically no difference between oat bran and other types of fiber, or even comparable amounts of low-fiber foods. What was Quaker's position on this?

The Question was the other shoe that Ink and everyone else at Quaker had been listening for, knowing with fatalistic certainty that it was going to drop sooner or later. Everyone working with oat bran knew the same thing: Anything that goes up that fast is going to come down. What no one knew was what the precipitator would be. Ink certainly had not expected it to be the Harvard study. He had seen the study's results more than two years before, when they were presented to a meeting of the American College of Nutrition, and he had dismissed them on several scientific counts shortly thereafter. To be honest, he had thought the study would never see the light of day. But it wouldn't go away. Not long before the Quaker press conference there had been rumors afloat, and someone in another department at Quaker had called Ink to ask, "Steve, do you know anything about some study coming out that will be negative about oat bran?" And the only thing he could think of was that two-year-old Harvard study by Frank Sacks—Frank Sacks who several years before had unsuccessfully petitioned Quaker itself for grant money. It can't be that study, Ink told himself. That's too old, too flawed.

But it was indeed the Frank Sacks study, and on that January day it looked as if it might be the harbinger of the inevitable backlash. Even at that moment, however, with the television cameras whirring for an evening-news sound-bite, there was room for hope: Perhaps, Ink thought, it's just a setback, a little plateau in the upward flow of oat's popularity. People will get over this; people will realize that one badly done study doesn't mean anything. But after Ink's "Nightline" appearance two days later—and the "Today" show appearance and the headlines in the *New York Times* and the *Wall Street Journal* and the *Washington Post*—it dawned on Ink and the others in the ever-expanding oat bran task force at Quaker that maybe this was, in fact, the end.

Five months later, combined sales of Quaker Oat Bran hot and cold cereals were down 50 percent. On May 21, 1990, the first six words of a front-page article in *Advertising Age* were: "The oat bran craze is over."[1]

There was no immediately clear reason, at the beginning of what came to be known as the oat bran phenomenon, why oat bran should grow and multiply like a mutant being in the marketplace; nothing really to distinguish it from the other earnest little substances that were discovered to have healthy pedigrees—olive oil, calcium, omega-3 oils from fish. All of those substances enjoyed greater sales when studies were released that seemed to link them to longer life, fewer heart attacks, stronger bodies. But when the good news about oat bran and cholesterol, which had actually been accumulating for decades, suddenly hit the media circuit in 1987, what happened was not just an increase in sales or a little frisson of consumer excitement. It was something more along the lines of an explosion.

Marketers later talked about it in paradigmatic terms: other promising food products came to be described as "another oat bran" or "the next oat bran." This one substance somehow seemed to sum up, near the end of the excessive eighties, many of the fears and hopes that had begun to catch up with us: creeping fears of decline, and hopes of redemption. Never mind that not everyone even had a problem with cholesterol; to be free of the stuff, to wash it out of your system with a dose of oat bran, sounded so good (and so easy). Oat bran seemed, too, so controllable and measurable: one bowl of oatmeal, one magic muffin, and the thing was done.

No one can exactly agree on the precise moment of oat bran's ascendancy, but it appears to have blossomed sometime between the publication of a book in 1987 titled *The Eight-Week Cholesterol Cure*, by Robert Kowalski, that remained on the best-seller list for more than a year, and the publication of an article in the *Journal of the American Medical Association* on April 15, 1988, detailing a study that suggested that adding oat bran to the diet was a promising alternative to drug therapy for people with high blood cholesterol levels. The two together—popular, self-help, commonsense advice on the one hand, and on the other the peer-reviewed imprimatur of one of the two most influential medical journals in the country—gave a powerful jump-start to a substance that had limped along, disguised in one of the less-glamorous grains, for centuries.

But there was one other force that defined oat bran's new identity: the U.S. government. In late 1987 the National Cholesterol Education Program, sponsored by the National Heart, Lung, and Blood Institute (part of the federal government's National Institutes of Health), proclaimed that one-quarter of the American population had dangerously high blood cholesterol levels, requiring at the very least dietary intervention. The wages of ignoring cholesterol were heavy: an elevated risk of coronary heart disease. The program recommended universal blood testing for cholesterol levels. It wasn't as if Americans had never heard of cholesterol and its dangers, but this was a big-time public-health push, and it planted cholesterol firmly in the public's consciousness.

The federal government was a factor in oat bran's success in one other way, albeit passively. The FDA, after decades of tight restrictions on food-packaging health claims, loosened its interpretation and enforcement of rules that had required any food making health claims to be treated as a drug and subjected to extensive testing. The timing, in the cosmic life of oat bran, was perfect: the fall of 1987. Suddenly there were no clear rules on claims, and the door was open to products that were essentially contradictions in terms—oat bran potato chips, for instance, or oat bran beer. One study showed that a significant percentage of the population would buy cola that had oat bran in it.[2] In 1989 alone, 218 new products containing oat bran were introduced to the market.[3]

If there were one company that would appear to have been in the catbird seat during this serendipitous conjunction of events, it would be Quaker Oats. Maker of the grande dame of hot breakfast cereals, one of the few food products to retain a classic package that evokes turn-of-the-century goodness and purity, Quaker would seem to be akin to the homesteader who suddenly finds that below his backyard lies a reservoir of oil. Quaker stood for oats, its name for many Americans practically synonymous with its product, like Kleenex and tissues, Xerox and copiers. Presumably, Quaker would have a large running start on capturing the oat bran market, and could only stand to gain from its primary product achieving sudden, glaring fame.

Strange, then, that one person at Quaker who saw the oat bran phenomenon happen calls it "a nightmare." Another says, "Oat bran was a very painful episode for Quaker." The oat bran story from the point of view of Quaker Oats is a different tale from the oat bran story as seen by the rest of the country. In that difference reside a few truths about how a food-and-health marketing fad—the fad of the decade—lived, breathed, and ultimately died.

Steven Ink, forty, a tall, willowy, earnest Midwesterner, came to Quaker Oats in January 1986 from a teaching position at the University of Florida. He had grown up in Minnesota and obtained a Ph.D. in nutrition from the University of Minnesota in Minneapolis, but his wife's career had helped lead him south to Florida and he began teaching and conducting nutrition research there. Ink liked the teaching, but the research was frustrating: good nutrition studies at the university level took so much time, sometimes decades, and he was impatient to apply the research to people and their eating habits. He discovered, he says, that he was a "people person" who wanted to educate people and help change their lives, who wanted to see the results of research rather than just the numbers. Quaker in the mid-eighties was an interesting place for people who wanted to do just that. "Anyone associated with our cereals division—the cereals marketing groups and cereals R-and-D groups—felt like this was exciting stuff and that we were really going to have an opportunity to communicate the benefits of our product in a meaningful way," Ink says in describing that time. In his upbeat vocabulary, "opportunity" is a word that crops up often.

Ink's job is to coordinate outside research, funded by Quaker, that deals with the nutrition and health aspects of Quaker products. He's also a nutrition cop of sorts, ensuring the accuracy of product nutrition information (the figures on the side of the cereal box) and evaluating product claims relating to nutritional content or health benefits. Quaker had seen a lot of promising research by the mid-eighties, when Ink arrived, and the company commissioned further studies to bolster what would eventually become an entirely new marketing direction. Quaker moved slowly and deliberately in those early oat bran days; there seemed, at first, no reason to rush and risk overextending into an unproven new area. In 1983 oat bran was so relatively obscure that when Quaker came out with its first hot oat bran cereal (as distinct from Quaker oatmeal, which had been around since the 1870s) it was devised specifically for health food stores. Called Mother's Oat Bran—not exactly a sexy sell—it did well enough to spur the introduction of a more mainstream Quaker Oat Bran hot cereal the following year, to be distributed in supermarkets. Quaker continued to tinker with new product ideas—flavored oat bran hot cereal; cold, ready-to-eat oat bran cereal—but without a great sense of urgency. "We wanted to develop these products well ahead of anticipated introduction to the marketplace," says Ink, "so that we could make sure that the taste and the texture considerations were met, and also to have enough time to ensure that the efficacy of the product was still there, even after heat-steam-pressure processing."

But there was one arena in which Quaker did manage to be ahead of the pack: In 1987 Quaker created a TV spot with a catchphrase that presaged oat bran's complex emotional/moral appeal. Quaker's surveys and focus groups had been indicating that the time might be right for a broad campaign focusing on health benefits rather than taste, and the company's answer was Wilford Brimley. Unglamorous and calculatedly nonglitzy, Brimley was just the right actor to tell America: "Quaker Oats—it's the right thing to do." In a time of moral uncertainty, intensified by the stock market shocks of October 1987 and a growing sense of guilt over the excesses of the eighties, the phrase worked. Even people who didn't like the campaign talked about it. And, more important from the point of view of Quaker, it sold oatmeal—Quaker Oats' sales increased 20 percent during the first year of the campaign. Once again, and perhaps never so blatantly, a link had been made between moral values and food.

By the end of 1987 it was clear that oat bran was going to be big. Quaker scurried to keep up with the explosion of products, but the company's most significant introductions—the flavored hot oat bran cereal and cold oat bran cereal—were not close to being ready. In fact, what Steve Ink remembers as being a high point in Quaker's oat bran campaign, the moment when the company was really riding the wave, occurred a year and a half later, in the summer of 1989. "We had been working on the ready-to-eat oat bran cereal for years," recalls Ink, "and we had finally just introduced it to one of the regional markets as a test—I think it was Arizona. And when we got the sales figures, as well as the sell-in figures to the trade—which shows the willingness of the retailers to stock the product—they really looked terrific. It was setting records for Quaker in terms of retailer interest."

But that triumph was overshadowed somewhat by the nagging fact that Quaker was late out of the starting gate—despite a head start in research and development—a point that would become increasingly salient as time went by. Even as Ink describes the pleasure of that moment he is compelled to add the inevitable modifiers. "We had done some clinical testing with the product,"

CONSUMED··· 93

he recalls, "and we were working with ways to incorporate as much oat bran as we could, and all that took time. The product had actually been under development for a number of years before the craze hit, well before we saw consumer interest start to swell. But as it turned out, we introduced it maybe a bit later than we would have liked to. It didn't coincide exactly with the huge increase in consumer interest, but nonetheless we were in there with what we thought was probably one of the best, if not *the* best, ready-to-eat cholesterol-reducing cereal products."

That last point was a critical one for Quaker. Although it goes without saying that company executives wanted to profit from the oat bran demand as much as the next guy, there was also an awareness of the Quaker position as the company with the highest profile and the oldest name in oats, and thus talk of producing "the best," or at least the most scrupulously researched, of goods. And that, perhaps, is why the company missed the point of the oat bran phenomenon, a point that had become clear in the year and a half that had elapsed between the original explosion of consumer interest and the moment of glory in 1989: The oat bran business was not really about being good, that is, healthy; it was about being perceived as good. This was a business for marketers, not scientists. A case in point: the biggest winner in the oat bran cereal business was probably General Mills, producers of the half-century-old Cheerios brand, which was catapulted to the position of number-one cereal in 1989.[4] But what made the difference was not the cereal's ingredients—Cheerios does not contain enough oat bran in one serving to have a proven effect on cholesterol levels—but the marketing: a bright red band across the front of the box that read, "Excellent source of oat bran!"

It is a continuing source of irritation and frustration at Quaker that it was for the most part the fudgers, and sometimes even out-and-out charlatans, who got rich selling oat bran. During the year and a half that Quaker was perfecting its new products (and, of course, making some extra profits on their existing oat products), the marketplace had become flooded with what were essentially pretender items. For every cereal or muffin that had a legitimate claim to health benefits, there were perhaps dozens that used oat bran more on their packaging than in their product. (Most studies have shown that two ounces of oat bran or three ounces of oatmeal daily—about the size of an average bowl of oatmeal—are needed in order to produce a lowering effect on cholesterol.)[5] Soon there were not only cold cereals that added a negligible dash of oat bran to their sweetened grains, but oat bran pretzels and potato chips, and oat bran breads and cookies and muffins whose generous amounts of butter or saturated fats completely canceled out any benefits from the bran. Bad enough, from Quaker's point of view, that these products were siphoning off oat bran interest, and profits, that should have come directly to Quaker. But it soon became evident that that was the lesser evil. What these products were really doing was fueling a marketing juggernaut that would eventually self-destruct; they were setting the stage for an oat bran backlash.

There were some at Quaker who had seen the backlash coming almost from the beginning. "People were genuinely excited," Steve Ink remembers of the early days of the oat bran surge, "but I think there were a lot of people that right away were very cautious about the whole situation, knowing full well that first of all this was a very difficult message to communicate to consumers—to let them know that certain products have a benefit while others do not. People here were concerned that if the craze were really to take hold, sooner or later consumers might become jaded or suspicious, and that wasn't going to bode well for our original intention, which was to see a slow increase in people's awareness of oatmeal and oat bran. Instead there'd be discontent and question marks in their minds, which is what happened." Ink describes the consumer confusion that Quaker saw, with shoppers calling or writing the company to ask basic questions about how oat bran worked and which products were useful. "We started to see the potential," he says, "that the consumers would doubt this whole proposition, simply because when you see several hundred new oat bran–type products introduced into the marketplace in a short period of time, obviously consumers will begin to see through some of that."

The media also figures as a major villain in the company's oat bran postmortem. The company wisdom, repeated often and heatedly after the fall, ran like this: Once the media got through with their exaggerated glorification of oat bran, they began an exaggerated witch-hunt, setting out to debunk their former darling and anoint a successor food trend, which they would eventually destroy in kind. Ink and the then-head of product management for Quaker cereal products even went to New York in the fall of 1989 to try to stem the media disenchantment by meeting with editors and writers. The problem, as Ink now readily admits, is that the story they were trying to sell had no angle—it was simply the "set the record straight" kind of update that news editors immediately shelve. The brutal truth was that Quaker was not going to be able to write oat bran's history; it was going to write itself, directed not just by the media but by the desires of the consumer. Because if the media did sanctify and then vilify oat bran, they were also reflecting an impulse that existed in the American public at large. Marketers and researchers who study the American consumer often remark on the all-or-nothing phenomenon that retailers encounter. If oat bran turned out not to be the absolute answer, to many Americans it was no answer at all.

Moreover, what much of the buying public loved about oat bran was the beautiful simplicity of it. The message that trickled down, distorted on the way, from news reports and marketing gimmickry was that oat bran was some sort of perfect health food—eat it and live forever, or at least longer than you would otherwise. Bake it into a delicious muffin and you could actually enjoy your medicine, too. When the inevitable complexity of oat bran became clear—that it must be part of an overall low-fat diet, that it is probably more effective, or at least more important, for people with higher-than-normal blood cholesterol levels—the easy fix was erased, and those who had looked for it returned to cheese danish or bagels or Cocoa Krispies.

As the backlash began, and as the market continued to flood with ever more absurd oat bran products, one more painful truth dawned upon the people at Quaker: The company's seeming leadership role in the oats market, which had never reached its full potential, was beginning to look strangely like a liability. If Quaker was synonymous with oats, it would be tarred with the same brush that smeared every dishonorable oat bran product. The Quaker name itself had already attracted what one person at the company called a "regulatory backlash." In the spring of 1988 the Center for Science in the Public Interest petitioned the Federal Trade Commission, accusing Quaker of misleading consumers and exaggerating health claims for oat bran. Although the FTC decided a year later, in June 1989, that the CSPI's case was not strong enough and that Quaker's claims were not out of line, by September 1989 there was another Quaker challenge. The Texas Attorney filed suit against the company along similar lines to the CSPI claims, but based on a Texas law that any health claims on a food product made it in effect a drug that must be tested. There were hundreds of companies to choose from in filing the suit, since by 1989 health claims on food products were ubiquitous, but Quaker was singled out. The case was finally dismissed in 1991, after moving slowly through the Texas and federal courts, but the public relations damage had been done long before.

It was a battle-scarred oat bran team at Quaker that limped into 1990, hopeful about the prospects of the newly introduced cereals but wary of further challenges by the courts or other oat bran competitors. Steve Ink's people in the nutrition department of Quaker had begun an attempt to take the initiative by convening a task force with the American Association of Cereal Chemists, with the goal of nailing down oat bran's true identity, physically and structurally. "We were trying to determine things like, what's the actual morphological definition of oat bran," says Ink, "and how can it be defined chemically and what are the analytical techniques needed to do that. The FDA had expressed interest in hearing more from us, and we had put that information together and were just about ready to go with it when the Sacks study began to break, and the whole thing became a little bit moot."

The Sacks study's effect was due more to timing than to science. The oat bran phenomenon had been pushed so far that any word about it was ipso facto news and, too, there were some who were happy to debunk what had begun to look like a fraud. Americans were ready to hear what seemed to be the painful truth about oat bran, and the press was ready to publish it. The study, conducted by Frank M. Sacks and Janis F. Swain, was published in the January 18, 1990, issue of the *New England Journal of Medicine*. In brief, it suggested that oat bran lowered cholesterol only about 7 percent (as compared to the 13 to 19 percent reductions shown in other studies), and that similar amounts of other low-fiber foods had the same effect, suggesting that the reduction in cholesterol was a result not of oat bran's magical metabolic properties but of simply replacing fatty foods with large amounts of starchy foods. Challenges to the study on scientific grounds focused on the small sample used—twenty participants—and the fact that they all had desirable levels of blood cholesterol to begin with, well below the cutoff of 200. ("It was like doing a weight-loss study of people who were not overweight," Steve Ink comments.) Also, the amount of fat consumed was not carefully controlled, so it was unclear what role that played in reducing cholesterol.

Even the press accounts of the study remarked on the intensity of the media reaction to the news. "While some in the scientific community pooh-poohed the findings because of the small sample," read an article in *Newsweek*, "the media response was near hysteria. The nightly news gave the oat-bran story equal billing with bloody battles in western Azerbaijan." The same article also suggested that the timing of Quaker's "educational" press conference on Monday, January 15, was no coincidence; that in fact Quaker had been preparing for the study's release for some time.[6]

Steve Ink is a little vague when pressed on the details of how much he knew and when, and certainly it is to Quaker's benefit to cast themselves as the wounded, unfairly surprised party—damaged by news reports of the study before other scientists had a chance to review and comment on its merits. That is a complaint that is often made by the victims of work published in the powerful *New England Journal of Medicine* or the *Journal of the American Medical Association;* the system at both magazines provides for release of study results to the media simultaneously with release to the doctors and scientists who are qualified to comment knowledgeably on interpreting the results. But there is no question that Quaker had some previous knowledge of the Sacks study, and had delegated Ink as its primary spokesperson in the storm that followed its release. That tussle was played out in what has in recent years become the primary arena for dispatches and battles on the nutrition front: "Nightline," the "Today" show, *The New York Times, The Wall Street Journal,* and every newspaper and TV show that feeds off those media giants.

The discussion between Ink and Sacks on "Nightline" the evening of January 17—the night before the study was formally published—was surprisingly sharp, almost bitter, with Sacks warning Ink that he was "on very shaky ground" and calling Ink's criticism of the study "absolutely unfounded from basic nutritional principles." Ink's tactic was to try to float above the fray and focus more on the big picture—talking about the plethora of earlier studies on oat bran and emphasizing the use of oat bran as just one element in a low-fat diet—although he did get into one tense interchange with Sacks about the methods of the study. Interestingly, although Quaker was on the defensive that night, Ink came off as lower-key than Sacks. His position was also enhanced when Ted Koppel grilled Sacks on his past relationship to the Center for Science in the Public Interest—Sacks had been on their advisory board—and what effect that might have had on his oat bran work. Sacks bristled, and for a moment it looked like Quaker might walk off that night with a definitive win. But after the customary summing-up the result was the usual "Nightline" draw: In this case, don't throw away your oat bran, but don't expect it to single-handedly save your life, either.

That balanced message in no way slowed the debacle that followed, with Quaker stock dropping precipitously on the New York Stock Exchange and sales immediately falling off—so immediately and so drastically that one brand-new product, the flavored hot oat bran cereal, was put out of commission within months. Clearly, the accusation of exaggerated health claims for oat bran was, to a public poised for such news, tantamount to a conviction. After all, the title of the "Nightline" segment had been "Does Oat Bran Work?", suggesting that one negative study was enough to call the whole concept into question. (Of course, it could be argued that those were the rules of the game all along—that a phenomenon could be created on the basis of one study. The "Nightline" segment reported that Quaker sold about a million pounds of oat bran cereal per year between its introduction in 1983 and 1988; the next year, after the JAMA study that suggested oat bran was implicated in lowering blood cholesterol, Quaker sold about 24 million pounds.)

But after a "Today" show appearance the morning following "Nightline"—again, with Dr. Sacks in attendance via the Boston affiliate station—Ink actually flew home to Quaker's headquarters in Chicago with a measure of hope. Granted, Bryant Gumbel had opened the segment by saying, "The latest research says [oat bran's] claims are exaggerated," implying that the latest word was, of course, the true word; and Sacks had gotten in a nasty dig to the effect that "the point here is that we need somebody other than company spokesmen to tell the American public what the scientific results are really saying," but the ending had, if anything, favored Quaker. Gumbel had asked Sacks if what the Quaker box said was true—oat bran "can help reduce cholesterol"—and Sacks had had to say yes, "it's quite literally true." Maybe, Ink remembers thinking, people will listen to the arguments, read past the headlines, and realize this shouldn't be the end of oat bran.

The first damage-control monitoring that Quaker did hinted that this would be the case. Early focus groups conducted by the company suggested that many people got the message that this was just one study, that it was controversial, that it wasn't the only truth. But as time went on the full impact of the Sacks study, flawed or not, controversial or not, became clear. "Those who were truly interested in diet and health were able to sort through the facts," Ink says now, "and did recognize that this was just one study that might not have too much relevance to them or their family members, and that there probably still was a bene-fit to eating oatmeal and oat bran. But the others—people that had just a passing interest in nutrition and health or were looking for quick fixes—remained confused enough to say the heck with it. We lost a lot of people who were just starting to get into un-derstanding this whole proposition but were willing to give it a try."

In other words, Quaker lost the chance to go mainstream with oat bran. They now find themselves, in effect, almost back where they were in the early eighties, with a core group of nutri-tion-savvy consumers who are going to buy oat bran no matter what. The push is off at Quaker to expand, to provide new prod-ucts with new flavors and more convenience; the company has the dubious pleasure of knowing that it is fully equipped to satisfy its entire corner of the market. Not that Quaker has completely raised the white flag. The company—and Ink in particular—is still looking to science as a way out of the confusion about oat bran, and Quaker created a flurry of attention in the spring of 1991 with the results of two studies it had paid for that showed a 7 to 10 per-cent reduction in cholesterol levels after an oat bran–supple-mented diet. (The studies were conducted with "no strings attached," according to the company, although inevitably kernels of doubt persist, rightly or no, about corporate-sponsored re-search.)

But if science might ultimately hold the key to selling oat bran, it could also, strangely enough, be seen as something of a culprit in oat bran's downfall. What emerges, finally, from Ink's postmortem of the oat bran roller coaster is not so much blame for the media or the public's fickleness or the oat bran charlatans as blame for science itself. Or, more specifically, for a debate among scientists, about what exactly people should be told about diet and health. The story of this debate shows one thing very clearly: Nutrition issues do not exist in a vacuum, and they are not "pure"—they are, rather, often dominated by marketing tactics and hidden agendas, even in the hands of those who don't have a product to sell.

Ink tells the story like this: The scientists working on cholesterol fall into two camps, the fiber camp and the fat camp. The fat camp is occupied by the movers and shakers in cholesterol reduction—the National Heart, Lung, and Blood Institute, the National Cholesterol Education Program, the American Heart Association—all, says Ink, "trying to educate people about the need to reduce total fat and saturated fat in the diet. That was their primary campaign. Reducing the level of dietary cholesterol or the level of dietary sodium, increasing dietary fiber—those were supporting stories, supporting advice. The major thing was reduce fat, and we had people who had built up their careers around supporting that type of advice with good research and a number of public health officials devoting a lot of time, energy, and resources to educating people about that."

Those people, says Ink, were not thrilled to have a cholesterol-reducing rival for the American public's attention in the form of oat bran. "They didn't want their story to be tainted or diluted by another developing scientific story," says Ink. He makes another distinction: that the researchers in the soluble-fiber (oat bran) area tended to be nutrition scientists, operating from a biochemical point of view, while the fat-reduction proponents tended to be physicians more accustomed to using drugs to lower cholesterol (and, he hints, more interested in a simple answer rather than "looking at diet in general and various components within the diet"). Not surprisingly, Ink puts Frank Sacks into the fat camp.

Ink is not the only scientist to talk about the juggernaut power of certain scientific ideas in the hands of the medical establishment. One professor of food-marketing research, John Stanton of St. Joseph's University in Philadelphia, puts it like this: "The implication, in talking about food and health, is that the government doesn't have vested interests. I mean, if you go to National Heart and Lung—the whole organization, billions of dollars, is based on the fact that cholesterol is bad for you—and you provide them with evidence that says maybe cholesterol's not the bad guy they said, what are they going to say? 'Oh yeah, well, you guys are right and let's disassemble our institute here'? Of course they have a vested interest in it."

Did the fat camp really kill oat bran? Nothing about oat bran is that simple, but the fat-versus-fiber fracas is a telling footnote to the demise of the most hyped foodstuff of the eighties. It also begins to explain why the American consumer finds it so difficult to pin down the truth in nutrition research—because there are many truths, and many parties who stand to benefit from their version of the truth winning out. Quaker, carrying the load of a famous name, gambled that it was better to be late but more believable, or at least more respectable. Perhaps their miscalculation was in overestimating the attention span of American consumers—or underestimating consumers' ability to finally understand that they were being manipulated, and their capacity for anger when they realized it.

At Quaker, the oat bran team has been scaled back, and some of the key people have been transferred to other parts of the company, to their great relief. Only the most upbeat of personalities denies that oat bran was a debacle at Quaker. One major oat bran–team player who has since moved on to another job at Quaker declined to be interviewed, explaining: "I don't want people to read this years from now and remember that I was involved with the oat bran campaign. I'd like it to be forgotten."

Steve Ink can't forget oat bran; it remains at the center of his responsibilities at Quaker. "Our goals are the same as they've always been—to communicate the benefits of our products," he says. "It's just more niche-oriented now. We hope it will expand eventually—but, obviously, more slowly this time."

Chapter Four

•

EATING YOUR MEDICINE

The Battle Over Superfoods

•

Humans have optimistically looked for medicinal value in foods for millennia: garlic as an antibiotic, yogurt for longevity, various herbal teas as cure-alls. Researchers can now foresee a more perfect answer: foods that are almost indistinguishable from drugs. A super-beta-carotene carrot might fight lung cancer; specially formulated sausages fortified with large amounts of omega-3 oils or other natural substances might prevent heart disease. But such rejiggering of nature's basic recipes has ended up raising some unexpected and fundamental questions about the identity of food itself.

What, exactly, is the true definition of food? What do we want from it? Is it simply fuel, or medicine to prolong life? What happens when we attempt to redefine food, to designate other uses that extend far beyond sating and pleasure? Even superfoods' keenest promoter, a man who is working to make such hybrids legitimate, betrays a sense of what is lost when food and medicine become one.

•

Dr. Stephen DeFelice has been trying to pin down the meaning of the word "food" for more than ten years. In 1983 DeFelice, a specialist in drug research and development, organized a conference at the University of Medicine and Dentistry of New Jersey called "Natural Substance: When Nutrition, When Drug?" in which a group of doctors, scientists, and attorneys attempted—and failed—to come up with a precise definition of food. Three years later he wrote about his search in *From Oysters to Insulin: Nature and Medicine at Odds*, a book in which he urged greater research into the medical uses of natural substances. He has combed dictionaries, and he has taken into consideration the legal definition of food established by the Food and Drug Administration (which is a combination of the obvious and the unexpected: "1: articles used for food or drink for man or other animals; 2: chewing gum; 3: articles used for components of any such article"). None of these efforts has yielded an answer. Instead, says DeFelice, most experts are ambushed by circular reasoning: Food consists of nutrients; nutrients nourish; to nourish is to provide with food.

Correcting this fuzzy thinking has become something of an obsession with DeFelice, especially since March of 1991, when he began actively trying to change the official identity of food; or, to be exact, of some foods—those formulated to prevent or cure disease in the eater. These might be called foods of the future—others have called them superfoods or designer foods—and DeFelice contends that their existence demands a new way of thinking about what food really is.

He described this idea to me over lunch, pausing at one point in midthought to consider how to improve the taste of the escarole before him. Knife in one hand, he carefully placed a substantial dollop of butter onto a forkful of escarole cooked in garlic and chicken broth. "Here, try this," he said, holding out the loaded fork. "Now, with more garlic, I can make it better than this . . . mm, love it!" We were sitting in a booth at Aperitivo Restaurant, on West Fifty-sixth Street in New York—the kind of midtown Italian restaurant that looks like it hasn't changed in twenty years: comfortable banquettes along the wall, pink linen tablecloths, artwork of dubious pedigree highlighted on the walls, waiters in white aprons who finish off pasta dishes in a movable chafing dish pulled up to your table. DeFelice has been coming here since the week the restaurant opened in 1968.

An energetic man in his fifties, DeFelice brings a lot of enthusiasm to things gustatory. "For me, eating is the total experience," he said. "This place may not have the absolute best Italian food in town, but eating isn't just the food. It's the ambience, the people, the whole experience of being there . . ." And, in fact, the process of ordering from the expansive menu so enchanted him that after we had made our choices he proclaimed, "I love to eat and drink!" He ordered a bottle of Pinot Grigio, and soon we had worked our way through the asparagus parmigiana ("They put a lot of butter, parmigiana, and bread crumbs on it—it's *good!*"), and began to seriously address our spaghetti carbonara (eggs, bacon, cheese), sole sautéed in bread crumbs, and the escarole. DeFelice, after advising me on how to eat my pasta ("Take it from the edge, where it's cooler—that's where all the good stuff collects, too") and telling the waiter to grate more cheese over it, reminisced about the family dinners of his childhood in an Italian enclave of Philadelphia. "Big meals—soup, meat, potatoes, salad, vegetables," he said. "It varied every night. We had red meats, fish, liver, kidneys, everything. We didn't worry about it. So now, when people talk about pork without fat, chicken breast with no skin . . . I like the dark meat! What do they serve in every restaurant? The damn breast, the dullest part of the chicken. It drives me nuts. And I want the skin—good stuff! I'm not a laborer, I don't eat just to survive—I eat for pleasure. Guys who don't eat any meat—we used to call those men sissies in my old neighborhood. My friends in Italy, when they have a pork chop they eat the whole chop—the fat, the whole damn thing. And the rate of heart disease in Italy is much lower than it is here. The argument against meat is so weak. I eat one steak, am I in jeopardy? Where's the data to say that? What people don't take into account with this worry about food is happiness. Everybody talks about heart disease, but there's a thing called happiness. I like living. I get up each morning, and I look forward to my work, to eating, talking to people. So I eat my cholesterol, and maybe I'll die four months earlier. I'd rather die four months earlier—four *years* earlier—than be a vegan, who doesn't eat meat or even dairy products, all my life. Life is wanting to live! Hey, I bet if you do a survey and ask people, 'If you could enjoy the pleasures of food and die three years earlier, or not enjoy the pleasures of food, which would you take?', they'd probably give up the pleasures of food, but I wouldn't."

As a scientist, and as an eater, DeFelice is a man of some ambiguities. Professionally, he is working to push food into the next century; personally, he's more steak and fries than New Age. Yet he appears completely sanguine about any contradictions between his championing of superfoods and his desire to see food purely as a source of pleasure. His work has made him literate in the new language of self-denial—low-fat, low-cholesterol, high-fiber—but it has also introduced him to an arena where science collides with folk medicine, and where the desire to rethink food impinges on the simple act of enjoying eating it.

DeFelice refers to the confusion that currently engulfs the whole business of food and health as nutri-babble, and it is tempting to see him as an embodiment of that confusion, or at least of some paradoxical thinking about food. Nutri-babble has a certain resonance when it comes to DeFelice's personality as well. He talks fast, almost telegraphically, words and ideas jumping ahead of each other, leaping into completely different subjects without pause, and as he speaks he leans in close to make his point. In the manner of a politician, he can sometimes manage to answer a question that has not been asked while skirting one that has been, but the irritant quality of that habit is tempered by an occasional wry self-awareness and frequent booming laughs. Full of theories and full of opinions, DeFelice operates along the edges of government, science, and the food and drug industries, both in his primary occupation as a consultant to drug companies and in his work with superfoods, which is an avocation—something he believes in but that brings in no money. His goal is, simply, to make superfoods legitimate, in the eyes of both the government and the scientific community, and to encourage their development by private industry.

Describing what exactly superfoods are is not easy, partly because not many of them exist yet. A superfood might be a vegetable juice formulated to prevent reproductive cancers in women, or a salad dressing or a bread made with ingredients that help prevent heart attacks. The identity of superfoods is so broad that DeFelice has come up with a new word for them: "nutraceuticals." His coinage grew out of his impatience with the existing definition of food. "You cannot define the difference between a food and a drug; it's impossible," he told me. "The Food and Drug Administration defines it legally: Food is something you eat, but once you make a claim that it works medically, it becomes a drug. What we have now are dietary supplements, brews, teas, extracts—all with claims for medical benefits. Are these foods?"

Not surprisingly, the solution to this problem—not a medical or scientific solution, but a linguistic one—occurred to DeFelice as he was lingering over a meal. "I was in Rome on business a couple of years ago," he said, "and I was drinking sambuca and thinking about this: Here we have nutrition but with a pharmaceutical use. Let's call it a nutraceutical. Let's create a word for this huge market, because the food and drug industries are going to be blurred in the future; people are going to eat their medicine. Everything from designer foods to dietary supplements to juices to ginseng tea. So I wrote an article about this new word, and now it's in the lexicon. There are nutraceutical meetings. It was in *Food and Wine*, as a new food buzzword. You know what that tells me? It's a need; people see it."

Having invented the word, DeFelice has earned the privilege of defining it, which he does as follows: "Any substance that may be considered a food or part of a food and provides medical or health benefits, including the prevention and treatment of disease. Such products may range from dietary supplements, diets, and isolated nutrients to genetically engineered 'designer' foods and processed foods such as cereals, soups, and beverages." He offers as examples of substances that he feels already qualify as nutraceuticals or potential ingredients in nutraceuticals such nutrients as niacin (shown to help prevent subsequent heart attacks in coronary patients), calcium (to treat hypertension or osteoporosis), vitamin A (to treat measles), and garlic (to reduce atherosclerosis). Those substances might be consumed in supplement form, incorporated into a food mixture (like a sausage), or concentrated in an existing food by means of biotechnology; DeFelice's example of this is "an engineered carrot, a fortified carrot."

DeFelice exhibits enough media savvy to understand the appeal not only of new words but of official-sounding names and acronyms. He has designated his effort to legitimize nutraceuticals the Nutraceutical Initiative, and in furtherance of it he has created NAG—the Nutraceutical Advisory Group—made up of what De-Felice calls "top legal and medical experts" from the Harvard Medical School, Tufts University, and Memorial Sloan-Kettering Cancer Center, and including two former general counsels for the Food and Drug Administration. The specific goal of the Nutraceutical Initiative is to convince Congress to create a special regulatory agency—a Nutraceutical Commission, or NUCOM—to oversee the licensing and marketing of nutraceuticals. Taking them out of the purview of the FDA, DeFelice believes, will encourage innovative scientific research into the potential of health-promoting foods. His contention is that FDA regulations are holding back such research. "Basically, the FDA is protecting people from knowing the truth," he said. "They're nice people down there, but they can't handle nutraceuticals."

The FDA attracts DeFelice's wrath for its bureaucratic caution, even while it has attracted applause from others for its latest effort to reform food regulations. That effort took the form of the Nutrition Labeling and Education Act of 1990, a broad mandate passed by Congress but left to the FDA to implement. The agency issued detailed proposals for how to fulfill the act in November of 1991, and after a yearlong period for review and public comment and an internecine skirmish between the FDA and the United States Department of Agriculture (which, in representing meat-industry interests, pushed for weaker regulations), the proposals were approved by the White House. The food industry has until May 1994 to relabel its products in accordance with the new NLEA rules. Those rules are designed to close loopholes in current food-labeling regulations that have allowed marketers to exaggerate the healthfulness of their products. Thus, for example, under the NLEA rules the words "light," "low-fat," "reduced," and "fresh" would be tightly defined for use on product labels; serving sizes for the purposes of nutrition labeling would be made uniform; and saturated fat, often a hidden contributor to high cholesterol levels in humans, would be required to be listed separately from other fats. And—of greatest concern to DeFelice—the FDA, after evaluating ten broader health claims for use on food labels, suggested approving four of those for general use: manufacturers could say that calcium intake may prevent osteoporosis, that sodium may contribute to hypertension, that dietary fats may contribute to cardiovascular disease, and that dietary fats may be implicated in the development of cancer. By the time the proposals were reviewed and approved, two more claims had been added: that fiber from fruits, vegetables, and grains may help prevent cancer and heart disease, and that antioxidants (such as vitamins A and C) may reduce the risk of some cancers.

"Historically, the NLEA is probably the worst thing that could happen in the field of nutrition for years, from my point of view," DeFelice said. "The people at the FDA feel that they're solving the problem of how to regulate food health-claims, but what they have done is to cement it. They're closing the door to research, to innovation. They're saying that you can make certain general claims, in certain categories—say, about low-fat diets preventing cancer. But anybody can make those claims. So if I'm a food company, I'm not going to do any research; I'm going to wait for somebody else to do the research. I'm going to spend my money on promotion instead—on selling my products. They just killed R and D. Killed it!"

DeFelice has little patience for the new crackdown on spurious food-content claims. "These regulations about the words 'fresh' and 'lite'—they're insignificant," he went on. "That's not the issue, that's peripheral stuff: chicanery, hookerism! It's always been around. So clamp down on it. Why does something like that get front-page coverage? What I want to know is what do the docs say, what do the experts say, about a particular kind of cereal, and what it might do for me. What the FDA is doing is saying, 'Shut it down; we can't handle it. Certain categories you can make a claim, anything else we're going to shut down.' The people at the FDA don't realize that the action is right before their eyes: vitamin A and measles, magnesium and diabetes, it's happening right under their goddamn noses. Every day: cranberry juice and urinary-tract infections, in the *New England Journal of Medicine*. And they're fighting this knowledge. They want to smother it. Folic acid and neural tube defects in kids—we have a new era in medicine. The FDA is not involved in innovation; they're anti-innovation."

Trying to influence public policy is not what DeFelice was trained to do, but he has found, over the course of a varied career, that he has something of an affinity for it. He often refers to himself as a "drug man," and it was his work on drugs that eventually led him to superfoods, and to his public campaign on their behalf. Trained as an endocrinologist at Jefferson Medical College in Philadelphia, he entered clinical pharmacology, becoming chief of clinical pharmacology at the Walter Reed Army Institute of Research, where he worked in lieu of going to Southeast Asia after being drafted during the Vietnam War. "They pulled me out of the Army computers because I was recognized as having drug know-how," he said. "I was part of a whole group of doctors who'd been drafted, and I was the only one who didn't have to go to Vietnam." At Walter Reed he developed antimalarial and antiradiation compounds for the Department of Defense, and began his education in the big business of drug research. After Walter Reed, he spent several years as the medical director at Pfizer pharmaceutical company, learning about the industry side, then started his own research company in New York City, called BioBasics. Pharmaceutical companies would come to him to arrange testing of new drugs they were developing, and DeFelice did everything from designing the studies to having them peer-reviewed. By the midseventies, he had built his business into what he calls an "empire" at the corner of Thirty-eighth Street and Madison Avenue, employing a hundred people.

But by the early eighties, said DeFelice, "It was no fun anymore—research had become more of a legal, bureaucratic thing, all paperwork. I wanted to get back to working with ideas." He scaled down and started working on his own as a consultant to drug companies in this country and in Europe, helping them to develop new drugs and get them approved—a style of work he says he prefers. "A drug marketer comes to me and says, 'I want to expand in Europe and increase my sales by five hundred million in ten years'; or, 'I'm trying to deal with this company and I can't get through to the old man'; or, 'My research is bogged down; how can I rev it up?' So I help them out." DeFelice now maintains a small New York office and another in Cranford, New Jersey, near his home in Westfield, and employs only two assistants.

DeFelice's first brush with health policy began with a research project in 1964, while he was pursuing a fellowship in clinical pharmacology at St. Vincent's Medical Center in New York, on the effects of carnitine on hyperthyroidism. DeFelice quickly became fascinated with carnitine, a compound that occurs naturally in the human body and is vital to cell metabolism. After several years of clinical testing in animals and humans, often conducted on his own time and with his own money (most of it borrowed), DeFelice became convinced of carnitine's efficacy in treating several health problems, from shock to angina pectoris and other heart ailments. The most debilitating of these was a little-understood and difficult-to-diagnose condition called simply carnitine deficiency, which affects children and is usually fatal if untreated. But when DeFelice attempted to obtain FDA approval for the use of carnitine as a drug, making it available by doctors' prescription, he came upon a bureaucratic snafu: Because carnitine was a natural substance already available in health food stores as a dietary supplement, no pharmaceutical company would fund DeFelice's new-drug application for its clinical use. There was no economic incentive for obtaining a patent to produce and market carnitine for prescription only when anyone could already buy it on the cheap. DeFelice was surprised to find that he would have had better luck with a completely new, artificial drug molecule that a company could easily patent and to which it could retain exclusive marketing rights; as it was, the FDA required just as stringent testing of a natural substance for approval as a drug, but without the promise of exclusivity.

DeFelice's long struggle with the drug-approval process eventually made him an activist. In 1976, still working on carnitine, he created what he calls "a nonprofit educational organization" that he named the Foundation for Innovation in Medicine. Its first focus was to help push for passage of the Orphan Drug Act, so called because it gives economic incentives to encourage research on drugs that combat rare diseases and are thus unprofitable to develop and market. The act was passed by Congress in 1984, and in 1985 carnitine was approved as an orphan drug, based on an application prepared by DeFelice and funded by an Italian company, Sigma Tauw, which now dispenses carnitine by prescription (carnitine is still available in health-food stores, but Sigma Tauw has the exclusive right to offer it by prescription and is the only company authorized to make health claims on its behalf). The Foundation for Innovation in Medicine still serves as a backdrop for DeFelice's policy efforts, and until now has run mainly on his own money and on contributions from friends both in and out of the health industry. "Mostly European industrialists," DeFelice said. "The people who've contributed to the nutraceutical push had no vested interests in it—they're friends, contributing as a favor to me." That may change, however; DeFelice is thinking of seeking commercial sponsors of his nutraceutical initiative.

The carnitine experience spurred DeFelice to expand his thinking beyond the world of drugs. "The promise of nutrition started to hit me—an old drug man," he said. "The public sees the possibilities, but the docs don't. There's misinformation out there, but the public really wants to know. What I felt from my experience was that regulation drove out the innovators, the bright guys." DeFelice's carnitine experience also gave him the idea to structure his nutraceutical commission on the Orphan Drug Act, which not only loosens somewhat the scientific requirements for a company's new-drug application, but also grants a seven-year period of exclusivity during which no other company may market the drug. "That act said, look, there is no economic incentive to develop drugs for these diseases, because the regulations for a new-drug application require too large an investment; it doesn't pay to fund the application. So our nutraceutical commission will diminish the requirements for a new-drug application, and we will give you seven years' exclusivity for your claim. You don't have to do all those studies that the FDA requires before a drug can be marketed. You do a few studies, show some reasonable data, we'll give you exclusivity. In the twenty or thirty years before the Orphan Drug Act was passed, only about twenty orphan drugs were approved. Since the act, over three hundred have either been approved or are in the hopper, the R-and-D pipeline. It works, the exclusivity issue."

DeFelice's nutraceutical initiative would end up having as much to do with business as with science. According to DeFelice, the problem with nutraceuticals in this country, and the reason he needs to champion them, boils down to this: Food scientists are rapidly approaching the technological capability to create these superfoods, but they are not allowed to market them. Or, to be more precise, superfoods can be sold, but not *as* superfoods, because the government does not recognize any such entity. A superfood manufacturer is allowed, on his food label, to say what his product is but not what it does; he may not tout its health benefits. And why, asks DeFelice, should anyone go to the trouble of creating such specialized products if he cannot earn an extra dollar by making them special?

After we ordered our dessert at Aperitivo—espresso, raspberries soaked in Grand Marnier, and for DeFelice a cigar, chosen delightedly from a selection proffered at our table—he sat back and laid out for me how his nutraceutical commission would resolve this impasse. "Since the FDA considers any food a drug once you make a medical claim about it, if you want to make that kind of claim you have to enter the drug system," he explained. "Well, the average cost of getting a new drug approved is two hundred million dollars, because of the extensive testing that's required. So if I wanted to say that cranberry juice helps cure urinary-tract infections, I'd have to submit a new-drug application, and funding the necessary studies would cost so much that once I had it approved I'd have to charge, say, a dollar for my cranberry juice. Well, the guy next door is going to laugh, because he can charge ten cents. He didn't spend the two hundred million dollars, but he can use my claim, because I have no protection for it. What we have is a non-research-driven nutrition industry.

"The FDA has created a big vacuum. Look at the drug system. How do we learn about drugs? The pharmaceutical companies sponsor the research, they have it published in the journals, they go to tell the docs about it, the docs learn about it before the public does. You get rid of the charlatans that way. Well, this is what I want in the food industry. I want a company that does research to be able to submit a claim to a nutraceutical commission made up of experts who review it. If that commission says that your data support the fact that magnesium lowers hypertension in diabetics—two or three clinical trials, something reasonable—then you would get exclusivity on that claim for seven years. This will create a boom, a research-and-development-based nutrition industry. It's as simple as that. You'll get the mainstream science out of the laboratories and to the people."

At a juncture when the FDA is very publicly tightening regulations on what food marketers can say on their packaging about the health benefits of their products, DeFelice is galloping in the opposite direction. But he feels that his timing is on the money: "I've sort of hit the right moment in history," he said. "We're in a flow where the old systems are breaking down. I'm saying, Hey, let's create a new thing in medicine like the biotech revolution, or like orphan drugs. We're at a point in history where people are asking questions. They want the benefits of nutrition. And we have the technology now to move ahead."

• • •

It is said that Marcus Porcius Cato the Elder, Roman states-
man of the second century B.C., was convinced that cabbage had
special medicinal effects, and prescribed it for his wife and son
when they fell ill with fever (the cabbage did not save their lives,
but that did not shake his faith).[1] Garlic has been a favorite cure in
many cultures, including the Egyptian, Roman, Greek, Chinese,
Japanese, and Indian. An Egyptian medical text from 1500 B.C.
prescribes garlic for headaches, throat problems, and weakness,
among other ailments, and folklore holds that the builders of the
pyramids were fed large amounts of garlic to keep up their
strength. Pliny's *Historia Naturalis* suggested a garlic cure for
sixty-one different illnesses, including asthma, ulcers, tumors, and
consumption; Hippocrates held that it worked against digestive
upsets and uterine tumors. Garlic has also been prescribed, in the
last two thousand years, to prevent heart disease and rheumatism
(in India), to treat high blood pressure (in China and Japan), and
as an aphrodisiac (sixteenth-century England). As recently as
World War II, the British were using garlic to prevent septic poi-
soning and gangrene in battle wounds.[2]

Garlic has one of the richest histories of medical use, but
many other foods have been credited as therapeutic, including fish
(for rheumatism, arthritis, gout, pulmonary consumption, and as
"brain food"); ginger (for nausea, whooping cough, fever); grapes
(liver and kidney ailments, fevers, tuberculosis, dyspepsia); yams
(for rheumatism, arthritis, colic, asthma); and yogurt (for bowel
problems, senility, and to promote longevity).[3] An article in the
August 1896 *North American Review*, entitled "How to Prolong
Life," describes how to eat for longevity and has this to say about
the apple in particular: "The apple is such a common fruit that few
persons are familiar with its remarkably efficacious medicinal
properties. Everybody ought to know that the very best thing they
can do is to eat apples just before going to bed. The apple is excellent brain food because it has more phosphoric acid, in an easily
digestible shape, than any other fruit known. It excites the action
of the liver, promotes sound and healthy sleep, and thoroughly
disinfects the mouth. It also agglutinates the surplus acids of the

stomach, helps the kidney secretions, and prevents calculus growth, while it obviates indigestion and is one of the best preventives of diseases of the throat. Next to lemon and orange it is also the best antidote for the thirst and craving of persons addicted to the alcohol and opium habit."[4]

Before this century, foods (and herbs as well) were put forward to prevent and cure disease for one reason above all: There was not much else to choose from when it came to easing suffering or warding off infection. The first vaccine—for smallpox—was invented in 1796, but vaccination was not practiced widely until late in the next century. Penicillin, the first antibiotic, was discovered in 1928, and came into use in the United States in 1940. Surgery was a painful and extremely risky affair before about the middle of the nineteenth century, when anesthetics and sterile hospital procedures were introduced. The practice of medicine was in large part guesswork; some would argue that it still is, but at least we have more tools at hand. The drug industry grew explosively in the first half of the twentieth century (aspirin was developed in 1893, phenobarbital in 1903, novocaine in 1905, insulin in 1921, sulfa drugs in 1935, streptomycin in 1944), and as it did the role of food shifted, becoming simpler and more fun. Curing could be left to the pharmaceuticals; food, besides sustaining life, could provide entertainment.

That thinking began to change again in the 1960s and 1970s, spurred this time by fear; the emerging environmental movement and the awareness of pesticides and preservatives that accompanied it made the words "all natural" the most popular phrase on food labels. Health food stores began to prosper, as consumers became suspicious of food additives and more open to the notion of certain foods as health-givers. But the big leap, according to DeFelice, occurred in the mid-1980s, with what he calls, in his shorthand fashion, "calcium–fiber–fish oil." "Calcium–fiber–fish oil changed the history of American medicine, not because of their particular value but because they made nutrition legitimate," he said. "For the first time, doctors joined the nutrition revolution. Without the doctors, who would believe it? Clinical data were published in reputable journals—*The New England Journal of Medicine, The Journal of the AMA*—and the health food industry was transformed forever. Instead of this mom-and-pop business—where it was really just the consumer and the proprietor figuring out what to eat—suddenly the doctors were involved, saying calcium may be good for you, fiber may be good for you. That to me was one of the biggest historical changes in medicine."

It was a change that, in DeFelice's view, left the FDA playing catch-up. Even as the media abetted this shift in medical knowledge, reporting on study after study that linked food and health—high-fat diets may cause breast cancer, fiber may prevent colon cancer, green tea may block the action of many carcinogens, oat bran may lower cholesterol and thus help prevent heart attacks—the FDA's official stance on how food manufacturers might use such information remained cautious. But in the context of the FDA's own history, that caution is not surprising.

The first laws to regulate the marketing of foods offered for sale in the United States were passed almost a century ago, when Congress approved the Pure Food and Drug Act of 1906. That act, enforced by the Bureau of Chemistry of the USDA, did not have as its primary focus health claims on foods; the greater problem with food at that time was purity, while it was the drug business that specialized in false claims for health benefits. The market was flooded with ersatz drugs, often called patent medicines—for instance, syrups for babies that contained narcotics. The food industry, similarly unregulated, was producing adulterated and unsanitary goods: Pickles and peas were often colored with copper salts, baking powder could contain ammonia, vinegar might include sulfuric acid. Conditions in meat-packing plants, described in stomach-turning detail in Upton Sinclair's novel *The Jungle*, were filthy. In 1927 the Food and Drug Administration was created within the USDA and took over enforcement from the Bureau of Chemistry; a year later Congress passed a revision of the 1906 guidelines called the Food, Drug, and Cosmetic Act, which remains the FDA's charter, with amendments added as food technology has evolved. For decades the FDA's position on health claims for foods was very clear and essentially unchallenged: Making a medical claim for a food item made it legally a drug, and the FDA would demand that either the claims or the product be removed in the absence of extensive testing for safety and efficacy.[5] The agency has the power to issue "cease and desist" orders against violators, or even to seize goods and bring the sellers to court, but usually the offending manufacturer quietly withdrew, unwilling to risk unflattering publicity.

That tidy system collapsed in 1984, in the midst of a general retreat from regulations on business in the Reagan era. In that year, the Kellogg Company started a new marketing and advertising campaign for their All-Bran cereal, featuring the headline: "Finally, some news about cancer you can live with." The copy, carried in print ads as well as on the back of the cereal package, went on to urge a high-fiber, low-fat diet as a way of preventing cancer, naming as a source the National Cancer Institute; the presumed message was that eating that particular cereal would ward off cancer. Here was a hefty health claim for a food, and the FDA decided to allow it. In fact, the agency decided to use it as a test case, assigning two of its consumer science specialists to conduct a study of "the effects of a health promotion advertising campaign on sales of ready-to-eat cereals."[6]

The FDA's compliance was not completely unexpected. The agency had been widely criticized for several years for the strictness of its health-claim regulations—especially in light of a growing body of scientific evidence, some of it the result of decades-long epidemiological studies, of the connections between diet and the prevention of chronic disease. The All-Bran experiment signaled the FDA's ambivalence, the first loosening of the bonds, but if the agency's leaders had expected a slow, careful expansion of health claims, what they got instead was an avalanche. The agency had tacitly acknowledged that the old regulations were too restrictive by backing off from enforcement, admitting in the summary of the All-Bran study that its policy of discouraging the use of health claims on food labels was "currently under review by the agency." But no new rules were yet in place, and marketers responded with a free-for-all—high-fiber doughnuts marketed as health food, cereals with minute amounts of oat bran touted as cholesterol-busters. The FDA's actions since then have been somewhat confused. The agency has issued new proposals for regulating food health-claims almost every year since 1987. Some excited so much confusion and resistance that they never made it beyond the proposal stage; others led eventually to the passage of the Nutrition Labeling and Education Act of 1990 by Congress, and to the proposed new rules that were hotly debated, almost derailed by the USDA, and finally approved by the White House in December of 1992.

The day after the first NLEA proposals had been released for public comment, in November of 1991, I spoke with Fred R. Shank, the director of the FDA's Center for Food Safety and Applied Nutrition. "Health messages are new to us, and we've opened the door," he said. "Are we satisfying everyone? Probably not. But at least we're saying that health messages on food labels are possible today. Eighteen months ago we weren't saying that. So it's an evolutionary process. Science is the limiting factor."

I asked for his opinion of DeFelice's idea for a nutraceutical commission to deal specifically with foods that purport to have medicinal value. "Separate commission—that's ridiculous!" Shank replied heatedly. "I mean, we've got foods here, we've got drugs here. And therefore, we should have the expertise to deal with the labeling, safety, and efficacy of those types of substances, once they are ready to be marketed. We don't need a separate commission, we need more science."

The "safety and efficacy" issue mentioned by Shank is at the heart of the FDA's approval system. When agency scientists consider a drug for approval, they split their investigations into two categories: tests for safety, and tests for efficacy. Is it safe, and does it work? When those standards are applied to foods that carry a health claim, it becomes clear why the FDA disapproves of DeFelice's proposals for a special commission to handle nutraceuticals.

"Basically, he would like the best of all worlds with the least interference," I was told by one FDA scientist. "Drugs require proof of efficacy and safety, but you can sometimes trade off safety against efficacy; for example, a drug like AZT, which is used to treat AIDS, can have serious side effects—that is, it can be less safe than we would like—but the condition it treats is itself so treacherous that the drug is worth approving. But foods must be safe, period. They are not being used to treat someone who has a fatal disease. We have no basis for risk benefit when we approve a claim for a food—it must be safe. But these people would like looser requirements for safety, *and* looser requirements for efficacy as well. And drugs are administered under medical supervision—something that would not be true of these foods. This idea of a separate system is driven by an unhappiness with having to follow the law in either category that currently exists, food or drugs." Questions of testing, of risk, and of benefit, are likely to be central to the future of DeFelice's nutraceutical initiative—and, by extension, to the development and marketing of designer foods in general. The American public may be, as DeFelice claims, eager for the advent of nutraceuticals, but it has also shown itself to be extremely averse to risk; consider, for example, the public response to nuclear power after the accident at Three Mile Island, and to apples treated with Alar. The public support of the FDA's crackdown on exaggerated health claims on food labels also suggests that consumers may not want to give superfoods a shortcut to respectability.

DeFelice's rebuttal to the FDA's reservations relies on what he considers to be common sense. In discussing questions of testing for safety, he pointed out that nutraceuticals are natural substances that man has consumed for centuries; a certain level of safety can be assumed to have been proven. And his standards for efficacy would be looser than those of the FDA precisely because nutraceuticals are *not* drugs. On the question of how much testing to require, he favors a policy of flexibility. "What's enough evidence?" he asked. "My commission might say, with regard to one nutraceutical, 'Give us another study.' Use the experts, case by case—every case is different, from flaxseed bread to chicken soup to extracts from a lizard's gizzard. So a food manufacturer will come to the nutraceutical commission with his scientific evidence—you would have some kind of formality for screening the applications—and you send the evidence out to the experts in that particular field, and the experts send back their opinion. The commission can overrule them, if there's a compelling reason. The commission may say, 'You must do more work, more studies.' Or it may say, 'This is so novel, so new, that it must be treated more as a drug; you'll need two years' toxicity studies.' Because the product is so concentrated, say—or because the animal data doesn't look good. But handle it case by case." DeFelice also feels that testing can be less rigorous if the health claim itself is qualified. "Put the qualifications on your label," he said. "Say 'There is some evidence that this product may be beneficial.' 'May'—that's all you have to say. 'This may help prevent lung cancer.' You don't have to say 'does.'"

But there is a problem here—one that even DeFelice acknowledges: It is very difficult to claim results when you are dealing with diseases that take decades to develop and may be caused by any number of environmental or lifestyle factors. Much of the evidence that indicates a preventive connection between diet and disease, for instance, is based on animal research—studies that may or may not be applicable to human beings. The question of whether or not a concentrated extract of celery juice that reduces mammary tumors in rats will do the same for women at risk for breast cancer will take years to answer. And even studies using humans—whether they are long-term epidemiological surveys that look at entire populations or shorter-term clinical trials that look at "markers" for cancer in a group of people at high risk for the disease—are often subject to wide-ranging interpretation. DeFelice himself is wary of epidemiological studies because they are so speculative. But he is nonetheless comfortable allowing a claim for efficacy that seems reasonable, even if all the evidence will not be in until sometime in the next century. What the FDA sees in such a shortcut, however, is a potential policy nightmare—a chaos of claims on everything from cookies to frozen pizza, the kind of thing DeFelice calls "hookerism." When FDA scientists and spokesmen talk about protecting the consumer, they are talking about protecting people not only from ingesting dangerous substances but from misleading claims from purveyors of modern-day snake oil in the form of super-beta-carotene muffins.

DeFelice reads more than simple protectiveness into the FDA's actions, however; he sees the agency's hesitancy in the context of what he considers to be a larger pattern of conservatism and tunnel vision in the scientific community. What we are thinking about food these days, he says, is based on very sketchy and inconclusive research, but that research is being presented as received wisdom. The result, according to DeFelice, is a nation of scientific followers afraid to challenge one another's thinking, and a nation of fearful and pleasure-starved eaters. "We're very paranoid and, let's say, desperate about what we eat," he said. He sees his nutraceutical commission as a way to throw open the windows and bring in fresh, unbiased ideas about food and health—and perhaps, paradoxically, free us to eat more pleasurably.

This is where DeFelice's philosophy makes its greatest stretch, leading, improbably, from the superfood revolution back to spaghetti carbonara and pork chops. His reasoning runs like this: the economic incentive provided by the bylaws of the nutraceutical commission will foster, as a byproduct of the rush to create marketable super foods, a much greater volume of research that will eventually answer all of our questions about eating and disease, presumably without the preconceived notions that he feels currently grip the scientific establishment. The ascendancy of nutraceuticals could, in this blueprint, also obviate the need for self-denial—hence DeFelice's refusal to give up his dark meat and pork fat. Perhaps, in DeFelice's view of the meal of the future, an appetizer of superjuice to prevent heart disease and cancer will clear the decks for a main course of steak and baked potato with sour cream.

Meanwhile, he is keeping his distance from many of the current ideas about food that are being disseminated by what he calls the "Savonarolas" of the scientific establishment (based on the fifteenth-century Italian monk and religious reformer whose faith never wavered, even when he was burned as a heretic). DeFelice's Savonarolas are hard-liners whose almost religiously held assumptions would, presumably, be challenged under a more entrepreneurial system. "Take the fat story, because the fat story is an example of what happens under the present FDA system, where entrepreneurial research is not being encouraged," said DeFelice. "The fat story was created. The docs believe it, everybody believes it. If I get up in a meeting and say to my colleagues that the dangers of dietary fat are overrated, they'll come down on me. Now, I know that they don't know the data. The data clearly say that we don't know enough yet about the connection between dietary fat and disease. The data say that there's an association between fat intake and illness in a small percentage of people. But we've made a lot of neurotics over this fat issue. The French eat more fat than we do, and they drink a lot, and they have less cardiovascular disease. Why?

"There's some really irresponsible medicine out there. Some of these advocates want to start taking fats out of kids' meals. But what's a high source of energy? Fat, when you're young. Fat delivers more calories per molecule than carbohydrates do. So they took bologna out of all the kids' diets. Bologna! You know, kids are not getting heart disease. We're finding that about eighty percent of the kids who had high cholesterol when they were seven or eight years old were normal by the time they became teenagers. You don't see that headline, right? And what are you doing to that kid's totality when you lower his fat intake? What are you doing to his mood, his energy? They're experimenting with kids—it's scary. But the advocacy out there—and the media don't attack these guys, they join 'em. The docs join 'em. It's becoming an industry.

"Take the cholesterol thing. I could introduce you to three top guys, all widely respected guys in the lipid field, epidemiologists, you couldn't get any higher than these guys—they will say to you that this fear of cholesterol is ridiculous. Ridiculous to the degree to which the message has been pushed, that is. There might be a certain percentage of people who have trouble with cholesterol, but not everyone does. These researchers used to get up in meetings to say this. They're not doing it anymore, though, because they've been blasted. If they go public, they're crucified. We have an intimidation system: You can't say anything bad about the cholesterol story, and you can't say that fat is good. Cholesterol is a very important ingredient in the body, you know—one of the most critical. But no one ever says, 'Don't eat too many low-cholesterol foods, because it could be bad for your health.' Here's my problem with this. Say there are risk factors associated with a condition like having high cholesterol. The next question is, what do you do about it? If you modify your diet, is that a help? *That's* where the data are weak, in fact nonexistent. And if you do lower your cholesterol, does it make a difference in when you die? No one knows this. It may be that only five percent of the population has to worry about dietary intake of cholesterol raising their blood cholesterol levels. But lowering dietary cholesterol is what's been sold, and that's what I'm against. The selling of that idea to the media, to academicians, with nonpeer data. This whole epidemiological area—handling large numbers of patients—it's very tricky. Even the experts disagree. Epidemiologists are like economists; you can look at their data from various points of view. It could be that diet is not that important. There could be other factors—the water we drink, or our emotions . . . the mind's never considered. All the great philosophies say that mind affects body, but we don't always look at mind factors. Maybe most of the people with high cholesterol who die from heart disease are the ones with depression. Maybe the French are happier than we are, and high cholesterol doesn't kill them. We don't know—that's what I'm getting at. And we're never going to find out, unless industry gets in there and starts paying money to do the studies."

One of DeFelice's favorite examples of the fallibility of the current theorizing about food and health—and of the way ideas about food quickly become truths in the eyes of the public—involves the Eskimos and heart attacks. The first suspicions that omega-3 fatty acids helped prevent heart disease emerged from studies of Eskimos, who consume large amounts of fat in the form of blubber and yet have much lower rates of heart disease than other Americans. Researchers began looking at the ingredients of the fat that Eskimos consumed and isolated omega-3 fatty acids, which they theorized had a role in protecting the heart. "The thinking is that Eskimos don't get heart attacks because of omega-3," said DeFelice. "Well, I could tell you it's because they don't have telephones. And that's not a joke. Have you heard of silent ischemia? Ischemia is lack of oxygen to the heart. Angina pectoris is a lack of oxygen too, but you feel the chest pain, you take a nitroglycerin and it dilates your arteries and does other things, and everything is fine. With silent ischemia you get no oxygen to your heart but you don't get the chest pain, so there's no signal. This is more prevalent than so-called noisy ischemia, where you do feel the pain. So they did a study of silent ischemia. When do you get it? Of course, you get it when you're exercising, but you are more likely to get it under psychological stress. The telephone is one of the major causes of silent ischemia. I'm serious now. The reason Eskimos don't get heart attacks up there is that they don't have telephones. Telephones cause ischemia, in our culture. I could say there's more evidence that telephone calls cause ischemia than that fish oil gets rid of it. But people have just closed their minds."

DeFelice sat back, empty espresso cup before him. "Nobody talks about pleasure—the need for it," he said. "The docs aren't telling them, the government's not telling them. Enjoy yourself. Nothing like good friends, good food, a bottle of wine. Don't say that fat has to be bad. Look at the French, the Italians—they're doing all right."

By this time, it felt like we had traveled far from supercarrots, but in DeFelice's complicated philosophy it is all one. All of these quandaries—the need for superfoods, the intransigence of the FDA, the overselling of the fat and cholesterol stories, Americans' loss of pleasure in eating—has a common cure: "an R-and-D-based industry," a phrase DeFelice repeats almost like a mantra. He sees himself not exactly as a guru but as a catalyst, a global thinker who will set the new nutraceutical industry on the right track. "I create, as Thomas Jefferson said, the mighty wave of public opinion," he declared. "The word 'nutraceutical' is out there now, people are using it." But as we pushed ourselves away from the table and prepared to leave the restaurant, it seemed clear that, despite the food-as-drug implications of his nutraceutical revolution, DeFelice has a keen sense of what is lost when food and medicine become indistinguishable.

Six weeks after our lunch at Aperitivo, DeFelice held a press conference in New York to present and discuss his white paper outlining his proposed nutraceutical commission. The conference was, appropriately, in a room just off the restaurant in the Omni Berkshire Hotel, with a couple of tureens of coffee set up and a view of scurrying waiters preparing for the lunch rush. It was the week before Christmas, and DeFelice's turnout was small: reporters from three food-industry publications, and an interview scheduled on the Cable News Network later in the day. This is not the "mighty wave of public opinion" DeFelice was anticipating, not nearly the level of interest that had been generated earlier in the year when he had released his new "nutraceutical" word. Then, his press conference had attracted about sixty reporters, and he had ended up being cited in stories in *Vegetarian Times*, *Longevity*, and *Health*, and had fielded calls from the TV show "20/20" and the *New York Times*.

At this press conference, he launched gamely into his presentation, but as it wound down, DeFelice became candid about the difficulties he is up against, acknowledging that his push is a one-man show. "There are vested interests against this, in the drug companies," he said. "I went to the supplement people, the vitamin people, to get their support, but they don't want to get behind this. They're afraid of change—of what new regulations might mean." Many of the questions from the reporters present focused on safety and efficacy problems. As the meeting neared its end DeFelice admitted: "If the media doesn't buy this, I go away. The media's got to buy this for it to work. But this is my hobby, not my life."

A few weeks later, I talked again with DeFelice, who was refusing to admit discouragement at the response to his white paper and press conference. "The first press conference got a big reaction, when I introduced the whole nutraceutical concept, but this was just a briefing—almost a rehash, just showing how we can implement the nutraceutical commission. This is all germinating. We got some newspaper stories going—in Dallas, San Francisco; the *Wall Street Journal* is interested. You see the word nutraceutical all over the place. But it's in limbo. I want to have a big media event next winter, have the Europeans and Japanese there, a big conference on the promise of natural substances, with audience participation. I'm good at running that, a think tank with the audience and a panel—a Socratic event." He also talked more about directly lobbying Congress—"not me, I'm not a lobbyist, it's not my temperament. But we need to find a leader down there, someone who knows his way around the Hill."

It has occurred to DeFelice that he is ahead of the game, but he sees that only in terms of international competition. "The Europeans and Japanese are competitive with us, and they're ahead of us in nutraceuticals, but nobody in the drug and food industry sees their head start as a threat," he said. "They're beginning to see the danger of lagging behind—they'll listen now—but they don't really see it." He has not extrapolated any further, to question whether the ordinary eater is ready to think of food as a collection of medicines. When I asked him about the future of food by any definition, he responded with a neatly packaged philosophical précis. "This is my theory now—you ready?" he asked. "Food has taken the place of God. Short term, religion is no match for technology. Religion has taken a beating, with the technological revolution. So God is gone, and food has replaced God. These people who are always talking about their diet, they don't want to die. So there's a hunger for the medicinal value of food. They want everything—give me pleasure, sex, drugs, food—and they don't want to die. Everybody's scared of it. I don't want to die, either. But I ain't gonna live my every goddamn day thinking about dying."

For DeFelice, food has already been transformed; all we can

do now is try to catch up to it, and manipulate that transformation into a shape that makes sense to us. As we talked, it became clearer that for him, superfoods will take the shape of a tablet: dietary supplements. Many supplements exist already, of course, composed of substances that some researchers feel prevent cancer and heart disease and other ailments: fish-oil tablets, fiber supplements, calcium pills, even beta-carotene tablets. But their labels cannot contain any claims for potential health benefits, for the same reason that nutraceuticals cannot make claims: a health claim would make the tablet a drug in the eyes of the FDA (dietary supplements are legally considered foods), subject to all the testing necessary for drug approval. (Many supplement-manufacturers step around these restrictions by making what are called "name claims," devising product names like Lung Care Tab, Masculine Drive Tab, and Cell Guard.) "Bottom line, it's not in the meal you sit down and eat," said DeFelice, "it's what you supplement over and above a normal diet—like a designer food, but also like vitamin C."

"When you talk about supplements, it sounds more like a drug than a food," I remarked.

"See, there you go!" DeFelice crowed. "Forget about your definitions. What is it? Create a new category, don't get involved with whether it's a drug or a food. If you read the medical journals, you see that all the action is in dietary supplements—carotene, calcium, vitamin A. That's where it's happening. But the FDA is going to release some new guidelines soon on the regulation of supplements, and they're going to try to put a clamp on any kinds of implied health claims. They want to limit dosing, they want to limit distribution, and this and that. I might get some media impact there, some publicity for the nutraceutical initiative."

He was already working over some related ideas that sounded like the next challenge for the Foundation for Innovation in Medicine, after nutraceuticals: the need for more freedom to conduct clinical trials (studies using humans rather than animals) for drugs and nutraceuticals. "The other evening I was sitting in a little cabin I own up in the mountains in New Jersey, and I was looking out at the beavers in my pond, and at the deer, and having a martini," DeFelice said. "And I was thinking, the FDA has really blocked the innovator when it comes to clinical trials. You need big bucks, you need a drug company or NIH to do clinical trials anymore. And you don't discover anything medically unless you test it in people. Beta-carotene, fiber, fish oil—all that means nothing until you put it in people and you show that it works. That's where the FDA has interfered the most."

DeFelice was giving himself another year to finish launching nutraceuticals. "Then I'm going to back off," he said. "Go on to other pursuits. The momentum's there. It's on the table. And the word's in the lexicon. I'm a media guy—I put the message out to people. The nutraceutical revolution has arrived. It's here. It's just not legal yet."

Chapter Five

•

DESIGNER FOODS

Making Breads with a Blueprint

•

Working out of a small, independently owned bakery in the middle of Wisconsin's farm country, a low-tech but New Age food scientist is touting breads made with a grain that he says is the next oat bran, only better. This wonder ingredient, flaxseed, has a steadily improving pedigree as research into its properties is showing that it may help prevent heart disease and cancer, and even promote bone strength and fertility. In fact, flaxseed has put the back-to-nature Wisconsin baker/scientist at the cutting edge of food technology, because it could be called the first designer-food ingredient.

Designer foods, most of which are still on the drawing-boards, would use natural substances to inhibit specific diseases—taking the form of, perhaps, anticancer juices and antiarthritis rolls—and if they overcome current hurdles in food regulation they could make the oat bran campaign look minor league in comparison. Like oat bran, designer foods work on the assumption that consumers will find the promise of magic ingredients—and easy answers to complicated health problems—irresistible.

•

Paul Stitt has been designing breads based on their health-promoting and disease-preventive potential for more than fifteen years, and now that his company—Natural Ovens of Manitowoc, Wisconsin—is finally on its feet he likes to tell the story of the cinnamon rolls, and of how he was widely vilified as a betrayer of the citizens of Manitowoc. He told the tale over breakfast at his home in Manitowoc, a city of 83,000 on the western shore of Lake Michigan, forty-five miles from Green Bay. On the table before us were waffles made from a mix created by Paul's wife, Barbara, who is the vice president of Natural Ovens. Paul and Barbara have packaged the mix, and it is sold as a Natural Ovens product. "Barbara Stitt's Pancake and Waffle Mix" contains oat bran, flaxseed, soy milk, and egg, and, for the benefit of those who feel they may have certain food allergies, the recipe omits any wheat, dairy products, or yeast. (Some nutritionists believe that allergies to wheat and milk are common and largely undiagnosed, and that consumption of yeast can lead to recurring yeast infections or other health problems; others believe such allergies have been greatly oversold.) In addition to the waffles, which were topped with strawberry puree and served with pure maple syrup on the side, breakfast consisted of pieces of honeydew melon, decaffeinated black coffee, and tall glasses of cold water. It was a model of New Age eating wisdom: no caffeine, no refined sugar, no milk products, no yeast, no wheat, very little fat, healthy amounts of fresh fruits.

"I decided to buy the bakery in town over fifteen years ago," Stitt told me. He is in his fifties, and his sandy hair, light blue eyes, and rather broad face announce his Midwestern heritage. "I already owned a cheese store, and I couldn't find any decent bread to buy for my store, so I decided to make my own. And the first thing I did, about two weeks after I took over the plant, was that I quit making cinnamon rolls. Now, these cinnamon rolls were Manitowoc's favorite junk food, and people here resented me for what I'd done. It got so bad I could hardly walk down the street. People would accost me and cuss me out, saying they wouldn't buy my bread if I wouldn't make the sweet rolls. And the banker canceled my loan—I had to find another bank. But I couldn't go back to making those rolls. It's totally against everything I believe in. All I could see in that product was just harm. So in short order, within a couple of months, my business in Manitowoc dropped drastically, because people would not buy any of my breads." As it happened, that may have been all for the best, because the shrinking of the Manitowoc market forced Stitt to sell his breads farther afield, leading, after some uncertain years, to the growth of a seven-million-dollar-a-year baking business that by the early 1990s employed a hundred and thirty people.

Stitt now sells his products in supermarkets in Illinois, Minnesota, Indiana, and all over Wisconsin, and conducts a mail-order business with customers in every state in the country. His breads bear no relation to cinnamon rolls. They are formulated to promote health and even extend life, to eliminate precursors to disease, to reduce the risk of cancer, heart disease, osteoporosis, arthritis. There are currently fifteen varieties of bread, and nine kinds of rolls and muffins, all of which achieve their purported effect through the use of an assortment of vitamins, minerals, and nutrients. The most promising of these ingredients—and the one unique to Stitt's products—is flaxseed, a rich source of omega-3 fatty acids, which are thought to provide protection against heart disease. Flaxseed also contains compounds called lignans, which early studies are showing may help prevent the development of cancerous cell changes. Flaxseed, Stitt says, is "going to be the buzzword of the nineties."

It is flaxseed that makes Stitt into something of a paradox. Although he embodies a deep respect for the natural order—he uses no artificial ingredients or preservatives, bakes his breads slowly rather than rushing them through as do other commercial bakers, raises farm animals to see how they thrive on his products, believes in eating close to the bottom of the food chain—he also stands close to the cutting edge of a new food technology. He has been called "the first real producer of designer foods in the United States" by the man who coined the term "designer food," a term and an idea that suggest a futuristic cuisine similar to that described by Stephen DeFelice, coiner of "nutraceutical." Designer foods, say the researchers who are trying to lay the scientific foundations for them, will be actual, concrete foods-as-medicine: they will be created specifically to prevent certain diseases, most notably cancers and heart disease. They will be, though no one wants to use the term, culinary magic bullets, swooping in to decimate disease-makers—rogue cells, gathering blood clots, free radicals. Flaxseed is Stitt's magic ingredient; with its anticancer, anti–heart disease properties, it turns out to be easily incorporated into all kinds of products—ice cream, salad dressing, even processed foods like luncheon meats. What's particularly incongruous in Stitt's status as flaxseed's first American promoter is that while he personally believes in adjusting our eating to match what we have learned about diet and health—whole grains, fruits and vegetables, little or no meat—the concept behind designer foods is the opposite: Rather than changing our eating to be healthier, we'll change our food itself.

Stitt's lifestyle in Manitowoc carries no suggestion of such high-tech aspirations. He has long since regained his standing in town, once the cinnamon roll furor died down, and now he and Barbara embody small-town success and prosperity. In 1988, the year he completed construction of a 28,000-square-foot baking plant outside Manitowoc to replace the old 5,000-square-foot building in town, he and Barbara won several regional awards, including the Industry of the Year Award from the Manitowoc–Two Rivers Area Chamber of Commerce, the Small Business Persons of the Year Award from First Interstate Bank of Wisconsin–Sheboygan and Manitowoc Counties, and the Small Business Persons of the Year Award from the U.S. Small Business Administration's Northeast Wisconsin Advisory Council. Next to their new plant the Stitts maintain a small "observation farm" that houses 150 pigs, 250 chickens, and 6 massive Belgian horses. Each year Paul drives the horses in various regional parades, choosing from among many invitations, while Barbara has founded a group called the Festival of Flowers that encourages the planting of flowers and gardens in Manitowoc's public areas.

As the three of us sat at the Stitt's dining room table, finishing our waffles and looking out at Lake Michigan through the expansive windows that lined two walls of the room, a Natural Ovens truck rolled by on the highway that skirts the lake. "Oh, that's Jodi, doing her early rounds," Paul Stitt said. It was 8:00 A.M. on a frigid, crystalline day in early November, and Manitowoc was in the midst of its first prewinter cold snap—temperatures of sixteen degrees (with a windchill of zero) and, the day before, a few flurries of snow. The lake, reaching to the horizon, looked deep gray-blue with touches of frost at the shore. As we watched, a squirrel perched in the bright early-morning sunshine on a feeding stand just outside the window, and a multicolored pheasant strolled into the yard, where the summer's rosebushes were covered with straw to protect them from the cold. Stitt was describing a recent experimental diet that he and Barbara tried out: as much bread as they wanted, and water (or herbal tea). (Paul laughed good-naturedly about the fact that this diet sounds reminiscent of prison fare—in the days before prison reform.) They followed this diet, along with four volunteers from the Natural Ovens staff, for three days. "What we were actually doing was satisfying an FDA request to determine the caloric content of two of our breads, Light Wheat and Nutty Wheat, by using a method where you measure calories going into the body and calories coming out," Stitt explains. "But we learned some things that surprised us—for instance, we found that none of us could eat more than about twelve slices a day; we had expected to be eating something like twenty. And after the first day or so we wanted less. It was just very filling and satisfying. Although we weren't doing it as a weight-loss plan, none of us would have minded losing a few pounds, and everyone did lose, from two to eleven pounds. It's been shown that if you eat bread with a meal you tend to eat more of the other foods rather than less; but with just the bread we ate less as time went on."

"It's also been found that people eat more when they're in a larger group," added Barbara. She is a little more sharply drawn than Paul, and a few years older. Her gaze is intent and her opinions strongly and sometimes sternly voiced, while his are tempered with occasional humor. Both the Stitts might be called global in their approach to food; just about every aspect of life is viewed through a framework of nutritional beliefs. Barbara's particular preoccupation is the link between food and behavior; Paul's is what he calls "solving world hunger."

Barbara's previous career was as a probation officer in Cuyahoga Falls, Ohio, but that changed when she began to develop theories about possible links between criminal behavior and an inadequate diet. Her first subject for study was herself. At the time, she was suffering from occasional blackouts, during one of which she left a courtroom after a case, descended in the courthouse elevator, and found herself out on the street with no memory of how she got there. She saw several doctors for this problem and for a host of physical ailments—including arthritis and symptoms of premature menopause—and being dissatisfied with their suggestions (which usually included the use of tranquilizers), she began to change her diet, switching from a candy bar–and-caffeine regimen to one that included whole grains, fresh vegetables, and fruit. When that turned out to be effective, she extended the same thinking to her clients, and began to put them on similar diets. Over a five-year period, she found that of the 1,100 people she counseled, 89 percent stayed out of jail. Her approach to changing criminal behavior eventually attracted the attention of the *Wall Street Journal*, and after an article about her methods appeared in June of 1977 she was featured on several television talk shows and eventually quit her job to become a lecturer on food and behavior. She met Paul Stitt in 1980, when she gave a speech at the Wisconsin Natural Foods Association Conference in Fond du Lac; he walked up to her afterwards and gave her a sample of Natural Ovens Sunny Millet Bread, which she loved. She wrote to ask for more of it, and became Natural Ovens's first UPS customer. She and Paul were married in 1982.

Paul Stitt, for his part, toys with the notion that the answer to world hunger is bread. "You could give people flaxseed, whole grains, a packet of the kinds of vitamins and minerals we use to fortify our breads, and they could make their own breads and really hardly need anything else to be healthy," he told me. He is by nature both an idealist and an experimenter, tinkering with new products, testing out current ones, and using himself, his wife, his staff, and the animals on his observation farm as guinea pigs. It was with that kind of work in mind that he obtained his master's degree in biochemistry from the University of Wisconsin in 1969 and entered the food industry. His first job was with Tenneco Chemicals in New Jersey, where his assignment was to create an inexpensive form of protein that would, of all things, help solve world hunger. The story of his journey from the mainstream food industry to the entrepreneurial world of designer foods is, at least in its early stages, a tale of disillusionment and frustration. Stitt had traced that transformation for me the day before, as we drove to Manitowoc from the Green Bay airport, across rolling dairy land studded with red barns, silver silos, and white-shingled farmhouses with front porches. "At Tenneco we were working on a process of taking methanol and feeding it to high-temperature bacteria, to come up with single-celled protein," he said. "In the sixties the big thing was to save the world, and we were window dressing for the company. I found out later it was the wife of one of the vice presidents who had this save-the-world attitude. She wanted the company to do something useful with its millions of dollars of profits. But the company also saw this as an economic opportunity: if we were successful, this product could be sold to developing countries. Well, we did succeed. We took two years instead of four, and we found a cheap way to manufacture a single-celled protein in powder form that could be incorporated into foods, like breads, to boost their protein content. So the chairman called us together on New Year's Eve—I thought we were going to get a bonus or something—and instead he fired the whole crew. He said, 'I'd end up with a pile of protein out back that I have no use for.' The problem was, when it got right down to it, he decided it wasn't worth the trouble.

"So then I moved to the Quaker Oats company, outside Chicago, in Barrington, Illinois. Quaker also seemed to want to do some idealistic things; I knew the company had worked on a project in Guatemala developing a grain-based nutritional product to feed to children there. I was working on making protein products out of the byproducts of oat manufacture, but instead of using them to feed the world's hungry the company plugged them back into their oats product. Then they found that the healthier the product was, the less of it people needed to eat. And, of course, they wanted people to eat *more*. So they put me onto finding ways to get people to eat larger and larger amounts of their products. I was working with flavor enhancers and various other chemicals. At one point my boss said to me, 'You're doing a great job, but let me give you some advice: Don't let your kids eat this stuff.' I just couldn't understand how people could do that; how they could produce food that's not good for you."

By this time Stitt was based in Manitowoc, where Quaker had a contract with a specialized research laboratory. When he couldn't live with the Quaker policies any longer, he quit and "fumbled around" for a while, conducting his own research in his basement and living off a small windfall from the sale of some land. "I was developing high-protein food products from cheese whey," he said. "It would solve the problem of waste control for cheese companies and at the same time it would create a market for their byproducts." But he couldn't afford to stay unemployed for long, and soon he bought a cheese store in Manitowoc. A year later, in 1976, the baking plant in town came up for sale.

"I worked with the previous owners for three weeks, to learn how they made bread," he went on. "Then I decided what I wanted the breads to contain nutritionally, and I just kept experimenting to find ways to get it in there, to get the levels of nutrients I wanted—trial and error, making small changes at a time, and trying not to make so many mistakes that we had to throw it away. I got about twelve or fifteen different vitamins and minerals worked into the bread, and it seemed like every time I improved the bread and made it more nutritional, more people bought the bread." A few years ago, Stitt began marketing a bread he called Arthritis Bread. He had become convinced that part of the best treatment for arthritis was dietary. "But the FDA came along and said you can't call it that," he said. "So we changed the name of the bread to Nutty Wheat Bread, but made it exactly the same way."

The turning point for Stitt was his discovery of flaxseed. "About six years ago, a doctor from Chicago called me up out of the blue and said, 'Paul, your breads are ninety-eight percent perfect. Why don't you go all the way? You're using refined and processed oil, and there are some hazards associated with using it.' At the time I was using peanut oil, after having tried corn oil and soybean oil, both of which had some problems associated with them. So I said to him, 'Well, I have to have some type of fat in the bread to keep it soft and moist; otherwise it just hardens up so fast you can't sell it. What do you suggest I do?' And he said, 'You're a biochemist, you figure it out,' and hung up. I had wanted to add an oil seed of some kind to the product, because I was beginning to realize that the problem comes often not in the oil itself but in the way it's extracted. So I looked at various oil seeds that could be ground up and added to the bread. I tried soybeans, and the bread tasted like paint. And then I tried sunflower seeds ground up, and that made the bread real crumbly. Then I tried flaxseed and it made the bread hold together very well. And I got to thinking, That's nice, but I wonder what else there is in flax? So I went to the library and put the word 'flax' into the computer, and it spit out practically nothing. But I did find out that there is a flax institute up in Fargo, North Dakota. I really didn't want to go up there—it was late November and already about twenty below zero in Fargo—but I thought I'd better check it out. And I found out a lot about flaxseed—for instance, that it contains fifteen to twenty percent omega-three, which was almost the same amount as in the fish oil they were touting for preventing heart trouble."

Flaxseed has actually been consumed by human beings for thousands of years. On a time line of human history that stretches across one wall of Stitt's office at Natural Ovens, the first evidence of human consumption of flaxseed has been marked with a yellow

Post-It note at somewhere between 5000 and 6000 B.C., the date of a bowl that contained an impression of a flaxseed on its interior. But although Europeans use flaxseed in some breads, in the United States the grain has been almost completely confined to animal use. After he had consumed large amounts of it himself, Stitt found, to his alarm, that American scientists had shown that flaxseed might even be toxic.

"I discovered that in flaxseed there's an anti-B_6 factor that had caused fatalities in baby chicks," Stitt continued. "After more research, I found that the way to overcome the anti-B_6 factor was to simply add extra levels of B_6. Another problem with flaxseed is that once you grind it, it tends to break down rapidly and become rancid. But I found that you could add certain compounds, like zinc, to prevent the breaking down of the flaxseed. Two months after my first trip to Fargo I went back to the flax institute to attend their annual meeting. I had been playing with flaxseed that whole time, and eating, some days, as much as a quarter pound of it, just to see its effects. At the meeting there was a fellow from the USDA, and he said, 'Oh my God, don't you know that flaxseed is toxic?' And I sort of gulped. I looked it up, and back in the literature of the twenties and thirties there were articles published showing that if you feed very high levels of flaxseed to animals it can be toxic. These articles weren't very detailed in their descriptions of the studies, but I got the impression that the researchers were feeding the animals moldy flaxseed, and at extremely high levels—sixty to seventy percent of the diet, which is absurd. That's when I started my farm here, and started feeding flaxseed to chickens to see what would happen. Well, I found out that the chickens ended up with bones that are twenty percent stronger than normal, and eggshells that are twenty-five percent stronger than normal eggshells. We think that's probably due to the presence of boron; in 1990 researchers at Grand Forks Human Nutrition Research Center found that flaxseed contains a high level of boron, and boron helps to lock calcium into the bone. It also helps to prevent osteoporosis in humans. We've had a good growth rate with the chickens, and we produced chickens that were lower in fat, and they laid eggs that were lower in cholesterol. I later did a study with swine and flaxseed, and had the data analyzed by the University of Toronto, and we found that by adding omega-three to the pigs' diet you would get high levels of omega-three in the animal tissues—the brain, liver, muscles, and other organs. We also found higher fertility rates, and the baby pigs were stronger, healthier, more resistant to disease."

Stitt was already putting flaxseed in most of his breads by this time. "It made a dramatic change in the health benefits of our bread, because not only did the flaxseed add the omega-three, but later on researchers at the University of Toronto found out that flaxseed contains lignans—compounds that help prevent mammary cancer in rats. And flaxseed has boron and lignans in high concentrations; it contains eight hundred times more lignans than buckwheat, which is the food that has the next largest amount. And the boron levels range from about thirty to about one hundred and twenty parts per million. Most foods contain only about one part per million."

Stitt has another, proprietary interest in flaxseed: He found that his method for stabilizing it was unique, and therefore patentable. In 1989 he was awarded patent number 4,857,326; an article in the *New York Times* headlined "Using Flax to Get Benefit of Fish Oils" described how Stitt's method could put "the health benefits of cod-liver oil—without its notoriously foul taste—into bread, cookies, salad dressings and even fruit drinks." Now Stitt sells stabilized flaxseed to several of the largest food companies, who are using it in various secret ways—"They won't say what they're doing with it," says Stitt, "but I've heard that there's going to be a major food company coming out with flaxseed in all kinds of products." He has also been approached by three diet-food companies to supply flaxseed for use in various weight-control products, and has signed a three-year contract with a Japanese company to be its sole supplier of flaxseed for use in several designer foods, including a flax-and-garlic bar for preventing cancer.

"Flaxseed is without a doubt one of the best new ingredients for making food," Stitt said. "Its big advantage is that you can mix it with so many kinds of foods. You could mix it into chocolate ice cream; you could mix it into any kind of salad dressing. You could put it into hot dogs if you wanted; you could put it, obviously, into breads and cookies and muffins." This is designer foods talk, but Stitt's characterization of designer foods is down-to-earth: for him, designer foods are part of an elaborate regimen of natural living and eating—just another way of obtaining the maximum benefit possible from one's food. When I asked him whether he would want to make superflaxseed, he protested that it was super already. "It's already so high in all these levels of compounds, you really wouldn't want it any higher."

Researchers and other food manufacturers might disagree. Part of the tantalizing prospect of designer foods is the idea of concentrating the power of a particular ingredient or chemical, taking it out of the realm of nature and into the lab. While Stitt is happy keeping his company at its present size and continuing to tinker with new products, the food giants, like the ones buying his stabilized flax, are thinking in much broader terms: "fortified" products, perhaps someday with health claims on their labels—cereals to prevent heart disease, juice drinks to prevent certain specific kinds of cancer. Two barriers lie in their way: definitive research that establishes the efficacy of flaxseed and other designer food ingredients, and food-marketing laws that allow their efficacy to be broadcast to a public hungry for potent formulas.

Work on the research problem began in earnest in 1990, when the National Cancer Institute announced it was funding a twenty-million-dollar, five-year project to investigate the potential of creating designer foods targeted for specific disease-preventive action. The project was the brainchild of an NCI toxicologist named Dr. Herbert Pierson, who has since left the institute to become a consultant to the food industry. The Designer Foods Project attracted a lot of attention—so much that at one point Pierson was putting journalists and representatives of the food industry on months-long waiting lists for interviews. Part of the public appeal of the plan derived from its name; it sounded particularly futuristic and trendy, almost chic. But the term "designer food" was not, in fact, Pierson's first choice, and it seems to have already, in the general excitement about the idea, slipped a little out of his control. "That term has evolved, independent of us," Pierson explained over the telephone before he left the cancer institute. "We played with a lot of terms—for example, 'experimental foods.' But if you use the word 'experimental food' when you're trying to recruit participants for a study, that'll scare 'em right off. They'll feel like guinea pigs. So we dropped that. Then we were going to use the word 'investigational food,' but that sounded mystical, almost occultlike. So after a lot of going back and forth, trying to describe the idea of a food designed specifically to help us study the relationship between phytochemical substances in the diet and cancer prevention, it seemed that 'designed food' turned into 'designer food.' But there are a lot of definitions of designer foods. Some people in the food industry feel that the term refers to taking products of biotechnological processes and then formulating those into processed foods. That's not how I'm using it."

The project Pierson initiated is essentially a vast information-gathering effort, in which about two dozen researchers around the country have been put under contract to study various substances such as phytochemicals (plant compounds) and antioxidants (chemicals that may block the formation of carcinogens by neutralizing free radicals, oxygen compounds that are thought to damage the body's cells). Their results are pooled and cross-referenced with a continually growing data base, which includes even anecdotal evidence from around the world about food's effect on health. The ultimate goal, Pierson said, is to take "the best out of Mother Nature" and form it into foods that can help prevent cancer in specific ways. The key to understanding how phytochemicals actually might block cancer is to look at how they affect various bodily processes. Pierson explained this to me in his characteristic language, heavy in scientific idiom. "I want to know how foods alter steroid metabolism in the body," he said, "how they alter prostaglandin metabolism, and how they alter the way we

detoxify and excrete pharmaceutical substances that are metabo-
lized very similarly to chemical carcinogens. So by looking at the
way these—what you might call phytochemically defined—foods
modulate these three metabolic pathways, you can get a feel for
the magnitude of changes that occur in humans as a result of consuming them."

I began to understand Pierson's rather labored explanation
only after I had spoken with another designer food researcher, Jon
Michnovicz, President of the Foundation for Preventive Oncology
and director of the Institute for Hormone Research, both in New
York, and a contributor to the designer foods project. Michnovicz
described the details of his work, which most recently has focused
on chemicals in the cabbage family and their effect on cancer, especially hormone-related cancers like breast, ovarian, or uterine
cancer. It became clear that it is easiest to describe how designer
foods might really work by using one example, because each potential ingredient will work differently, and on different diseases.
Garlic might retard tumor development, for instance, in a fashion
completely unlike that of parsley, and may work on one type of
cancer but not on another. "We have isolated a small molecule
called indole carbinol that occurs in high concentrations in the
cabbage family," Michnovicz explained. "This compound has the
ability to alter the way the body handles the hormone estrogen,
and we believe, with growing evidence on our side, that this alter-
ation is beneficial. There is a particularly problematic form of estrogen that might be what causes breast cancer; we have a lot of
evidence to that effect. What indole carbinol seems to do is promote the breakdown of estrogen into its most benign form rather
than into this troublesome form."

Michnovicz divides designer foods into two possible forms—
one a food in which the active ingredient has been concentrated so
that, for instance, one designer orange would have the vitamin C
level of four normal oranges; and the other a new kind of dietary
supplement, in which a potent natural substance is extracted from
a food, purified, and then used in a specially formulated health bar
or drink. "You could take a few swigs of a future version of V-8

and know that you'd got a couple of hundred milligrams of some compound X," he said. "In effect, a drug—but a preventive drug. And when you think of V-8 juice, you realize that this really isn't far off at all. But V-8 exists just to have a lot of vegetables in a juice form; in the future we might have V-2, or V-3 or V-4, with just the concentrated vegetables you need for a particular disease. Maybe indole carbinol and something else. In its refined stage, that kind of food is years off, but the research is already in motion."

Pierson had given me an example of a product along these lines that was currently being test-marketed: a juice called Fruition, made by the Nestle company from apricots (some varieties added oranges, pineapples, or passion fruit); Nestle advertised it as "naturally rich in beta-carotene." (The ad also read, "The Surgeon General's report states that foods high in Beta-Carotene may protect against a variety of cancers.") "Nestle's Fruition juice is basically a designer food, if you want to look at it that way," Pierson said. "It's formulated to be rich in carotinoids." Both Michnovicz and Pierson gathered rhetorical steam when they talked about the future. Michnovicz mentioned "some very tantalizing clues" with licorice root extract and envisions a world stocked with designer foods that is "both near and, still, far at hand." "When programs like mine start showing that garlic does this to your metabolism," said Pierson, "and that licorice root does that to your hormones, and citrus fruits do this to the way we detoxify things, you're going to see a wave of industrial activity. These particular foods are going to be touted or formulated into a lot of things; you're going to see an explosion revolutionizing food products. Conceivably, any prototype food, like a tofu, allows itself to be formulated with materials that are known scientifically to be healthy, and I think we're going to be living in interesting times not too far down the road."

Those interesting times were filled in further by a researcher at Tufts University, Jeffrey Blumberg, who is associate director of the United States Department of Agriculture's Human Nutrition Research Center on Aging at Tufts and is also an editorial advisor to the Tufts University Diet and Nutrition Letter. Blumberg described a commercially appealing rendition of designer foods, in which health benefits are delivered in the form of dietary indulgence—chocolate-chip ice cream, perhaps, drained of its dangerous fats and infused with licorice root extract or some other phytochemical to make it a cancer fighter. Blumberg worries that the fascination with food-as-medicine might tend toward the neurotic, but in an interesting twist, he wonders if the cure for overvigilance about fats and other dietary dangers might actually lie with technology: changing our foods, he suggested, might be easier, on many levels, than changing our eating.

"If we can provide to the consumer a large variety of healthful food choices," said Blumberg, "so that—now, I'm being a little idealistic here—so that all their choices are going to end up being good ones, then they don't have to be so neurotic about it. The fact that people are going a little crazy about it, and thinking of food in medical terms, doesn't change the fact that if we could actually market products that are fortified with chemo-protective agents—it's just in their doughnuts and bologna and baked goods or whatever—then, gee, maybe they won't have to be so concerned if they're not eating carrots but beta-carotene, and not drinking milk but calcium. Let people choose the things that they already have preferences for, but just make those more healthful choices.

"I think that's one direction designer foods would lead us in; as opposed to saying, 'Oh, you have to change everything you want to eat and how you prepare it and eat it,' we could say, 'Okay, what we've done is created within the dietary patterns that you already have a more healthful diet.' We actually have the food-technology capability today of taking a nice steak, extracting all of the saturated fatty acids and replacing them with omega-three polyunsaturated fatty acids. We are not doing that, but the technology actually exists. I don't know if it exists to do it with such great success that it's still going to taste exactly the same, but it is not a farfetched notion." Blumberg, meanwhile, has his own way of hedging his bets: he takes a multivitamin and a vitamin E supplement every day, as a possible cancer- and heart disease preventive.

• • •

Paul Stitt supplies the Designer Foods Project with stabilized flaxseed to use in experiments, and the project has, in turn, ended up providing some direction for Stitt. When we met he had just brought out a new bread called Seven Grain Herb Bread, which according to Stitt contains almost two hundred phytochemicals, many of which are being studied in the Designer Foods Project. "These compounds appear to help prevent cancer in one way or another," Stitt explained. "That's the reason I chose the herbs that I did to put into this bread. I wanted to pack in the maximum number of cancer-preventing compounds. Besides, it just plain tastes good."

After our breakfast at the Stitt home, Paul and I drove out to the Natural Ovens plant to look over the operation. Over its front entrance towered a nine-panel, fifteen-foot-high stained-glass window, commissioned from a local artist, that depicted various scenes: a farm haloed by a rainbow, a harvest scene featuring a horse-drawn reaper, a baker sliding breads into a brick oven, and a family eating breakfast around a table covered by a checkered cloth. All day long the building sends out the aroma of freshly baked breads; Stitt maintains that you soon learn to distinguish which bread is baking on which day by scent alone.

Stitt asked his secretary to bring us some fresh Seven Grain Herb Bread to sample. He broke open a package and we each bit into a slice—it was fragrant and savory, almost peppery in flavor. "This bread makes a great stuffing for chicken or turkey, because it has sage and tarragon and rosemary in it," he said. We were sitting in his office, in a corner of the vast building. Through one window, we could see Stitt's observation farm, the pigs and chickens housed in stone buildings put up by German farmers in 1910. One of the barns also houses Stitt's collection of antique tractors and horse-drawn farm equipment. "I'd like to make the whole place a farm museum at some point," Stitt said. In a corral next to the farm buildings Stitt's six Belgian horses were munching contentedly on a special mixture he has created for them that contains hay, oats, and flaxseed. Stitt claims that a flaxseed diet cured their split hooves and improved their coats, and he now markets a flaxseed product for horses called Horseshine.

It was in Stitt's office that we began to talk about the second hitch in the designer food business, even after the problem of adequate research is resolved: the law. Stitt's Seven Grain Herb Bread may have been designed to prevent cancer, but there is no indication of that fact anywhere on its label. Stitt seemed resigned to that reality. "The sad thing is we know how to make designer foods, but we don't know how to label them," he said. "I think historically people have always felt that food is medicine, and medicine is food. It's only in the last fifty years that we've gotten away from that idea. Our ancestors knew all about this and they never questioned it. It was gospel to them. And now we are in a kind of stage, it seems, where we're going back and saying, well, is this really true and will this work and so on?"

About his own products, Stitt had few doubts: "There are some people who have been using our products for years, and we can say with a fair amount of confidence that eating our products—along with the rest of the diet being halfway smart—you will no longer have high blood pressure, you will not have high cholesterol levels, you will not have arthritis, you will not have osteoporosis, you will not have symptoms of diabetes. Using our products will go a long way toward preventing heart disease and strokes, and eliminating cancer in young people and in people in the prime of their lives. It may not eliminate cancer forever. You may get cancer when you're ninety or ninety-five. And all of this requires some prudence on the part of the consumer. People have to exercise more, and cut down on the excess fats in their diet."

Stitt touts the advantages of his products in ways that slide around the FDA regulations. The labels on his products open up to create a sort of brochure, and while the part of the label that's visible on an unopened package simply lists the ingredients, as well as the amount of fiber and omega-3, the inside says much more. "Inside our labels we report studies that other research laboratories have done, with beta-carotene or with omega-three and so forth," he explained. "And so far, anyway, the FDA has not said anything;

we're simply quoting other people, as to what they have found that these ingredients do." The brochure for Seven Grain Herb Bread says that it contains 197 cancer-fighting compounds—a claim that could not be made on a food label. But Stitt goes easy on the FDA. He has what he calls a "good working relationship" with people there; he trades information with scientists in the agency's Experimental Nutrition Group, which is part of the Center for Food Safety and Applied Nutrition—the arm of the FDA that actually analyzes food products and ingredients, while the rest of the agency regulates their sale. "The FDA is over-whelmed," he said. "They can't do much of anything because they're so understaffed; the food industry has seen to this on purpose, by lobbying against any new appropriations to the agency. They want the agency to be as strapped as possible—after all, how fast can you go down the road if there's no policeman? I've found that things go better with the FDA if you don't confront them. For instance, when I started using flaxseed in the breads I had to prove to them that flaxseed was a food, since it hadn't been used that way in the United States—flax had been used in fabrics and so on. So I got together the scientific literature, and all the evidence I could find that it's been used as a food for thousands of years, and I just kept feeding the people at the FDA this information. And they approved it."

One reason that Stitt was not overly concerned with labeling was that his sales were going up—20 percent over the last year—and he felt that he was doing well enough without saying that his anticancer bread really *is* anticancer bread. "The fact is that people are buying Seven Grain Herb Bread because it tastes good," he said. If a few of his more well-informed customers know that there are other benefits to eating his breads, well, fine. After more than fifteen years of very up-and-down business, including five close brushes with bankruptcy, he was not about to tinker with his success. He was even a little afraid that making health claims would drive customers away—that they would assume that food so good for them couldn't taste good.

Despite his philosophic acceptance of the FDA's controls on

claims for foods like his Natural Ovens products, Stitt was full of plans for more research and new products that—quietly and tastefully—prevent disease. "I'm excited about what they can do with licorice and licorice root extract, which is one of the things the Designer Foods group are looking at," he said. "I think there's a real potential for using those kinds of products in things like cookies. Licorice root is a natural sweetening agent, and it's very potent at very low levels. I'd also like to test out the Seven Grain bread. Feed it to rats with high cancer rates—there are strains of rats that they use for research that get spontaneous cancers. Feed it to them, comparing it to a typical American diet and to a standard rat-chow diet. But what I want to do most is research on dietary factors that affect learning ability, because I think the ability of children to think, to remember, to learn, is the most crucial issue affecting our country." Stitt has already taken a first step in this direction: he has developed a drink mixture called Right Start, which he created especially for pregnant women. Containing mainly flaxseed but also zinc, magnesium, iron, and B vitamins, it is geared to promote brain development in fetuses—although, of course, it doesn't say that on its label.

Despite his restless experimenting, however, Stitt's focus will remain on his breads. He has found something he does extremely well, that matches his global philosophy, and that people are happy to buy, and that seems to be enough. His status as the first designer-food maker will probably never be a headline maker, even if flaxseed explodes into a fame that makes it, as he predicted, "the buzzword of the nineties." In fact, for someone with such grand ideas about saving the world from hunger and saving Americans from disease, his reach is surprisingly modest. He has not thought of competing with what he calls the "big boys" to keep his claim on flaxseed intact, for instance. "If flaxseed really took off, the big boys would just snow me, push me out of the way so fast," he said imperturbably. "They just have so much more clout in advertising and marketing. The way the big boys do it, they sit back and let people like me take the risk, and then if it works they just come in and take it over—or try to." One reason for his sanguine acceptance of this business reality is that he knows he has created a niche market for himself. "If some company like General Mills goes in and sells a hundred million pounds of flaxseed, I'm still going to have my little market that I can live with," he pointed out. Underlying his confidence is an idea that may have much to do with the eventual success or failure of designer foods themselves, because it might get to the root of what people truly want from their food—whatever their guilt or anxiety tell them they want. "The only route to get people healthier," Stitt said at our last meeting, "is, number one, to make food that tastes good. And number two, make foods that make people feel good after they eat them."

Chapter Six

•

FEAR OF FATS

The American Diet on Trial

•

Today, even the most casual grocery shopper knows that fat is to be avoided at all costs; that message is encoded on countless labels proclaiming "low-fat," "no-fat," "fat-free." Fat has replaced cholesterol as the number-one dietary nemesis for most Americans. Some doctors and scientists have extended this mass-market advice to its furthest reaches, suggesting that for health reasons we should consume no dairy products, no meat, no chicken, no fish, no vegetable oils. Many other health experts feel that such renunciation is not only unnecessary but dangerous. How much fat is really optimum? Can one ever again eat a hamburger? The answer is easily obscured by the seductiveness of absolutism—by the logic that says that if less fat is better, none at all must be best, and the comfort that can come from concentrating all of one's worries on one source. The voices of moderation are easily lost in the resulting rush to the moral high ground—and the hunger for a guarantee of prolonged life.

•

Neal Barnard seemed, in his very serious way, to be enjoying himself. He was stirring his linguine with tomato sauce (no meat, no Parmesan cheese, and no oil used in its preparation), recalling his days before he went to medical school, when he was working as a morgue attendant at a hospital. "I tell you, it's a very graphic experience to open up a person's skull, take the brain out, and find a hole as big as a Ping-Pong ball, and then find atherosclerotic plaque in the carotid artery or somewhere else," he said. "We saw coronary arteries filled with plaque, colons filled with cancer. When you read about it in a book it's one thing; when you hold it in your hands, when you smell it, when you see in graphic detail what it does, it is very striking. For these autopsies, you have to pull out a section of ribs to examine the heart—a big pie section of ribs—and then put it back. One day after an autopsy, I went up to the cafeteria for lunch and what was offered to me was ribs. You really lose your appetite for things when you associate them with death."

He took a bite of his linguine. I continued to devour my gnocchi al pesto (with fresh Parmesan on top). I had chosen a meatless entrée in unspoken deference to Barnard's fervent vegetarianism, half afraid he would be unable to speak to me if I were displaying a dead carcass on my plate. Barnard is the president of the Physicians Committee for Responsible Medicine (PCRM), a nonprofit group he founded in 1985, and it is one of the tenets of his work and life—and he hopes someday of everyone's life—that he eats no animal products and very little fat of any kind, even vegetable oils. Barnard feels so strongly about this dietary regimen that in April 1991 he issued, under the auspices of PCRM, a proposal for four new food groups, to replace the traditional four that had stood for decades (which were grains; fruits and vegetables; dairy products; meats and fish). PCRM's new grouping was: whole grains, vegetables, fruits, and legumes (nuts, beans, and their derivatives—tofu, soy milk, peanut butter). Meats and dairy products are grudgingly admitted as occasional options, but Barnard personally believes humans should not touch them, and says he will never do so again. A number of public health officials, even some of those who agreed with Barnard that Americans must shift their diets away from meats and fats, expressed alarm over what they perceived as the extreme nature of PCRM's suggestions. In September 1992 Barnard augmented his dietary recommendations by holding a press conference to warn against consumption of cow's milk, especially by children. He cited milk's high fat content as well as asserting that milk can produce iron deficiency in infants, cause diabetes in children with a genetic predisposition to the disease, and cause colic, allergies, and digestive problems; many doctors and nutritionists took issue with at least some of these conclusions. In a move that demonstrated considerable public relations savvy, Barnard invited Dr. Benjamin Spock, the best-known child-care expert in America, to sit on his panel at the press conference (although Dr. Spock later clarified that he agreed with only one of Barnard's assertions against milk—that breast-feeding is the best method of infant feeding and that whole cow's milk should not be given to infants under one year because of the risk of anemia).

Barnard had agreed to describe his dietary convictions to me over lunch, and we had walked two short blocks from the small suite of PCRM offices in northwest Washington, D.C., to a storefront Italian restaurant. At thirty-eight, Barnard looked fit if nondescript: medium build, regular features, short dark hair. At our lunch there was an impatience and something a little ill-at-ease in his manner—as if he were aware that his views may appear extreme, and that rankled him. He spoke quickly, articulately, with few shifts in inflection. One sometimes gets the feeling he has said these words and phrases before, and in many cases he has. Within PCRM he has almost single-handedly built a mini-industry of nutrition information, and one way he has accomplished this is through repetition. He has published two books, *The Power of Your Plate* and *A Physician's Slimming Guide*, made a cassette tape called "Live Longer, Live Better," and puts out a bimonthly magazine, *A Guide to Healthy Eating*, that covers much of the same ground as the books.

It very quickly becomes clear in speaking with Barnard that

he has few, if any, doubts. Although his medical training was in psychiatry, he has reached some unshakable conclusions about diet through, as he describes it, "spending a lot of time in the medical library, reading literature, and a lot of time writing and speaking and advocating." He sprinkles his speech with references to various studies—of cardiovascular illness in the Soviet Union, of vegetable oils and breast cancer, of cancer rates in China in relation to fat consumption, of osteoporosis and intercranial hemorrhages among Eskimos. In his book *The Power of Your Plate* he interviewed many doctors and researchers who are experts on heart disease, cancer, weight control, and food contamination, and although most of them do not go as far as Barnard in advocating renunciation of all animal products, he dismisses those conclusions that do not match his own as simple failures of will. "Doctors recognize that it's not a good idea to smoke, but many of them do smoke; they have trouble breaking that habit," he commented. "Your habits are ingrained long before one learns the health consequences of one habit or another, and changing those habits can be easy or difficult depending on your social milieu, your own interests, and so on." Opinions that directly contradict his own run the risk of being bluntly called "stupid." When I asked him to comment on the fact that some people find his dietary recommendations too restrictive for feeding children, he responded, "Stupid people do. Stupid people who haven't read the literature and are wedded to their own preconceived notions, yes." And what, I asked, did he think of the new so-called food pyramid, put out by the United States Department of Agriculture, calling for a greater dietary emphasis on grains, fruits, and vegetables, and less on dairy and meat products? "Stupid. It still says you should dose yourself two or three times a day with an animal tissue and two to three times a day with a mammary secretion. And that's ridiculous."

Barnard's dietary recommendations, his direct challenge to the USDA, have succeeded in drawing considerable media attention. At our lunch he described the rationale for his food plan. "The traditional four food groups have stuck around for thirty-six years now, despite thirty-six years' worth of science that has shown those to be a real mistake. It makes absolutely no sense to teach kids at age ten or twelve in school that they should eat meat two or three times a day, and dairy two or three times a day, when the rest of your time is going to be spent trying to get the cholesterol out of their bodies, to avert one of the four thousand heart attacks that occur every single day in the United States, to diminish the toll of breast cancer, which kills another woman every twelve minutes. And we know that these are linked to, particularly, meat and dairy consumption. That's a gross oversimplification, but it's a fact, nonetheless. There is a tremendous amount of scientific data showing that there is essentially a dose-related response. The more meat you eat, the lower your life expectancy, the higher your cholesterol, the greater your risk of cardiovascular disease and malignancy. There's just no question about it anymore."

Barnard delivered this pronouncement with a mixture of earnestness and a certain sternness, but with just the barest hint, too, of perverse pleasure, perhaps at being the voice of reason and discipline in what seems to him a world of self-indulgent and therefore somewhat childish gluttons. This schoolmasterlike side of his character emerged in stronger shades when I pressed him on whether a careful eater could slip in a piece of meat, say, once a week. Barnard admitted that there was not yet any scientific evidence to explicitly prove that such a moderate level of meat consumption would be dangerous. "However," he said, "I think that's a useless question. Many people raise this point, and I think it's a useless thing to pursue, because I don't believe there is such a person, who would eat one serving a week. It's like one cigarette a week: there really isn't any data to show that a cigarette a week is dangerous, but people tend to not be able to restrict themselves to that tiny amount. Same with meat—once-a-week becomes leftovers for the next day, and it keeps the taste of these foods in one's psyche, it causes you to feed them to your loved ones, it keeps them in your lifestyle, in your recipe box. It's a teaser diet."

Barnard includes in his ban fish and chicken, which he feels have gotten a false reputation as being relatively healthy—after all, he pointed out, even with no skin and at its leanest, chicken is about 20 percent fat, as opposed to 4 percent for black beans and 1 percent for a potato; and fish is simply protein and fat, about which he has nothing good to say. "We've long ago established that we don't need the protein of animal products, we're better off without it. And the omega-three oils that were so much in vogue years ago—there were a couple of letters in the American Journal of Clinical Nutrition about a year ago, saying it is better to get your omega-threes from vegetables and legumes."

In all of Barnard's well-informed talk about what people should eat, however, the notions of taste and pleasure do not often arise; they seem almost beside the point. And in fact, in his own life Barnard appears curiously remote from the romance of food. He admitted that he is not a "foodie," that when he goes home alone to eat a homemade dinner (he is single) it is something "really simple—for me a nice meal is a lot of brown rice, some black beans and some vegetables; some carrot juice." But, he insisted, he loves food, especially ethnic cuisines—Ethiopian, Indian, Mexican—and he strenuously denied the notion that cutting out animal products cuts out any pleasure. "To me that's a rather parochial viewpoint—people who think that are people who by and large may not have tried other kinds of things to eat. When I was growing up in North Dakota eating pork chops and roast beef, nothing I ate would grace the pages of Gourmet magazine. Now, if I sit down to, say, some Indian spinach-potato curry, or jalapeño burritos, or Szechwan bean curd . . . there's just no way I'd go back to that other way of eating."

But Barnard is aware enough of how austere his regimen sounds to hesitate at first in describing his own progress from meat-eater to vegan (pronounced vee-gun, it denotes someone who consumes no animal products at all). "In about 1977 I became an ovo-lacto vegetarian," he said, meaning he consumed eggs and dairy products, but no meat, chicken, or fish. "Then in roughly 1984 I became a vegan. Shortly after that I eliminated vegetable oils from my diet, almost completely. And I continue to change my diet. I'm now eating more whole grains as opposed to flour and pasta and things like that. More vegetables that are uncooked. I don't use salt anymore. I haven't bought a stick of margarine in years. I don't talk about these things too much, because people will think I have an extremely ascetic lifestyle. As you can see, I don't. But it's hard for people to imagine that."

Perhaps one reason for what appears to be a certain dissonance between Barnard's intense involvement with food in the abstract and his much cooler approach to eating in its physical, gustatory reality may be that there is another, wholly distinct reason for his denial of animal products: PCRM devotes much of its time to lobbying for animal rights and against animal experimentation and livestock farming. Barnard does not see this issue as completely separate from that of diet, and he professed not to understand the concern of critics who are disturbed that his dietary recommendations might not be based solely on nutritional science. "When we proposed the new four food groups, it was entirely and completely from a health perspective," he said. "But if you recognize that what you're doing by eating animal products is destroying the environment as well as your internal environment, you have more reasons, more motivators, to adopt a healthy diet. I'm saying there's no good reason to eat livestock products, whether it's humane, health, environment, whatever."

No one would argue that Barnard is mainstream. Although many doctors and nutrition researchers would agree, for example, that Americans should lower their fat intake, perhaps even drastically, few recommend a complete abstention from fats of all kinds. But Barnard's position stands as a sort of logical extension of an attitude that has been gathering strength for several years: the villainization of dietary fats. Some scientists speak of a steamroller effect, similar to the cholesterol frenzy of the 1980s, in which any evidence pointing to the dangers of fats is embraced while contradictory ideas are not encouraged by the scientific establishment. One need only look down a supermarket aisle to remark how quickly the food industry has embraced the saleability of the "low-fat" and "nonfat" concepts.

The fact that Barnard stands for complete renunciation, a clean break and therefore a pure conscience, is an example of a way of thinking that has a powerful appeal to many Americans. The clearest expression of this thinking can be seen, as is often the case, in marketing terms: in the fact that Nabisco brought out a "fat-free" Fig Newton even though an ordinary Fig Newton has only one gram of fat; that Dannon does a huge business with its "nonfat" fruit yogurts even though its regular "low-fat" fruit yogurts contain only three grams of fat, and with those three grams produce a far superior flavor and texture. *Perhaps*, the seduction of this thinking goes, *if low-fat is good, no-fat is better?* Why leave any ambiguity when you could deny yourself everything and be completely sure? There is, in our current thinking about food, an attraction to absolutes, a righteous pleasure in abstention. Barnard's philosophy of eating, which puts this dietary response into dogma, raises the question not only of whether such a response is necessary, but also whether it is entirely good.

Researchers have been documenting a connection between dietary fat and various diseases for decades—for instance, a pioneering study that showed a relationship between dietary fat and breast cancer was published in 1953—but their findings did not begin making an impact on the public consciousness until the late 1980s. That change was effected first by official agencies, with the media, as usual, aiding the effort. The 1988 Surgeon General's Report on Nutrition and Health concluded that of the ten leading causes of death in the United States, five—coronary heart disease, certain cancers, stroke, diabetes, and atherosclerosis—are associated with diets high in fats and cholesterol. In late 1987 a nonprofit organization called the Henry J. Kaiser Family Foundation began a public-service campaign to reduce fat consumption in the United States, dubbed Project LEAN (Low-fat Eating for America Now). By 1990, a group of thirty-eight federal agencies and organizations of health professionals endorsed a new report issued by the National Heart, Lung, and Blood Institute that called for everyone over the age of two years to lower their fat intake from the current average of 37 percent of calories to at the most 30 percent of calories.[1] The message resonated: A year later, a Food Marketing Institute survey found that 42 percent of Americans ranked fat their number one nutritional concern, up from 29 percent two years earlier.[2] Newspaper and magazine writers took it from there, adding nutritional breakdowns to recipes, telling home cooks how to replace the fat in recipes with mashed prunes or bananas, headlining that "gourmets and nutritionists join in a drive against fats,"[3] offering up "the skinny on no-fat sweets."[4]

Marketers of fast-foods and prepared foods responded as quickly as recipes and packaging could be rejiggered. According to Gorman's New Product News, a trade publication based in Chicago, the number of new low-fat products doubled between 1989 and 1990.[5] Products that had always been low in fat appeared with new labels exclaiming "Fat Free!" The highest-profile move came from America's preeminent fast-food chain: In April 1991, McDonald's introduced the McLean hamburger, with less than half the fat of a quarter-pounder. (Industry analysts estimated that the company spent $50 to $70 million developing the McLean technology.)[6]

Amid the new fat frenzy, so reminiscent of the excitement about cholesterol in the late 1980s (which has since quieted considerably), came the first challenge. In the June 26, 1991, issue of the Journal of the American Medical Association, an epidemiologist and statistician at the University of California, San Francisco, named Warren S. Browner reported that if everyone's diet contained no more than 30 percent of calories from fat, the average American life span would be only three to four months longer. For individuals at higher risk for coronary disease, the benefit would presumably be greater, but based on pure statistical analysis the news did not look exciting for the average meat-eater. Six months later, JAMA published four full pages of outraged letters from doctors and researchers taking issue with Browner; several suggested that fat intake might in fact have to be considerably lower than 30 percent before a larger average benefit could be shown.[7]

No one is about to argue that the dietary-fat-and-disease issue is complete bunk. The evidence against fat is two-pronged: Both large-scale epidemiological studies involving fat intake in various cultures around the world, and laboratory studies with animals that look at dietary fat and the development of cancerous tumors or heart lesions, point convincingly to some relationship between a high-fat diet and disease. Probably the most-cited epidemiological example concerns Japan: The daily fat intake in the United States is about twice that of Japan and the breast cancer rate here is more than four times higher, while the colon cancer mortality rate in U.S. men is more than three times higher. And when Japanese emigrate to the United States, their cancer risk quickly comes to resemble that of Americans, either within the same generation or in the next, presumably because their diet comes to mimic that of most Americans.[8] That pattern is echoed in other countries, from Argentina to Thailand, with all showing a positive correlation between fat intake and cancers of the breast and other organs as well.

But within all of the studies there are many unanswered questions. The same paper that outlined the breast cancer statistics raised the question of whether increased cancer risk might be more closely related to high-calorie intake rather than fat intake, since some animal experiments showed that a high-fat diet, when the amount fed was restricted, produced fewer tumors than a low-fat diet when the amount was unrestricted. Perhaps, some researchers believe, it only *looks* like a high-fat diet is to blame because a high-fat diet tends to also carry more calories. But the most nettlesome question is what some researchers call dose-related: How much fat is too much; how much fat is optimum? This is where many scientists diverge from Barnard.

Although federal agencies have set a goal of 30 percent of calories from fat, there is a growing body of doctors and researchers who feel that this level is not low enough. An overview of studies conducted with heart patients in which they reduced the fat content of their diets to about 30 percent (the American Heart Association's recommendation) showed very little improvement in the state of their arteries; in fact, in most cases patients' arteries were *more* occluded after a year on the 30 percent diet.[9] John H. Weisburger, senior member and director emeritus of the American Health Foundation, a research institution in Valhalla, New York, has conducted clinical trials to determine what level of fat intake is healthiest. "In 1982, when we testified before a National Academy of Sciences committee," says Weisburger, "I felt that the Heart Association recommendation for cancer prevention—thirty percent of calories from fat—just wasn't right, but we didn't have any data. So we set out to do research here, using animal models. We demonstrated in very carefully elaborated models that animals eating thirty and forty percent fat had the same high incidence of cancer, and that the twenty and ten percent animals had a much lower incidence. Also, Dr. Walter Willard at Harvard has been documenting the fat intake and disease rates of sixty thousand nurses, and has found that there was no effect regarding breast cancer risk between women who ate forty percent fat and those who ate thirty percent—thirty was clearly not low enough. On the other end, we found, in our animal models, that there was no difference in cancer rates between the animals eating twenty percent and those eating ten—so here at the foundation we recommend a twenty-percent-fat diet, which will appreciably reduce the risk of cancer and heart disease."

Many other researchers have been slowly gravitating to the figure of 20 percent of calories from fat, but hesitate to actually recommend such a number for fear that it would require too great a leap for the average American eater to make. Thirty percent, many feel, is within reach. One problem is the difficulty of translating these percentages into real life—into a plateful of food. How much meat or chicken or fish would 20 percent allow? Some dieticians recommend thinking about it in terms of actual fat grams: For the average person consuming about two thousand calories a day, a 20-percent-fat diet would allow consumption of about 44 grams of fat. Considering that a container of yogurt usually contains 3 grams of fat, that sounds pretty manageable—until you start counting McDonald's quarter-pounders (20 grams of fat), an average piece of old-fashioned apple pie (19 grams), an Almond Joy candy bar (14 grams), or an eggs benedict breakfast at a Denny's restaurant (36 grams). Of course, counting fat grams assumes a fair amount of vigilance on the part of the consumer—it may be more trouble than many people want to go to—but it's also becoming easier to do as food packaging and fast-food restaurants begin to offer nutritional breakdowns of their products. Such a system also allows for substitutions, along the lines of: I had 10 grams of fat from my chicken thigh, so I'd better steam my vegetables and eat my potato without butter.

Weisburger's suggestion is to set up what he calls a "new dietary tradition," making substitutions for high-fat items. "Such a diet would be composed of mainly rice, pasta, or potatoes without fatty sauces; cereal-bran fiber; and fruits and vegetables," he says. "And the food industry now is making available low-fat equivalents of standard products—skim milk, nonfat yogurt, low-fat or nonfat cottage cheese, turkey and other meats with less fat, frozen yogurt instead of ice cream." He cites a by-now familiar list of substitutions: whole-grain bread for white bread, jelly or marmalade for butter on toast, low-fat yogurt on a potato instead of sour cream, baked potatoes for french fries, herbed low-fat yogurt for mayonnaise or dressings, smallish servings of lean cuts of beef, pork, lamb, veal, skinless chicken or turkey, and fish (not fried) in place of fatty meats, frankfurters, and sausages. Moderation is the byword.

But, in the extremely relative world of dietary philosophies, what seems moderate to Weisburger looks restrictive compared to the heart association's 30-percent rule and quite liberal compared to the 10-percent/no-animal-products rule espoused by Barnard. Despite the ongoing discussion of the relative merits of 10 or 30 percent fat, however, few scientists go as far as Barnard. Among the handful that do are two researchers who have both, in contrast to Barnard, carried out extensive first-hand research in diet and health. Interestingly, one has focused on clinical research and the other on epidemiological data.

The first is Dr. Dean Ornish, a researcher in cardiology at the University of California, San Francisco, and author of *Dr. Dean*

Ornish's Program for Reversing Heart Disease. That program, which Ornish claims actually opens clogged arteries, involves following a diet of 10 percent fat and almost no cholesterol (although Ornish does allow two types of animal products—egg whites and one cup daily of nonfat milk or yogurt), as well as exercise and regular stress reduction through techniques like yoga and meditation. Ornish has documented his results with test groups, comparing them to control groups that followed American Heart Association guidelines and experienced a worsening of their condition, and he presents his program as an alternative to drug therapy or heart bypass surgery.[10] While many doctors have embraced his findings, others are more skeptical, awaiting corroborating evidence. Some point out that there can be a sort of placebo effect, in which a dedicated researcher, through charisma, selection of patients, and sheer enthusiasm, comes up with results that can't be reproduced elsewhere; others quibble with Ornish's method of measuring arterial improvement.[11] In any case, Ornish's research was conducted solely with heart patients who already have severe arterial blockage, and although he recommends a slightly looser "prevention diet" for others, it's questionable whether his work is yet completely applicable to the general public.

Another researcher squarely in Barnard's camp, nutritional biochemist T. Colin Campbell of Cornell University, does extend his dietary recommendations to everyone, from children to the elderly; the main limitation on his research is that it is completely epidemiological, meaning that it is based not on lab results but on comparisons of the diets and disease rates of different cultures. The central problem with this approach, according to many researchers and statisticians, is that it is suggestive rather than conclusive. But Campbell nonetheless feels that his results show compelling evidence, and he has spent the last decade working on what he calls the China Project on Nutrition, Health and Environment—a massive survey of diet and health that involved about 10,000 people from various areas of China. "What's unique about the China study is not the number of people, actually," says Campbell, "it's the number of things we studied. We looked at almost all the nutrient characteristics of a person—fat and fiber and minerals and vitamins and all the rest. We also considered virtually all the diseases that were reported in China, so we were able to look at the relationship between diet and disease in a far more comprehensive way than simply looking at, say, fat and cancer, which is such a narrow picture. Basically, the Chinese are very healthy, so it obviously prompts us to want to know why."

What he has found has convinced Campbell that "a 10-percent fat diet, more or less, without animal products, is the ideal diet." One general rule, he says, stood out: that the more a particular region's diet mirrored the standard American diet—high in fat and animal protein, low in fiber—the higher the rates of "diseases of affluence": cancers, heart disease, strokes, diabetes. From the China data he uses the example of breast cancer, because it is "one of the more responsive cancers to fat intake. If you look at the relationship between fat intake and breast cancer, what you see is a continuing reduction in risk from 24 percent of calories from fat all the way down to a diet of 6 percent of calories from fat. That's pretty remarkable, because what it's saying is to get it down even to 24 is not enough to achieve the optimum benefit; you have to go lower than that."

One of Campbell's responses to his work was to adopt a vegan diet for himself and his family, but he is less doctrinaire about choosing to do so than is Barnard. "Whatever people eat, that's their business, not mine," he says. "Do you need to go the whole way to 10 percent fat? It's really all a question of probabilities. There certainly are people who can live to be eighty or ninety and eat all the wrong things, or even smoke till they're ninety and not get lung cancer. The explanation for that, I suspect, is individual genetic susceptibilities—there are certain individuals who seem to be able to withstand the barrage of all the wrong things. But overall, clearly, a 15-percent-fat diet is better than a 40-percent-fat diet. It's sort of like whether you bet on the horse with two-to-one odds or the one that's ten-to-one. If you really want to play it safe you obviously bet on the horse that's guaranteed to win, and that would be staying at around a 10-percent-fat diet. Whereas if you want to have a good bet but not necessarily have the same guarantee you might be around 15 to 20 percent."

But it is that very idea of a "guarantee" that disturbs others in the field of disease prevention. Dr. Thomas N. James, a cardiologist, president of the University of Texas Medical Branch, and a former president of the American Heart Association, is so irked at such claims that he calls the drive against fat in the diet "a hideous scam." His conviction that the influence of fats and cholesterol on heart disease has been overestimated, at least as the current evidence stands, has, by his own account, not made him popular. "In my presidential address to the Heart Association in 1980 I warned them not to keep telling people that we could prevent coronary disease," says James. "At the very best we might reduce the risk, but to tell them we could prevent it was not telling the truth, and people have a long memory. They got mad as the dickens at me; they practically drummed me out of the corps."

One thing that bothers James is what he sees as the wholesale approach of the American Heart Association and other groups such as the National Cholesterol Education Program. "A relatively small percentage of the population has a problem regarding cholesterol, saturated fats, and such things," he says. "Most people handle those things quite well. I think having a meat-ax approach to this, eliminating everything for everybody, doesn't make sense. I particularly regret the terror this is striking into the hearts of older people, and I just find reprehensible this dictation to people of exactly what they can eat and what they can't eat. It's the epidemiologists and the statisticians, or the physicians who are enamored of that evidence, who've been the voices who've carried all of this business. But as a physician, I find little of this very helpful. It may be true that the average cholesterol level in Hungary or Timbuktu or someplace else is slightly less and that coronary disease is slightly less because of that—they say—but when you try to apply that to an individual it doesn't work, at least until you get into huge elevations of cholesterol. An awful lot of folks have high cholesterol and go along and never have coronary disease, and an awful lot of people who have normal cholesterol have severe coronary disease. When you back these doctors and researchers into a corner about that they admit it doesn't apply to individuals, but they want to apply it to whole populations, in fact the whole world. I find that very troubling."

Most telling, says James, is the zealotry he observes. "Those advising these various diets, they don't say try this for a few weeks or a month and see how you like it. They say, this is what you absolutely must eat or turn into a frog and die or something. And then they never back off. They never say do this in moderation. And the weakest part of that entire argument is how angry any of them get when you challenge the dogma. They descend to rude tactics of various kinds. I've gotten threatening letters, I've gotten warnings of one kind or another from the proponents of these diets. They can't stand criticism; they get very angry."

One statistician whose conclusions are closer to James's than to Campbell's or Barnard's is Paul Meier of the University of Chicago, who has consulted with the National Heart, Lung and Blood Institute and the Food and Drug Administration and has participated in many randomized clinical trials dealing with the question of heart disease and its relationship to fats and cholesterol. A deliberate and careful speaker, he admits that when it comes to diet-heart trials, he feels that so far not very much has been proven. He gives as an example the so-called MRFIT study, which stands for Multiple Risk Factor Intervention Trial and which compared two groups at high risk for coronary disease. One group made lifestyle changes including switching to a low-fat, low-cholesterol diet, the other group made no changes in their eating habits. "That trial really showed no difference at all in mortality," says Meier. "Generally speaking, experimental intervention, whether with drugs or diet, has so far been unsuccessful. I'm inclined to believe that the animal fat–coronary disease parallel is real, but the experimental evidence is weak. I think the epidemiological evidence is strong enough to justify stocking the store shelves with much lower fat materials than we have today. But I'm appalled by anyone who says we ought to get fats down to ten or five percent. I know of no diet like that. And in general I resist extremes. There are many groups with many objectives who start with a conviction and gather what they call evidence to support it—and there's enough variation in the world that you're bound to find some."

A realistic question here, perhaps, is how much evidence do you need to adopt a diet that seems fairly harmless? What could be wrong with following T. Colin Campbell's example and mimicking the vegan diets of other cultures, hoping to mimic also those cultures' lowered risk of certain diseases? Few doctors and scientists would argue that eating more fiber and more fresh fruits and vegetables is a bad idea, and if other people get along fine without much fat or any animal products, why not Americans as well? This notion carries a simple and seductive logic, but that logic is marred by a few disturbing findings—findings that seem to point back to moderation (that is, a diet that includes a little bit of everything).

One concern is the effect of very restrictive diets on children. Although Campbell points out that all five of his children grew up on a nearly vegan diet and "were not compromised in the slightest," many others worry about a lack of protein and fats in children's diets. "In children, macrobiotic or vegan diets have been demonstrated to be harmful," says Weisburger of the American Health Foundation, "because they don't contain essential proteins for kids to grow. Children won't grow—this has been documented—because such a diet is incomplete." This idea is echoed by Dr. C. Wayne Callaway, an endocrinologist with George Washington University and a member of the advisory committee for the 1990 USDA dietary guidelines for Americans. "Many third-world countries are trying to get their level of fat intake up from about eight to ten percent to about twenty percent," says Callaway, "because kids just can't grow at that lower level; the food's just not calorically dense enough to get enough calories."

Callaway's assertion was put to the test in this country by Theresa Nicklaus of Tulane University in New Orleans, who compared diets of 871 ten-year-olds in an ongoing Bogalusa, Louisiana, heart study. About 1 in 7 were on low-fat diets, defined as less than 30 percent of calories from fats, and Nicklaus found that those children's overall diets were compromised. They were less likely to get enough of certain nutrients, such as vitamin B_{12}, niacin, and riboflavin (70 percent were deficient in vitamin B_{12}, which is found in meats and dairy products), and they obtained 25 percent of their calories from sugar, compared to 14 percent for the children on higher-fat diets. Nicklaus found that because the children's low-fat meals were less calorically dense, they tended to snack more on less nutritious foods.[12]

Neal Barnard, not surprisingly, is not impressed by such studies. "You can have a horribly balanced diet on any kind of diet," he points out. "Having said that, you are much safer as a vegetarian than as a meat-eater. Because by the time these kids with high-fat diets are eighteen or nineteen years of age, they'll have fatty streaks in their coronary arteries. That's what's going to kill them. They're not going to die of a riboflavin deficiency. What's going to kill them? Cardiovascular disease and, especially for the women, one in nine will get breast cancer."

The assumptions Barnard makes about childhood diet contributing to later disease are supported by many large groups like the National Cholesterol Education Program, which advises a low-fat diet beginning at age two, but Thomas N. James feels those assumptions are not yet warranted and may be harmful to children. "Children need foods that have cholesterol and saturated fats in them to grow normally," says James. "Those who now are saying that atherosclerosis begins in childhood have not mounted a persuasive case. They've done epidemiologic studies on cholesterol levels and on things like the autopsies of Korean and later Vietnamese soldiers who died, but nothing much there is clinically impressive. One would have to follow those children and their families and siblings for thirty or fifty years to know whether any of this means anything or not. The extrapolations that are being made from that constitute, I think, rather a thin case."

Another rogue element in the philosophy that lower fat and fewer animal products is always better concerns women, and in particular their reproductive capabilities. Claude L. Hughes, Jr., a researcher and professor of obstetrics and gynecology at Duke University, has conducted several animal studies that point to an odd occurrence: certain plant compounds, called phytosterols and phytoestrogens, may when eaten in large amounts cause sterility in female animals. "When humans eat a diet rich in these compounds," says Hughes, "the same physiological mechanisms are probably at work, inhibiting reproduction. Vegetarians have phytoestrogen levels one hundred times higher than people on a typical Western diet." The list of plants and vegetables that contain phytoestrogens is long, and includes such popular items as apples, carrots, French beans, and soybeans. Normally such foods are not a problem, says Hughes; it is only when they are consumed in quite large amounts—when they become staples—that they may have an effect on hormones. "That could affect not only fertility but early osteoporosis as well," says Hughes, "since an estrogen imbalance can promote thinning of the bones and fractures." The therapy Hughes recommends is, in a word, moderation. "I would caution against a radical change in diet for anyone," he says. "An ideal diet includes a diverse collection of plants and animals, grains and protein sources. That diversity protects against the chance of ingesting too much of any particular compounds that might have a hazardous effect."

The case for moderation received evidence from a surprising quarter in 1992, when studies began suggesting a disturbing conundrum regarding blood cholesterol levels. While high cholesterol levels (more than 240 units) were associated with higher risk of heart attack, very low levels of cholesterol (less than 160 units) were associated with higher risk of death from other causes, including strokes, certain cancers, suicide, homicide, liver disease, and lung disease. In fact, mortality rates for those with extra-low cholesterol levels equals the rate for people with very high cholesterol. According to the editor of *Circulation*, a medical journal where one of the studies on low cholesterol appeared, the safest cholesterol levels for overall survival seem to be moderate ones: between 180 and 200 or 220.[13] Some of the studies seemed to demonstrate a higher level of aggressiveness in the low-cholesterol groups, leading researchers to speculate that lowering cholesterol may affect mood or intellectual patterns. If true, that finding would be of special concern to children, both because their learning ability might be affected and because they are at much higher risk of death in accidents (which might be influenced by mood or aggressiveness resulting from low cholesterol) than from heart disease (which may be promoted by high cholesterol). In other words, these statistics raise the possibility that very low cholesterol may be of greater harm to children than very high cholesterol.

The new cholesterol findings point up the problems in extrapolating from incomplete data in order to prescribe wholesale and extreme shifts in dietary habits. What these studies indicate, according to some doctors and researchers, is that public health officials may have jumped the gun on cholesterol reduction, or at the very least applied their evidence too widely. Despite the fact that cholesterol is, in the words of one researcher, "absolutely necessary to every cell in the body,"[14] few scientists seem to have considered the question of whether you could drive cholesterol levels too low. It appears a singular case of tunnel vision, but it fits neatly into the same pattern that has made such a success of nonfat food items: If lowering high cholesterol is good, then lowering it almost out of existence must perforce be even better, safer, healthier.

"There's a supermarket chain here in Washington," Neal Barnard recalled at our lunch, "that did a promotion recently saying that people should not be afraid of food. That they should not worry about that bit of cholesterol, that they should not worry about that lean meat. And that is just out-and-out garbage. Because there isn't any data that suggests that eating a little bit of cholesterol is as good as avoiding it. And there are studies showing that people who consume lean meats are not as healthy as ovo-lacto vegetarians, and that ovo-lacto vegetarians are not as healthy as vegans."

While Dr. Thomas N. James describes a steamroller effect to

promote low-fat, low-cholesterol diets, Barnard describes a steam-roller moving in the other direction, toward indulgence in fatty diets, a steamroller financed by agribusiness. "I am an extremely small David, and there are lots of other little tiny Davids out there trying to fight an enormous Goliath that says, 'Don't worry, just buy it.' " In Barnard's fight there are no compromises. "I don't like fat substitutes because they reinforce the taste for grease," he said. "What we have to do is learn to live without it. You can adjust your taste for fat up or down. The way to do it is not to have chemical grease half the time and real grease the other half of the time, the key is to lose that taste. I believe that meat is something that primates tend to crave when they have access to it. So if you're trying to use meat in small amounts, as a condiment, peo-ple tend to not stick to that, they tend to use more and more. And the easiest way to break any habit is to get away from it. To many people meat then becomes revolting."

Barnard does his best to promote that transformation, al-though occasionally he steps back and disclaims his role as prose-lytizer. "I don't tell people what to do," he said as our lunch ended. "What I do is try to tell them their risks. My point is not to pre-scribe diets to people, but to say, here's what I think is the best, and here are the ways people can take advantage of it. I think that's my approach, rather than bringing in things like guilt and proscription." But a moment later he couldn't resist a parting thought, directed toward the most emotionally freighted element of the dietary debate, the element that provokes the most guilt and the most anxiety about where our changes in eating might take us. "I think there will come a time," said Barnard, "when we will look upon raising children with regular meat in the home as being to a certain extent abusive. Because you know that two out of three of these children are going to die prematurely of cardio-vascular disease or malignancy, and that's no treat. McNuggets on a birthday might seem like a treat. It's not such a great treat when you end up having a stroke." Shortly afterwards we left the restaurant, leaving behind us at our table his half-eaten linguine, my cleaned plate, and our unused wineglasses and coffee cups.

Chapter Seven

•

FOOD CONTROL
An Epidemic of Disordered Eating

•

Obsessing about food is more than a national pastime; it's on its way to becoming a national disorder. Dieticians are beginning to jettison ideas of "eating normally" in the face of almost universal dieting and a pattern they term "restrained eating"—eating not in response to natural cues of hunger but to external cues of will and self-control. Indeed, control is key in this new way of eating; food is transformed from a source of pleasure and sustenance to a test of resolve and a wellspring of power, moral superiority, even class status.

Food itself has become an active adversary: butter must be categorically rejected as a temptation, refrigerators must be kept clear for fear of binges, restaurant dishes must be inspected for lurking oils. Behaviors that were once considered symptoms of exotic and extreme eating disorders—anorexia nervosa, bulimia—are inching their way into everyday life, as more and more Americans seek in the taming of their appetites for food a mastery over not only their bodies but their lives.

•

Laurel Schiller* is making herself dinner on a warm July got evening in New York. She feels good, but hungry; when she home from her sales job at a cosmetics company she did a fifty-minute workout, including aerobics and calisthenics, and it is now close to eight o'clock. "The McNeil-Lehrer Newshour" is blaring on the television as she tosses together her ingredients, and her mind is automatically clicking off the calorie counts. Fifty for the lettuce, another fifty for the cucumber, say forty for the tomato. Mushrooms—those are good, hardly any calories; carrots, alfalfa sprouts. Dressing: balsamic vinegar mixed with mustard—almost no calories. Two hundred total, and no fat. Schiller used to consult a well-thumbed calorie counter almost constantly, but she hardly needs to do that anymore; the counts are internalized. But while calories are important to her—she sticks to a precise 1,400 per day, including even the stray stick of gum (15 calories) in her count—it is fat that is the greatest adversary. For that, however, she needs no counter: There is simply no fat in her diet. She has rounded it up and chased it off, and now she can't even remember the last time she ate peanut butter or pizza (real pizza, that is, not the kind she makes at home with pita bread, tomato sauce without olive oil, and fat-free mozzarella cheese). Even skinless chicken breast and fish are outlawed; they're lean compared to other sources of protein, but they do contain some fat.

Schiller sits down to eat her salad alone. Her sister, with whom she shares the two-bedroom apartment, is out for the evening, and she flips through a magazine over dinner. Then the salad is done and it's time for the pièce de résistance, the 370-calorie topper. Schiller splits a banana lengthwise (average calories: 100), puts it in a bowl, and starts spooning over it Dutch Chocolate American Glacé frozen dessert (an ice milk that has 270 calories per carton and zero fat). With that kind of calorie count, she knows she can (and will) eat the entire carton—a thought that never fails to give her a little frisson of pleasure.

*This is not her real name, and some identifying characteristics have been changed. She prefers to use a pseudonym, because however dedicated she may be to her dietary regimen, she is also embarrassed by its severity.

At the end of the carton Schiller is pleasantly (but not guiltily) full, her body still buzzing from her workout. She starts thinking about what she will eat tomorrow: fat-free wheat flakes and skim milk for breakfast, a plain bagel and a salad dressed with vinegar for lunch, intermittent snacks of jelly beans or Gummi Bears or nonfat frozen yogurt from the machine at the deli. Then she'll have to be very careful, because she's going out for dinner—maybe she can talk Shelly into going to Loulou's, where she knows she can get steamed vegetables that she trusts to have no fat (sometimes you can't be sure that the waiter is telling the truth, and she often finds herself squeezing her baked potato to be sure it doesn't have any oil or butter on it). By the time Schiller goes to bed she has the next day's eating mapped out. But as she turns out the light and puts her head on her pillow, she wishes it were morning already, because she is feeling hungry again.

"I used to be an enormous junk-food eater," Schiller says. She is in her late twenties, with long chestnut hair, light brown eyes, a wide smile, and an engagingly unaffected manner. "I was never overweight," she continues, "but I was never thin-thin." "Thin-thin" is a conjunction that comes up often in her patter about food. It seems to denote just the right level of thin—not merely a kind of natural slenderness, which is what Laurel has had most of her life but which is a size 8 rather than a size 6; thin-thin is something that works with clingy black skirts or tight stretch pants. Once she became thin-thin, Schiller says, "I could wear all these things I'd always wanted to wear and never wore. For the first time I felt very happy about the way I looked and very confident." It did not bother her that friends and family wondered about her health. "At work people were saying I was getting too thin. When I went home for Christmas everyone was saying, 'Oh my God, you're so thin.' That made me so happy. Isn't that sick?"

Schiller became thin-thin originally as a fluke, on what some women call the heartbreak diet. Her fiancé, Aaron, whom she had dated for three years and then lived with for the next three, had a sudden epiphany that all their plans were a mistake, that he wasn't ready for marriage, and moved out. For a while Schiller simply couldn't eat. "I just didn't have an appetite, and I was always crying, always had a lump in my throat. I think also when you're so upset and nervous you burn up more of your food, because even when I did eat I kept losing weight." Schiller didn't own a scale so she doesn't know how many pounds she lost, but she clearly lost a lot: clothes fit differently, and people noticed. The weight loss was one of the few bright spots in what was a very dark time.

Then Schiller found something else that made her happy, if only for a few minutes a day: exercise. She tried a videotaped home-aerobics routine and, she says, "I found that right after the exercise I felt really good, and it was the first time in such a long time that I had felt good about myself. Even if it didn't last that long—it was just that immediate high after you exercise—I was so happy to be happy for a little while. So I got totally addicted to it. I was doing it every single day." Eventually, she got happy enough to start putting weight back on, despite the exercise. She saw thin-thin slipping away. "I couldn't figure out how to get back to what I used to be. My clothes weren't fitting the same anymore, I thought my legs were getting heavy—muscles were building up. I wanted to get back to the skinniness that I had been."

That was when, for the first time in her life, Schiller thought about consciously dieting. She began to diet-shop, trying one, then another. The one she eventually found was actually presented to her with a sort of anti-recommendation; Schiller was immediately attracted. "A friend of mine was telling me in a very negative way about this other friend of hers who wouldn't eat any fat, not a gram of fat," she says, "and I thought, oh, that's the best idea! Then I found a book that was all about fat-free diets, with recipes and stuff. It became my bible; it lists tons of fat-free things, with brand names and everything." At about the same time she obtained, from a magazine article, a formula for figuring the lowest number of calories per day you can eat without slowing your metabolism, and came up with the magic 1,400.

Those two concepts—no fat, 1,400 calories per day—became

the constructs for a new life. One of the most delightful and unexpected benefits of that life was the gratifying sense of control Schiller felt. "I remember thinking, God, I have such willpower—if I set my mind to something I can do it," she says. "Watching other people who said, 'Oh, I want to lose weight,' but they couldn't stop eating and start dieting, I'd think, how come I'm so strong?" Her workouts, too, which she almost never skipped, made her feel strong and resistant. She sometimes felt that she could do anything.

But with that surge of control came some darker elements. It was, for instance, impossible for her to be sure of maintaining her regimen if she went out to restaurants, so she began to constrict her social life. "Every time I'd make a plan I'd think, I don't want to do this because there's nothing for me to eat there. So I wouldn't want to make plans, or I'd make plans not involving dinner. Or I'd just make sure we went to a restaurant where I knew there were things I could order. But I used to love to go out to good restaurants, and at a certain point I realized it was kind of weird that I was staying home just so I could eat what I wanted."

Then she began to be concerned about her health. The first worrisome sign was the disappearance of her period (a low-calorie intake and/or high level of exercise can disrupt the hormones that trigger ovulation). "I remember one morning waking up thinking that I felt really skinny," Schiller says. "I totally had lost my chest—I was completely flat-chested—and my hair was not in good shape, and I thought to myself, This is disgusting, I'm just ruining my body." But she stayed on the diet.

The most disturbing moment came at Thanksgiving. Schiller had been strictly following her diet for several months, and she went home to visit her family in a suburb of Washington, D.C. She decided that for Thanksgiving dinner she would allow herself to eat what she calls "normally," that is, without restrictions. So she began—and she couldn't stop. "It was horrible," she says. "It was disgusting. It's the joke of my family now. I ate all the dinner, with about three helpings, and then dessert—I must have had fifteen desserts. I was just thinking, this is so yummy, I love this, I haven't had this in so long, I never eat it, I deserve it. It got to the point where people—even my mother, who thought I'd gotten too thin and was too restrictive—were saying, 'You have to stop, you're going to get sick.' But I couldn't control myself. It was scary."

Schiller had just had, for the first time in her life, a certifiable binge. The next day, she was back on her diet.

Students of eating disorders have begun to understand a central fact about them: they exist on a continuum. No longer do anorexia nervosa and bulimia—respectively, self-starvation and binge-and-purge disease—comprise the entire definition of eating disorder; they are simply the endpoints of a long range of behaviors that begin with compulsive thinking about food and progress toward greater obsessions. What all eating disorders share is a search for control through food—control of one's body, one's desires, one's fate—and a process whereby food becomes symbolic, coming to stand for something other than simple sustenance or taste. In any eating disorder, food is likely to acquire the stature of an adversary.

In anorexia, the enmity for eating is extreme: the clinical definition describes someone who will not maintain body weight over 85 percent of normal for her height, who has an intense fear of fat and distorted body image although she is underweight, and who misses at least three consecutive periods. Anorexics tend to think about food constantly (some may cook avidly, and feed others), but they eat hardly anything; in extreme cases, without intervention or forced feeding, anorexia can lead to death. Bulimia likewise has a formal definition: the bulimic has a minimum average of two binge-purge episodes a week for at least three months, uses vomiting, laxatives, or strict diets to prevent weight gain, and is overly concerned with body shape and size. Bulimics hate food perhaps even more than anorexics, because they feel less in control of it—their periodic binges are humiliating failures of will.[1]

Those two conditions are the extremes, and eating-disorder specialists estimate that only 2 to 5 percent of young women (almost all anorexics and bulimics *are* women) fit those definitions.[2] But what could be called disordered thinking about food on a lesser scale is so common that by the late 1980s specialists were beginning to describe another, much larger category: subclinical eating disorder, or SED. The hallmarks of SED can include chronic undereating, overexercising, and binge eating that results from undereating. Results of this behavior include scant or nonexistent periods and the effects of low metabolic rate from undereating (fatigue, cold intolerance, depression, dizziness on standing, constipation). SED can also produce a sort of catch-22 of dieting: If a dieter chronically undereats (that is, eats less food than she needs for energy requirements) and combines that with large amounts of physical exercise, her metabolism may slow down drastically to conserve more energy from the available food. This results in a weight stasis: A dieter may be consuming as little as 800 to 1,000 calories a day (for most people normal intake is closer to 2,000 or more) but not losing weight because her body assumes that she is starving. It clings, in its infinitely self-protective wisdom, to every calorie. One clinician who runs an eating disorders counseling group estimates that 80 to 85 percent of women fall into the category of "disordered eating—people who are obsessed about weight and body image," at some point in their lives.[3]

Obsessiveness is as key to subclinical eating disorders as it is to more extreme cases. Dr. C. Wayne Callaway, an endocrinologist at George Washington University who has looked extensively at SED, says some of the psychological patterns of SED include "having cravings for food, having great difficulty controlling food intake, being obsessed with food, starting to dream about food, thinking about food well in advance of meals." That kind of thinking promotes a loss of perspective, a skewed view of what normal eating is—and an elevation of food to a position of extreme power. "If you ask people like this, what did you actually eat? they'll say, 'Oh, I binged yesterday,' " says Callaway. "And you say again, what did you eat? and they say, 'Gosh, I had a peanut butter and jelly sandwich,' or 'I had three pieces of cheese.' That's somebody who's not bingeing but who does have a distorted view of eating."

That distorted view, and the behavior that it leads to, has as its trigger the struggle for control that is at the heart of all obsessive thinking about food; in researchers' terms, that struggle is expressed in a phenomenon they call "restrained eating." A restrained eater is a chronic dieter, and her eating patterns are therefore always controlled. When and how much and what she eats are not determined by hunger or desire but by external factors: how many calories something contains, or what she ate yesterday, or some complicated calculation of guilt, sacrifice, and indulgence: "I skipped breakfast so I deserve this ice cream cone" rather than "I am hungry for this ice cream cone." It is a measure of how far we have traveled from that latter sentiment that restrained eating is so common it is considered "normal," at least in the definition of normal used by researchers. That is, it is the norm; it is more common than "natural eating," which is eating according to one's internal cues of hunger and satiety.

Researchers Janet Polivy and C. Peter Herman, of the University of Toronto, first advanced this idea in 1987 in an article in the *Journal of Consulting and Clinical Psychology* entitled "Diagnosis and Treatment of Normal Eating." " 'Normal' eating for North American women is now characterized by dieting," they wrote. "It is now 'normal' for individuals in our society to express concern about their weight and to engage in fitful attempts to change it. . . . Normal eating now requires periodic dieting." They ascribe some of the motivation for this behavior to the fact that thinness "connotes power, health, and other contemporary values" and that thinness "reflects the sort of self-control that is presumably required to achieve and maintain slenderness." Thus, they conclude, "the meaning of a phrase such as *normal eating* is no longer obvious."[4]

The kind of "normal" eating that Polivy and Herman describe eventually leads to a more-or-less permanent dissonance between the cues that lead to eating and the act of eating itself. Humans develop early in life a system for regulating food intake, based upon physiological needs; we must actually learn how to recognize when we're sated, because there is a time delay between the point at which we are full and the point at which we *feel* full. Thus, we construct an intricate and unconscious choreograph of cues to tell us when we've had enough—and even what types of food we should eat. For instance, studies have shown that young children will, if presented with a variety of foods, eat a naturally balanced diet within the course of a given week. They may eat all starches one day and all fruits the next, but over the course of several days they take in a diet astonishingly similar to our educated idea of "healthy" and "balanced."[5] Restrained eating disrupts this system, sometimes irreparably.

"People who don't diet remain reasonably well in touch with the natural signals that nature built in to regulate eating," says Peter Herman. "That is, their bodies tell them with reasonable, not perfect, efficiency when to eat and when to stop eating. A diet proposes different ideas, and the ideas are cognitive, not physiological. It's our belief that a reliance on those sorts of unnatural signals undermines one's ability to know when one is truly hungry or when one is truly full, with the result that the regulation of eating in the normal course of affairs becomes entirely dependent on these fairly arbitrary mental rules of what to eat. Mostly these rules are telling you: Don't eat even though you might be tempted to."

This sort of self-imposed system leads to some peculiar and illogical behavior. Herman describes a study in which groups of subjects were given varying amounts of milkshake, then later allowed to eat as much as they wanted of several flavors of ice cream. Subjects were divided into restrained and natural eaters, based on a questionnaire called the "restraint scale" (which asked how often the subject dieted, how much her weight fluctuated, how much time she spent thinking about food, whether she felt guilty about what she ate, and so on). What they found was that when the natural eaters (nondieters) had a small "pre-load" of milkshake, they ate a larger amount of ice cream later; when they were given a large pre-load, they ate relatively little ice cream later. They seemed to base their eating on overall amount, and if they were full of milkshake, they didn't bother with more ice cream.

The restrained eaters showed a fascinating, and completely illogical, pattern. When they were given a small pre-load, they ate
only a small amount of ice cream later. But with a large pre-load,
they ate much *more* ice cream later. Herman calls this behavior
"counter-regulation," and he describes it like this: "When the restrained eaters were given a small pre-load, their diet stayed intact; their whole goal is to eat little and we hadn't done anything
to undermine that. Whereas when they got the large pre-load—
well, once you've blown your diet or had it blown for you somehow, then all bets are off, and the diet is ruined for the day, might
as well pig out and start again tomorrow. In the context of what is
supposedly a well-regulated system—the feeding system—it's really pretty interesting.

"The question for us is, How can nature, which is built to
prevent this sort of nonsense, allow it? And our thesis is that nature is ruined by dieting. Ultimately the dieter has a great deal of
difficulty even knowing when she *is* hungry; she loses touch with
her internal signals. This is exaggerated, of course, in clinical eating disorders, but it occurs as well in what we call normal dieting
or restrained eating." Once that connection with internal signals is
broken, says Herman, it is hard to repair—partly because of the
dieter's own reluctance. "Most people don't break out of this. Once
you get into the dieting rut it's statistically unlikely that you're
going to escape. We've tried some programs to get people to stop
dieting and get back in touch with the natural physiological signals of hunger and satiety. Most dieters are reluctant to do that;
they don't trust their own bodies." What restrained eaters are left
with is a cruel snare: In attempting to completely control their
eating by putting it under their conscious manipulation, they are
unwittingly committing themselves to an eventual loss of control.
Bingers have been known to consume multiple bags of cookies,
doughnuts, several pizzas, gallons of ice cream. Bingeing, it seems,
is the body's revenge for tampering.

Restrained eaters, by definition, think obsessively about food,
simultaneously craving and reviling it. What's particularly striking is that this process can be entirely conscious and yet not lose

one iota of its power. One woman told *New York Woman* magazine, "I was wishing for that innocent time the other day—for when food was just food." "Even 'normal' women have completely lost their perspectives," the article goes on. "The average woman—and what she weighs is irrelevant—is actually twisted in a web of tangled habits and impulses, sunk in a mire of lusts and prohibitions about what she eats, how she eats it and with whom." The writer goes on to describe various women's internal guilt monologues about the frozen bonbon they ate after lunch or the relative size of the piece of lasagna they ate for dinner. One woman comments: "In order to impose discipline on myself, I've had to keep an empty refrigerator."[6]

All of this obsessiveness about eating—and particularly about body size—seems very modern, a product of the twentieth-century ethos that equates thinness with power, attractiveness, and self-control, but in fact women have been denying themselves food for various reasons for centuries. In medieval Europe it was not uncommon for women to fast as a way of proving their religious faith and demonstrating a holiness that could rise above needs of the flesh, a phenomenon that eventually came to be known as *anorexia mirabilis* (miraculously inspired loss of appetite).[7] In the nineteenth century, fasting enjoyed a strange little burst of publicity, as a series of "fasting girls" captured popular attention. These girls, unlike earlier religious fasters, usually did not have an underlying philosophy for refusing food; they seemed, rather, to enjoy the fame that came to them as a result of their claims to exist on virtually no food. Mollie Fancher, a New York woman who claimed to stop eating in 1866 at the age of nineteen, maintained her hold on celebrity for decades as a "fasting girl"; despite challenges by doctors, no one ever proved that she ate a bite.

But concurrent with the fasting girl phenomenon a new diagnosis was coming into vogue, that of anorexia nervosa, named and described in the 1870s. Anorexia nervosa seemed to strike upper-middle-class girls, and social historian Joan Jacobs Brumberg outlines in her book *Fasting Girls* her theory that the disease was intimately related to the bourgeois family system that was being created by the industrial revolution. What's particularly interesting about Brumberg's analysis is her contention that anorexia nervosa originally preceded any preoccupation with dieting and slenderness, and instead was tied to other aspects of late-Victorian society: intimacy and material comfort, parental love and expectations, sexual division of labor, and ideas about gender and class. "Among the middle class," writes Brumberg, "it seems that eating correctly was emerging as a new morality, one that set its members apart from the working class."[8] And, perhaps even more powerfully, in the Victorian age the open enjoyment of food was symbolically linked with sex and carnality; thus, proper young women were expected not to exhibit much appetite. "In Victorian society," writes Brumberg, "food and femininity were linked in such a way as to promote restrictive eating among privileged adolescent women. . . . Female discomfort with food, as well as with the act of eating, was a pervasive subtext of Victorian popular culture."[9] The taboo against women eating meat—considered too "stimulating"—was so pervasive that chlorosis, or iron-deficiency anemia, was quite common among young girls; the skin pallor that it caused was, in fact, considered attractive.[10] "Over and over again," according to Brumberg, "in all of the popular literature of the Victorian period, good women distanced themselves from the act of eating with disclaimers that pronounced their disinterest in anything but the aesthetics of food. . . . The woman who put soul over body was the ideal of Victorian femininity. . . . To be hungry, in any sense, was a social faux pas. Denial became a form of moral certitude and refusal of attractive foods a means for advancing in the moral hierarchy."[11] And the social hierarchy as well: true "ladies" had few carnal appetites of any sort, and one's style of eating was a clue to social status.

It is a short step from those ideas to the ones that, unconsciously or not, constrain women today. Thinness and fatness, as the Duchess of Windsor so pithily pointed out, are construed as signals of class, and it's a rare woman today who does not apologize for exhibiting signs of a powerful appetite. If, in Brumberg's words, "in the 1980s anorexia nervosa constitutes a modern credo of self-denial,"[12] the same might be said in the 1990s for restrained eating.

Laurel Schiller had warned me in advance, laughingly, that I might be embarrassed by the way she orders her lunch. And, indeed, when the waiter came she entered into a discussion: Could she have the mozzarella and tomato salad, except without the mozzarella, and with mustard and balsamic vinegar on the side? And the steamed artichoke, could that be served with no sauce? We were at a chic little French brasserie where tables were lined up on the sidewalk to take advantage of the August sunshine. The menu featured many light entrées—seafood salads, chicken niçoise, grilled vegetable plate—but in Schiller's book all of these were flawed. "I never get grilled vegetables, just steamed," she confided, "because they always put oil on the grilled ones."

When her food arrived it looked rather stark on the huge bistro dinnerware: alternating slabs of bare tomato and purple onion on one plate, an unadorned artichoke marooned in the center of the other. But Schiller dug in happily, mixing the mustard and balsamic into a paste that she used for dipping artichoke leaves, and eating a little bread on the side (not the slices that featured nuts and raisins, though—and no butter on top). "Some people just can't stand to eat at restaurants with me," she said cheerfully, "because my ordering is so involved, and I'll send things back if I think they have any oil on them. I've found a handful of restaurants in the city where there were things I could order, like big salads or steamed vegetables and rice or baked potatoes. Things that I could eat. For a long time I just didn't want to go out much because I was worried about what I'd eat. That's when I realized there was something a little wrong with this—that it probably had a lot to do with control. Aaron moving out was completely *out* of my control, and it was so awful. And then there I was all of a sudden living alone in New York, and I felt I had to prove I could be a grown-up. This eating thing showed I really was in control. It felt good."

One curious aspect of Schiller's dedication to her calorie- and fat-deprived regimen is that she realizes it is not "normal." In fact, the words "eating normally" crop up often in her speech. At the infamous Thanksgiving, she had decided to "eat normally." On vacation, she "ate normally." When she goes out with her boyfriend, she (sometimes) "eats normally." She sometimes binges on an entire Entenmann's fat-free cake and then thinks: "This isn't normal, this can't be normal." But knowing that her current diet is not normal does not abate her interest in it in the slightest. Any foray into eating normally actually worries her greatly; she lives in fear of a terrible regression to the way she used to eat and a dread size-8 body. "It got to the point where, everything I put in my mouth I thought, am I going to gain weight from this?" she said at lunch. She claimed to have become more moderate since then, but her moderation is a relative concept. "Now I break my diet all the time," she said, "but every time I break it I want to go back to the way I used to be, when I never went off the diet. When I was the most obsessive about this, I started to get scared that if I stopped even a little bit then I would start to gain and go back to my old way, so that kept me really strict. Now I don't feel thin at all anymore. I try on clothes sometimes at night just to make sure they still fit the same way they did when I was really thin." (The fact that they still do is one clue to how strict her diet remains.)

Schiller's "old way" was completely unrestrained. In fact, there is no hint of deprivation or calorie-obsession in her upbringing or even in her college years, the time when an estimated 80 percent of women flirt with disordered eating behavior. "My house, when I was growing up, was never the type of place where you couldn't eat between meals or anything," she said. "We had a ton of junk food in the house, and even today there are drawers filled with every kind of potato chip, every kind of candy. I was always allowed to eat whatever I wanted. And I ate a ton of it—barbecued potato chips, Slim Jims, chocolate. I ate red meat a lot, and I always ordered desserts in restaurants. It's disgusting now, the thought of it, but I would eat steak and my favorite part of it was the fat. You know how prime rib has that whole rim of fat around it? I loved that."

Despite those habits, Schiller was never overweight. "I guess I was normal—about a size eight. But I always felt I should be thinner. Always. I didn't think of myself as slender. But it never crossed my mind really to diet or exercise. I just thought, oh, this is the way I am." When she set up housekeeping in New York with Aaron, whom she had met at college, she reproduced the diet she knew best: "I made steak a lot, and lamb chops and things. My refrigerator and cabinets were always full. I tried to make it as much like home as possible, because I was so homesick."

Then came the traumatic breakup, and Schiller's subsequent transformation. Now she is an aficionado of fat-free specialty foods and cooking methods, and a veritable dictionary of food calorie- and fat-counts. But she has substituted other indulgences for the Slim Jims and prime ribs of the past. The premier one is sugar. "I *crave* sweet things," she said. "I always ate a lot of sweets, but I eat much more now than I ever did. There are so many things you can buy that satisfy those cravings for sugar, but without fat. I live on Skimpy Treats and jelly beans and Gummi Bears . . . " The other indulgence worries her a little: She has a tendency to binge on certain items, especially sweets. "I never had that kind of problem before, where I couldn't stop eating. I mean, I always ate a lot, I was always a very big eater, but not to sit down and eat a whole cake." A fat-free cake, of course.

Schiller's largest concession to "normal eating" now takes the form of an institutionalized binge. One day a week she allows herself to eat normally—whatever she wants, not thinking about the diet—and her behavior on that day tends to illustrate the "counter-regulation" Peter Herman observed in his experimental restrained eaters. Because it's her one day of free eating—a broken diet, essentially—she eats more, without regard to internal hunger cues. "I'd think, this is my one night, I'd better get it all in," said Schiller. "So I'd eat whatever I wanted, and it wouldn't even be a question of hunger. I'd just think, I might as well have this because it's going to be another week." Every time that happens, the link between hunger and eating becomes weaker, the dedication to external controls stronger. In fact, hunger is almost beside the point in Schiller's life. "I'm always hungry," she said at one point. But that hunger has little to do with what she eats (except for the sweets, which are fat-free and therefore guilt-free). Schiller's diet is in many ways an unconscious echo of the Victorian woman's dainty regimen: sweets and salads in place of meats and hearty fare.

The recent (slight) loosening of her rigid diet rules has coincided with the entry into Schiller's life of a new man. Now she coordinates her night of normal eating with date nights. "When we first started dating, he would pick a place where there wouldn't be fat-free food—like one time he picked this Mexican restaurant—and I would feel kind of foolish saying I can't eat there. But I would be upset, thinking about it all week, wondering what am I going to eat there? I was more nervous about what I was going to eat than about going on a date. Now, when I go out to dinner and I absolutely can't order fat-free things, I'll just go ahead and get regular food, but I won't feel as bad about it as I used to."

That is as far as Schiller will go toward "eating normally." She hopes to stick with her restrictions forever, through marriage and having children. "I think it will be much harder," she admitted, "but I hope I'll be able to do it." Schiller is, with thorough good humor, in love with her chains; their limits somehow, in some wordless fashion, confer a measure of strength and confidence. "I used to just eat whatever I wanted, whenever I wanted," she mused over black iced coffee, no milk. "Now I can't believe that I'm this way; people who knew me in college can't believe it. But I don't miss that old way of eating. Because it wasn't that I was *able* to eat whatever I wanted; it was that I just didn't care."

Chapter Eight

•

PUBLIC EATING
Serving the Food Phobes

•

Few acts so distill and display our ideas of what we should and should not eat as that of ordering a meal in a restaurant. The menu is a minefield, and more and more diners are questioning not only the basic healthfulness of the foods they order, but the way those foods are prepared. These anxieties have led to a new age of restaurant dining. No longer is eating out inherently a moment of relaxation and pleasure seeking; it is often transformed into simply another task on the way to dietary correctness.

This philosophy has also redefined the role of the chef, who must not only foresee and accommodate rapidly changing culinary darlings and bêtes noires—low-fat goat cheese is in, full-fat brie or camembert is out; grilled and oven-roasted are in, sautéed and fried are out—but turn on a dime in the kitchen to reconfigure favorite recipes for the ever-increasing number of diners with special requests. Their reward: an intimate view of how Americans really eat.

•

The big wall clock in the cramped, steamy kitchen of the Blue Ribbon restaurant was inching toward eight on a Friday evening, and things were beginning to accelerate. Escargots simmered with bacon and apples in a reduction of veal stock and red wine (soon to be enhanced by a sizable hunk of butter mixed with herbs and garlic), salmon and steak sizzled over a grill, huge pots of gravy and broth issued wisps of steam, a whole trout bubbled in a deep fryer. The three chefs in charge of all this—Eric and Bruce Bromberg, brothers and co-owners of the restaurant (with Eric's wife, Ellen), and sous-chef Kris Polak—moved among the various pots and sauté pans with a frenzy that seemed partly balletic and always on the verge of dangerously chaotic. Bruce flipped and salted the contents of several frying pans in one swift movement; Eric slathered grilled vegetables with oil, then spun around to pare delicate slices from a fat-topped hunk of duck breast; Kris deposited pieces of steaming-hot fried chicken on a plate with bare fingers, wincing with each one. Shawn Sant Amour, the waiter who served as liaison between the dining room staff and the kitchen, emerged slightly breathless at the window—the counter between the kitchen and the waiters' station—and shouted "Ordering!," slapping down two written orders. "And fire tables ten and twelve," he added. "Firing" is the kitchen's signal to put the entrées on to cook; a sign that the customers at that table are winding down on their appetizers. "Okay," Eric called out to the other two chefs, "we're going to go on it all now. You ready? Stay with the program. Want me to call them one more time? Okay: two paella, one London broil, one tofu ravioli, one turkey, two catfish, one rack of lamb." Bruce and Kris responded silently, spinning for new pans, reaching for another clump of butter.

At Blue Ribbon, a small (sixteen-table) restaurant in the heart of SoHo, New York's hip, downtown neighborhood, the kitchen is located at the bottom of a steep flight of stairs. This setup can appear a little Biblical at times: upstairs all is calm and cool, in a dining room bathed in a warm yellow light and decorated in rose tints and wood, small enough to be intimate and not too loud; downstairs is a cramped, harshly lit, steaming room easily twenty degrees hotter, filled with clangs and shouts and crashes, a seeming hell of cookery. But in another sense the atmosphere, on that Friday night the week before Christmas, 1992, was positively jubilant. Blue Ribbon had opened barely more than a month before, on November 3, and the restaurant was already packing people in. That very Friday Blue Ribbon had received a short but positive review in the *New York Times*, in the newspaper's "$25 and Under" slot, and the night before they had served dinner to a table hosted by Gael Greene, restaurant critic for *New York* magazine. In a business renowned for its brutality and its many failed establishments, Blue Ribbon was enjoying a very promising start.

But beneath the jokes exchanged between kitchen and waitstaff, most of them about the fact that many people were ordering exactly what was mentioned in the *Times* review (potato pancakes, escargots, beef marrow with oxtail marmalade, paella, salmon) ran a very serious concern: How were people liking their food? Plates that were completely cleaned were displayed proudly to the chefs; one half-eaten plate of paella prompted a somber postmortem. Eric Bromberg, at thirty-one an experienced, Cordon-Bleu-educated chef and spiritual head of the Blue Ribbon kitchen (its name is the English translation of Cordon Bleu, where Bruce also took his degree), wants people to like the food he makes for them, and in pursuit of that goal he will cook whatever his customers want to eat. That is not to suggest that he does not have a point of view about food. He has, in fact, very strong opinions about what he likes, but they are matched by a strong opinion about service and the notion that people who are paying for their food deserve to get exactly what they ask for.

Bromberg has attempted to serve both himself and his customers by, quite simply, cooking for others the food that he likes to eat himself. He first got a chance to create a menu that truly reflected that at a New York restaurant right across the street from Blue Ribbon called Nick and Eddie, where he was a co-owner. (Before that he had worked at several high-profile New York restaurants, including three years at the American Hotel in Sag Harbor, a resort community on Long Island.) Nick and Eddie, which opened in 1990, was one of the best of a miniboom in "new American" restaurants that found interesting, sometimes European-inspired ways to present some classic American foods—catfish, hamburgers, mashed potatoes, leg of lamb, pork loin, hot fudge sundaes. Opening when Americans were becoming ever more concerned about meats and fats, Nick and Eddie bucked the trend and served food that just happened to be deliciously sinful to capacity crowds.

Blue Ribbon opened to an even more diet-concerned clientele, in an age when meat-and-potatoes are considered déclassé and many restaurants feel compelled to offer at least some "spa cuisine" or "heart-healthy" entrées (even Nick and Eddie had, by this time, added two dishes adorned with a heart motif on the menu to signify low-fat and low-salt). Bromberg's concession to such societal pressure was to offer tofu ravioli on a plate heaped high with glistening grilled and steamed vegetables, his single vegetarian entrée among twenty-two others that included beef stew, fried chicken, sesame-glazed catfish, rib steak, swordfish, leg of lamb, choucroute garni, hamburgers and turkey burgers, and a paella filled with clams, shrimp, salmon, sweet peppers, turkey sausage, and saffron rice. He soon sensed the need for another nonmeat dish and added vegetable fried rice; both the rice and the ravioli became good sellers.

Bromberg seems completely sanguine about offering such a full-bodied menu, and part of his unconcern may derive from this knowledge: Some people are going to ask him to make changes in what he cooks, no matter what he offers. If this era is diet-obsessed, it is also unashamedly activist. Almost every magazine article or book about changing one's diet includes advice about eating out: Request your food cooked without oils, sauces on the side, balsamic vinegar in place of mayonnaise, salt banished. Eating out is no longer automatically an occasion for indulging, eating something you wouldn't cook at home, or even trusting a chef to prepare his or her dishes in the best possible way. Paying for one's food to be prepared by others now rivals home-cooking—in

1990 Americans spent 42.5 percent of their food dollars on meals away from home—and the result is a new tradition: second-guessing the chef. Why go off your diet, runs the reasoning behind this, simply because you're in a restaurant? This attitude has brought a new, perhaps not too inviting, day for chefs. It also means that chefs have a unique insight into the way Americans truly eat: they see how people request their food (and therefore how they imagine or idealize it), and they see what actually gets eaten. There is often a sizable gap between the two.

Bromberg has a layered reaction to the new wave in restaurant ordering: While he professes himself happy to make any changes his customers desire, he regards many of those changes as misinformed and rather silly. He described these particular culinary trials to me on a sunny October day about a month before Blue Ribbon opened. Because the restaurant was in the midst of renovation (all accomplished by Eric, Bruce, and a few core members of the staff) and choked with plaster dust, we sat in a nearby park. It was an unseasonably warm day and Bromberg wore roomy California-surfer shorts and a T-shirt. He is slightly heavy-set (he confessed to being on a diet himself), with dark, longish hair just beginning to be touched with premature gray, and a face that can look a little cherubic, especially when flushed pink with the heat of a kitchen. His manner is brisk and straightforward; when he talks about food and how people eat, opinions and judgments come flowing out. "I got into this business because I love to cook," he said, "and I love to make stuff that people like. And if that means putting fish and one piece of broccoli in the steamer and the person that eats that says, 'That was fantastic,' I'm just as happy about that as I would be to make foie gras with filet mignon in some very fancy French preparation."

But, Bromberg has found, there is a recurring problem with that scenario: People don't always like what they think they *ought* to eat. "Why do you go to a restaurant in the first place?" he asked. "Because people have said the food is good, in one way or another. Now, some people go to that restaurant and then say, 'I want my fish steamed, I want my vegetables steamed, I want my sauce on the side or no sauce at all, I want a side of balsamic vinegar'—all of these are common orders. But then when the food gets there, some people end up saying, 'This was bland and really not very good. I don't know why everybody thinks this restaurant's so good.' There's a real contradiction here. I do think customers should have exactly what they want. But when people get too aggressive and too picky, it affects the flavors. I wouldn't suggest that a piece of steamed fish and some steamed vegetables isn't delicious, because I think it is, and it's natural flavors. But many people are bored with those flavors; they've grown up eating food that's been seasoned, that has salt and pepper, that has herbs, cooked in butter or oil, and then they order something with none of those ingredients and say, 'This doesn't taste great to me.' And I think another thing that occurs to them is that they could go to the supermarket, get some vegetables, go home, put them in a dish with a little water, plastic-wrap it, put it in the steamer or microwave, and have the whole thing for two dollars instead of seventeen dollars."

While Bromberg professed an unending willingness to rearrange his menu for customers with special requests—"demanding customers is what the business is all about," he said—several aspects of the current rage for such rearrangement clearly stick in his craw (in addition to the one he just described, being judged as a chef on food that he prepared to someone else's specifications). One is the irritating habit some customers have of making menu changes and not recognizing that the kitchen will need extra time to accommodate them. "If someone wants their mashed potatoes with skim milk or olive oil, that's fine," said Bromberg, "but it's going to take an extra fifteen minutes or so to cook the potatoes, get a new thing going. Most customers understand that, but a reasonable amount would also say, 'Where the hell is my food?' That's kind of a dangerous trend in terms of where restaurants are going."

Then, too, he is annoyed—but also sometimes amused—by the huge volume of misinformation that permeates his customers' desires. "We get some pretty strange orders," he said. "Like: 'I'm on a diet so I don't want mashed potatoes, I want french fries.' Or, 'I'd like my burger with no bread, and a double order of mashed potatoes.' Or people don't understand that while olive oil has no cholesterol, it has just as much fat as butter, just as many calories. So someone will say they're on a diet and they don't want butter but they do want olive oil. Or they ask for their salad dressing on the side, or just oil and vinegar on the side, and then they end up putting three or four or five tablespoons of oil on their salad and think they're eating healthy. The American public gets fixated on words and specifics. We see it immediately in the kitchen, an absolutely up-to-the-minute response to health news. There could be a report on the 'Channel Seven News' about polluted waters at six o'clock, and at eight o'clock people are asking us, 'Is this polluted fish? Where does this fish come from?' Every health item in the *New York Times* has an instant response, too. As a chef you either stay up-to-date or you don't know what you're talking about."

Bromberg felt that health concerns were so central to his work that in the fall of 1991 he spent several weeks at the Duke Fitness Center at Duke University in Durham, North Carolina, one of the nation's leading diet and nutrition centers. "I studied heart disease and cholesterol and obesity and every other issue pertaining to food and human beings," Bromberg said. "I learned that going over the edge—like no fat, no meat, limiting your diet completely to vegetables—is less beneficial than moderating. Now, I'm sure I'd get a pretty good argument about that from macrobiotic people, but this program said that for healthy eating you should have a balanced intake." Bromberg has translated that idea of moderation into a theory of restaurant eating based on twin notions of enjoyment and self-control. "Once you get into a good, high-quality restaurant," he said, "I think health concerns are so apparent now that, even if you get a cream sauce on a fish dish, you're talking about maybe an ounce or so of sauce. Now, an ounce of cream—I don't know the exact number of calories, but it's not a lot. It's on your fish and you eat your fish, and usually there's some sauce left on the plate when you're done. Now, you have the option of sopping that up with your bread or leaving it on the plate. Or, for instance, take the mashed potatoes we make; they have cream and butter in them, but realistically in a single serving the amount you're getting may be a teaspoon of cream and a teaspoon of butter. Not an enormous amount. I think moderating your intake is the key. If you like bacon and you want to have it, have a piece—about seventy calories, not a big deal. If you eat twelve pieces of bacon every morning, you're probably running some kind of risk. But I think substituting your taste sensations and enjoyment from food now, so that you'll sustain yourself for another year and a half or two years down the road . . . well, I think it would be nice to have enjoyed your meals along the way."

What seems to Eric Bromberg a simple matter of moderate self-knowledge and self-control—leaving a little rich sauce on the plate if one is concerned about fats, for instance—seems to constitute a significant challenge to many restaurant patrons, however. Restaurants seem to be, in fact, the ground upon which Americans duel most fiercely with their conflicted impulses toward renunciation and indulgence. Part of the reason for this may lie in the very public nature of restaurants—where else does one have to speak aloud one's choices for a meal? These days the social pressure is on to show one's nutritional correctness, which can be indicated not only by opting for seafood or salad but by specifying "sauce on the side" or "no oil used in preparation." And yet this choice is made especially difficult by the immediate juxtaposition of the tempting and forbidden: steak au poivre and fettuccine Alfredo offer themselves up right next to the grilled scallops on a bed of radicchio and the boneless, skinless breast of chicken. An increasing number of people split the difference; many chefs tell of serving meals that begin with a light salad, dressing on the side, and end with the double-chocolate mousse surrounded by raspberry crème sauce. If this schizophrenic response threatens to dull the pleasure of the chef's job—which has traditionally been defined as serving others the tastiest dishes one could devise—it could also be perceived as a challenge to be more inventive and more flexible.

But even those chefs, like Eric Bromberg, who strive most of the time to treat their patrons' food-health sensitivities as an opportunity to be more creative find themselves losing patience when customers' zeal outpaces logic, when the perception of what is healthiest or most abstemious overshadows the reality of what a meal is all about.

When the National Restaurant Association conducted a nationwide survey of restaurant-goers in late 1989 that would assess "consumer attitudes toward nutrition in restaurants," the researchers found that almost everyone fell naturally into one of three categories. First there were the "unconcerned patrons"— self-described "meat-and-potatoes" types who eat whatever they feel like eating and whose most frequent orders in restaurants include steak or roast beef, fried chicken or fish, premium ice creams, and rich, gooey or chocolate desserts. At the other extreme were the "committed patrons," who believe that diet plays a role in the prevention of illness and whose restaurant food choices reflect that belief; their favorite orders are broiled or baked seafood, poultry without skin, raw-vegetable appetizers, fresh fruit, vegetables seasoned with only herbs or lemon juice, whole-grain muffins, and low-fat frozen yogurt. Between these two groups an almost equally large eating-type emerged: "vacillating patrons." The vacillators are concerned about health and nutrition, but when they eat out they are what the survey calls "taste-and-occasion-driven." Their restaurant choices are all over the map: they're likely to specify lean meats, food cooked without salt, and caffeine-free coffee, but they also favor steak or roast beef, fried chicken or fish, premium ice creams, and, like the unconcerned eaters, "rich, gooey or chocolate desserts." They are also much more likely to eat differently in a restaurant than they do at home.

These groups divided the population almost exactly into thirds, although the committed patrons are on the rise (moving from 35 percent in 1986 to 39 percent in 1989) and the unconcerned eaters are waning (from 38 percent in 1986 to 32 percent in

1989). All of this means that two-thirds of all restaurant-goers—the committed plus the vacillating—make at least some of their food choices based on nutritional concerns. That's why the National Restaurant Association also offers a nutrition guide to restaurateurs to help them modify recipes and menus to meet the demands of their concerned eaters, as well as offering a nutrient-analysis service that uses computer software to calculate the nutritional content of recipes.[1] That's also why when the *Zagat* restaurant-review guides conducted a survey in 1990 of 8,500 of their participants, that asked, What will be the food trends of the nineties?, two suggestions that came up were "The No's—no salt, no fat, no cholesterol, no oil, no butter . . . " and "The Free's—bacteria-free, additive-free, hormone-free, nitrate-free, pesticide-free . . . " (along with other such items as nonfat ice cream, macrobiotic African dishes, seaweed, rice bran, "listing nutritional contents on menus," and "appetizer-dessert meals—no entrées").[2]

These numbers and lists and predictions all point to the same unassailable fact: restaurant eating is undergoing a metamorphosis. Two changes have coincided—people eat out more often, and they are more concerned about what is in the food they eat. The result is a lessening of the distance between chef and customer and an almost unconscious effort to make eating out more like eating at home, where one's meal is not a special occasion and where one has complete control over what goes into the pan. Consider, for instance, this restaurant ordering advice from *Dr. Dean Ornish's Program for Reversing Heart Disease*: "If you eat out frequently, get to know the chef and maitre d' at two or three favorite restaurants. . . . Spend a few minutes with them at an off-peak time and explain the guidelines of your dietary preferences. . . . When you eat at a new restaurant, call ahead if possible and explain your dietary requests to the chef or maitre d'. Is the food made to order or is it a 'we heat 'em, you eat 'em' place? Baking, steaming, boiling, and poaching don't require the addition of oil—can the chef prepare something for you in this way? Will he or she cook something for you without butter and oil? Will they put the sauce on the side? Does the restaurant offer fruit for dessert? Or a fruit sorbet? . . . If you see an interesting item on the menu, ask if the chef could modify it for you. For example, if the restaurant serves mushrooms sautéed in butter, ask if the chef could sauté the mushrooms in wine instead. . . . In almost every fine restaurant, the chef will prepare for you a vegetable plate, fruit plate, or a special salad, even if these are not on the menu. If you order a vegetable plate, ask the chef to steam, boil, bake, or grill the vegetables and specify that he or she not use any oil or butter in preparing them."[3] One chef commented to *Allure* magazine in 1992: "You think, my God, why do these people come to a restaurant?"[4]

Mark Miller, an anthropologist by training who is now owner and chef of three high-profile Southwestern-style restaurants (Red Sage, in Washington, D.C., and two Coyote Cafes, in Santa Fe and Las Vegas), is, like Eric Bromberg and most other chefs, happy to give people what they ask for in the name of service. But he sees in the restaurant-worries of eaters a serious misperception not only of nutrition but of the fundamental meaning of food. "People in America have dietary problems not because of what's done in restaurants," he said recently, "but because they continue to consume junk, and too much animal protein. There really isn't a good understanding of nutrition in the United States. Someone in one of my restaurants will tell me, 'I'm on a diet,' and then sit there lapping up olive oil, which is one hundred percent fat. And then I make them a tamale with one teaspoon of lard, and they say, 'Oh, I can't have that.' But, for instance, one tablespoon of duck fat in a sauce that gets spread out among twenty people, that's inconsequential. These people aren't fat or having health problems because they ate one-twentieth of a tablespoon of duck fat in one dish two weeks ago. And they don't have a respect for what one tablespoon of duck fat can give to a sauce."

That lack of understanding and, especially, respect is, to Miller, a key to American problems with food. "People are not taking food seriously in America," he said. "We need to take ourselves and our culinary history seriously, but instead we're caught up in misconceptions, in convenient eating, and in placing blame on the wrong things. Lard is not the problem. Too many of our food choices are being driven by psychological perceptions of what the food is about, and ideas of status. People feel that olive oil has higher status than lard, so it's okay. But what's happened is that we don't have rituals with food, we don't understand the importance of food, we've lost the connection with farms, the connection of food with the land and the sea. People don't really want to discuss food. We don't have a food culture. It goes back to the Puritan days when people were put in the stocks for having spices in their kitchens. It's turning away from life. Food would make you sensual, it would make you real, it would make you alive." Here is where Miller draws upon his earlier training: he can't help but see his customers from the point of view of a psychological anthropologist.

"Food also feeds the soul," he continued. "But we are isolating ourselves from those 'soft issues' of food. Living longer doesn't make any difference. Anthropologists rank societies based on their aesthetic levels, not on science—not on how long they live and their health programs. Do you fulfill your human potential by living longer, or by being more creative and more experiential? Food is part of the availability of richness in life, richness that adds to enjoyment and pleasure in life. Most cultures have nurtured that sense of the value of experience, but what we're doing is denying that. We've got a scientific way of looking at things, and it's not a qualitative, cultural, experiential way of looking at things. If you feed the body and starve the soul, you still have a dead spirit."

This way of looking at food—coldly, with distance and distrust—becomes self-perpetuating, according to Miller. "Our current situation is not going to lead to furthering the enjoyment and experience of food. And that's a real problem, because the experience and acknowledgment of food brings you more self-awareness, and self-awareness will bring self-control. With self-control you will basically be able to have a correct diet. The moment people stop buying potato chips is when the potato chips will disappear from the supermarket." He gives as an example dietary traditions in Japan, where he has served as a restaurant consultant. The exquisite, marbled Japanese beef that floors Americans by costing fifty to one hundred dollars per pound is enjoyed—every mouthful—in serving sizes of one to three ounces. In fact, the average Japanese serving size in general is three ounces; the average American serving is at least eight. (Miller feels that we should all be "reverting back to the historical diets that were nutritionally and culturally correct." He includes in these the Mediterranean and Asian diets. "The new food pyramid doesn't tell us anything that these societies didn't know and practice. And that didn't happen randomly.")

Miller's prognosis is not promising for the American diet. "We're not developing a food culture that is rational and sensible and that can create a nutritionally balanced diet while also being part of the great enjoyment of life. We're cutting ourselves off from food experience, which is worse for our soul upkeep. For instance, most chefs I know are probably a little overweight. Do they have stressful lives? Yes. But do they enjoy life? Have they had more experiences? If you added all the experiences and enjoyment they've had out of life, they've had seven or eight lifetimes. I think more people should pay more attention to their psychological health than their physical health. But instead we're starving ourselves for real experiences. I feel that there's this whole existential starving going on out there."

In the steamy, sticky belly of a restaurant kitchen, one fact is quickly evident: oils and sauces and salt are the essential glues and flavor-conductors of cooking—especially fast cooking that places a premium on taste. Over a high flame, oil in the pan is almost a necessity, barring a few foods that can cook in their own juices. But there is one thing about oil that nervous restaurant-goers overlook: a well-trained chef can use just enough to coax the most pungent flavors out of a dish without drowning it. Eric Bromberg explained this process on another evening in the Blue Ribbon kitchen, this one in early January, after the holiday rush. "If things are cooked well, and you cook them in oil," he said, "the amount of oil absorbed by the food is very low. Maybe a table-spoon here or there, and in the context of an entire dish and an entire meal, it's not a dangerous thing." His sesame-glazed catfish was a case in point; while it appeared to be sautéeing in a consider-able amount of olive oil, when the fish was cooked he threw most of the oil away. And although he makes a habit of brushing olive oil on meat that he is about to grill, most of it, he pointed out, drips off into the flames. "Now, that doesn't happen with vegeta-bles," Bromberg continued, pointing out the mushrooms and pep-pers, burnished with olive oil, that sat on the grill. "Vegetables just soak up oil like crazy, especially mushrooms, eggplant—like a sponge. Most people don't realize this, but I bet you get *more* oil with grilled vegetables than with a lot of other dishes. They think they're ordering healthy."

Oil and herbed butter and cream, even on the lightest dishes in this enlightened kitchen, are constant presences. The butter fin-ishes the sauce on the shrimps Provençale and the escargots; the oil annoints everything that alights on the grill, soaking the leeks thoroughly before and after cooking; the cream enriches the mashed potatoes, acorn squash, and mussel soup. According to any government study, this is not the way one should eat every night of the week. But once you begin to try to shift the balance that is created by knowledgeable chefs, you run into instant con-tradictions. "Post-holidays, a lot of people have been asking for sauce on the side," said Eric Bromberg, working over the grill. "It's like that's the thing they know to ask for: sauce on the side. Well, it annoys the hell out of us. You know why? Because nor-mally we put about an ounce of sauce on, say, a piece of fish. But when you put it on the side, you have to give them about four ounces, because one ounce looks skimpy sitting in a dish. Well, every time, they eat the whole four ounces! And we go through a lot more sauce." It's a truth universally acknowledged by chefs: Put anything on the side, and customers will eat a lot more of it.

The orders on that January night were subtly different from the ones coming in before Christmas. Many more listed only en-trées, with no appetizers—what the waiters and kitchen staff call "o.p.u." for "order pick up." "What is all this o.p.u. stuff tonight?" someone called out in some irritation; making meals without "aps" throws off the kitchen rhythm somewhat. More customers were also trying their hand at rehabilitating the recipes. One man requested a change in the collard-green brochettes that accompany the grilled swordfish—little packets that look like stuffed grape leaves but are instead collard-green leaves wrapped around a mixture of goat cheese and camembert, grilled on skewers with mushrooms and onions. He wanted the brochettes, but without the camembert. Eric got to work constructing new brochettes from scratch. (Bruce and Eric Bromberg had already noticed an interesting fact about the camembert: when they had recently rewritten the menu to list only the camembert in the brochettes, orders for that dish had fallen off; when they added the mention of goat cheese back in, orders rebounded. Goat cheese, it seemed, had a better image than camembert, perhaps because it is perceived as less rich.)

Another table ordered the pu-pu platter appetizer—an eclectic mixture of international morsels that includes fried chicken wings, potato pancakes, barbecued ribs, pierogies, and grilled shrimp—but wanted to "stay on the light side." Thus, they specified no wings and ribs, "nothing fried," but wanted to keep the potato pancakes and pierogies, both deep-fried. This occasioned a brief conference in the kitchen, complete with a few ironic comments. "Oh, I get it—nothing fried, except the fried stuff," said Bruce. "Maybe I should send it up like this," said Kris, holding up the wooden pu-pu platter decorated with a bed of shredded lettuce and nothing else. After some discussion, they decided on making special grilled skewers with mushrooms and scallops to replace the offending items. Those, of course, as with anything grilled, were coated first with oil. The same customer who had ordered the pu-pu restrictions had as a main course the swordfish with plain couscous, without the collard-green-camembert brochettes. Little patterns in the special ordering were discernible to the chefs. Bruce, for instance, noted that "sauce on the side" was almost always for salads and fish; almost no one made that request for the sauces on the London broil or duck. (The latter orders come, per-haps, from the "unconcerned patrons.") All of the special requests were knit somehow into the controlled chaos that peaked at about 8:45: "Ordering three times!" "Rack of lamb on the board." "I need sesame and scallions—now!" "Vegetables, looking for rice." "Firing tables fourteen and eleven." "Picking up a duck and a Lon-don on the super-fly." "Let's get some of this stuff out of here—are you listening?—we're going with fifteen, thirteen, thirty." "Scallops looking for greens!" "Bruce, I need that London. All the other food is up at the table." "Twenty, twenty-two, and ten, as fast as humanly possible."

Dessert, it seems, calls up its own second-guessing. Just de-ciding to indulge doesn't end the matter: control can still be ex-erted. "Ordering a Chocolate Bruno, but without the ice cream." (The dish, named in honor of a French chef who trained both Eric and Bruce, consists of a little ramekin of something akin to choco-late mousse, surrounded by three scoops of ice cream and a drizzle of chocolate sauce.) This order occasioned another conference: how to make the dish look inviting when it had only the ramekin ma-rooned on a plate? Another order came in: "A very thin piece of cheesecake." Another discussion: What's very thin? Kris cut one and it looked *too* thin; he made another pass at it. The very thin slice of cheesecake lined up in the window next to a huge sundae drenched in chocolate sauce, strawberries, nuts, and whipped cream.

All of these special orders are not simply verbal; they are translated into an arcane code on the written orders, which come down to the kitchen looking like hieroglyphics. Several years ago Eric designed an order-writing system for the waiters to accom-modate the growing numbers of special requests, and he now hands out an instruction sheet several pages long that outlines the rules. Every possible variation is provided for: Two people order the same dish and both want to delete, or "86," the mashed pota-toes but each asks for a different substitution; or, both want lamb, one medium, one medium-rare, one wants a substitution, one wants sauce on the side ("SOS"). A strong distinction is made between "no butter," "no oil," and "no fat." If the customer asks for no butter, the waiter must ask: "Is oil OK?" If so, he writes "no butter." If not, "no fat." Sometimes even this complex code fails to fully enlighten the chefs. "What is this about the artichoke?" Kris asked one of the waiters. "Oh, with balsamic vinegar on the side. Okay."

"It's been my mission to get the waiters to absorb as much information from the customers as possible," Eric explained as he turned brochettes and scallops on the grill and whipped open the oven door to bring out a pan holding a duck breast sizzling in its own fat. "If the customer has requested something special, I'm going to make it the best I can with those restrictions, but I don't feel compromised by that. In fact, a lot of times I come up with new things because of special requests. Five or six years ago someone wanted salmon cooked with absolutely no butter, no oil, anything. All I could think of to do was put it in a nonstick pan without any fat at all, and it cooked perfectly—you get a beautiful crisp skin. It was a neater way to cook it. I started cooking it that way all the time. I grew up with a grandmother who doesn't eat anything and my mother who doesn't cook or eat anything, and friends who were picky about one thing or another, and my brother who wouldn't eat tomatoes—I'm used to it, it seems completely normal. I don't feel, as a chef, that my job is to force anyone to do something they don't want to do. That's not the reason I got into this business; I didn't do it to flex my muscles or prove to anyone how great or cool I am. No matter what kind of cultural era you're in, no matter what the issues are, you have the customer to please and the ingredients to concoct." He began to slice precise, thin pieces of duck, topped with a beautifully browned ridge of fat, and lay them gently on a plate.

The next time I was at the Blue Ribbon, it was to eat. It was a frosty Wednesday night in late January—not prime restaurant time—but we got the last available table for two. The dining room at Blue Ribbon is small, essentially a storefront, and the sense of intimacy is enhanced by the colors: brick walls painted in rose, yellow wall lights, a wooden mirrored bar. There was something of the sense of being at a small cocktail party; undefinable, slightly abstract rock music played just loud enough to raise everyone's voice one level, wine corks popped, candles flickered, the bartender occasionally rattled a glass cocktail shaker and poured mysterious drinks, the scene at the bar shifted as those waiting were seated and others scanned the menu, deciding whether to stay. At the tables people leaned to converse across trays of raw oysters, sampled each other's foie gras and steak tartare appetizers, smoked cigarettes, sipped wine.

I knew my apple-and-leek potato pancake appetizer achieved its delicious light crust in the deep fryer, and on the plate the pancakes were topped with a good-sized dollop of sour cream, but I also knew I had had nothing else from a deep fryer in recent memory. Then my sesame-glazed catfish arrived, lightly browned and glistening on its bed of mashed potatoes. I could picture exactly how it had looked going into the pan—soaked in olive oil, enhanced by a sizable blob of herbed butter toward the end of cooking—and I had seen much of that oil go into the garbage pail after the catfish was lifted out of the pan. The toasted, almost burnt, sesame coating contrasted beautifully with the fresh, light taste of the fish itself. I ate every bite. And I remembered Eric Bromberg describing his personal feelings about food—not just cooking it but living with it. "One of the greatest pleasures I know is eating," he said. "And I don't mean just eating indiscriminately, I mean the flavors and the tastes and the enjoyment that that can bring you. To deprive yourself of that for some future benefit—I can understand the thinking, but I think we've gone too far over the edge of restricting. I'm not saying everybody should just sit down and gorge themselves until they die; I'm not suggesting a solely hedonistic approach to life. But taste is one of your greatest senses, and you should allow yourself to taste, and to appreciate."

Conclusion

•

A NEW (AND OLD)
WAY OF EATING
Rediscovering Pleasure

•

Amid the cacophony of voices and arguments over what and how we should eat, there exists one message in unison: Americans are not eating right. Our many contortions in the face of our food—self-denial, fear, obsessiveness, hope for magical salvation—all spring from attempts to redress that same wrong. But the true cure for our dietary sins may lie in an almost opposite direction to that prescribed by the nutrition cognoscenti: not in claiming more control, but less; not in taking power away from food, but giving it back; not in fear of death, but in love of life. Somewhere in the ancient love of food and its rituals lies rationality and reverence for natural things and a balanced sense of how much is too much—colored by scientific knowledge, but not ruled by it. A price is exacted in this new way of eating. We must give up our hunger for certainty, and for power over what remains the essential mystery of our lives and our deaths. The reward is large: a chance to live in harmony with our food, rather than to struggle against it.

•

Jacques Pépin refuses to suffer about his food. It's a philosophical decision that begins with simple concepts—he enjoys eating and drinking—and ends with much deeper ones. He believes
that enjoyment of food (and the rituals that codify and often in-
tensify that enjoyment) is knit into the very fabric of society, act-
ing as a civilizer, a bond between peoples, a celebration of life
itself. But as someone who makes his living teaching and writing
about cuisine, what he sees around him in his adopted American
culture is a veritable sea of suffering about food. His word for this
is, in the style of someone to whom English is a second language,
a little-used form of a common word: "punition." Pépin sees punition at work in, for example, an American magazine advertise-
ment for running shoes that claims: "I believe calories *do* count on
vacation." "That's completely ridiculous," he exclaims. "It's the
idea of punition and suffering, and it is no good. People have a
guilty complex if by chance they eat anything that tastes good, a
guilty complex that something is going to happen to them. They
are very furtive, like someone who stole something. I don't want
to have any of that feeling. I want to sit down with my family and
enjoy a great meal. Even if I eat too much, I say, 'I know it; I'll eat
a bit less tomorrow.' "

Pépin's rejection of punition does not perforce throw him
into the camp of unbridled hedonism. He has written several
cookbooks on special diets—for cardiac patients and for weight
loss, among them—and knows how to cook and eat with less fat,
sugar, salt. Instead, he chooses his indulgences, opening the door
to dietary extravagance and then gently closing it again. Remi-
niscing about a summer trip to France—a cruise from Bordeaux
around the Iberian peninsula to Barcelona, followed by a lecture
tour with a group from Boston University from Alsace to Bur-
gundy, with stops to see friends in Lyon—he says: "After that
type of marathon of eating I've put on a few pounds. But I'm not
going to have a guilty complex or get terrorized when I'm there,
because it's that type of trip. I know that I will put on a few
pounds. And I know that afterwards I have to cut down and lose
weight a little bit, progressively. So, likewise, you live in a way

whereby on an everyday level you watch a bit more, you're careful. And then when the weekend comes or when your friend is coming to visit, well, then you open a bottle of champagne, you have a lot of wine, you have a lot of food, and you know that it's a lot. But that's fine; you know that that's what life is all about. One day a bit much, and you're not going to die because you splurge one day."

This is not a particularly American way of thinking, although it's a useful way of thinking. It doesn't have the aura of Puritan penitance or the gleam of scientific certainty; it doesn't bring the smug satisfaction of moral one-upmanship. This way of eating is in fact controlled, but not in the way Americans usually think of control—that is, not every calorie is accounted for, and the grams of fat and ounces of alcohol probably sometimes exceed the daily recommendations of nutritionists and public health officials. It is controlled by being sometimes uncontrolled; it finds a balance, over time, by occasionally allowing things to get out of balance. In so doing, it implies a self-confidence—a self-trust—that often feels out of reach to Americans who fear that if they let themselves go they might find themselves, a hundred Big Macs later, completely beyond the pale, lost in a devouring maw of forbidden desires. Such thoughts tend to be self-fulfilling prophecies: by living in fear of what food will do to us and therefore making some of it untouchable, we strip away the natural controls that come with moderation. The piece of chocolate cake that we really "shouldn't" eat might become two or three pieces because we think: I won't ever eat it again, might as well load up this last time.

The truth that lies behind such anxious vigilance and ambivalence is that the fate we are seeking to outmaneuver—death by chocolate, or by steak—remains a stubborn mystery. Not only is it dispiriting to think of living one's life dodging one's death, but there's also no percentage in it. Despite our rapidly accumulating knowledge about food and disease, we are far from knowing what really kills us. Robert Ornstein, a psychologist who has written several books about the nature of consciousness and the chemistry of the brain, illustrates the enduring mystery of disease in his 1988 book *The Healing Brain*: He suggests looking not just at "risk factors" and at who actually gets sick, but at who *doesn't* get sick. That process, he says, reveals the depth of our ignorance. For instance, there are three key risk factors for heart disease: cigarette smoking, high serum cholesterol in the blood, and high blood pressure. People with one factor have 2 times the risk of heart disease; those with two factors have 3.5 times the risk; those with all three factors, a 6 times greater chance of heart disease. But, paradoxically, knowing if someone has these risk factors does little to predict who will actually have a heart attack. Combining the data of the six largest heart disease projects, he found that of 7,300 men in the studies, 600 had high values for all three risk factors. Of the 600, 82 had a heart attack in ten years of follow-up. That means 86 percent did not have a heart attack; of those who had two risk factors, 91 percent had no heart attack. "This is not to suggest," writes Ornstein, "that smoking, elevated cholesterol, or high blood pressure are not important, but only that they do surprisingly little to predict who stays healthy and who becomes ill."[1]

Ornstein's example is not a license to live solely on hamburgers and fried eggs, but it is a reminder that nothing is a guarantee. Here's another way to think about it: even the numbers that come from those most vociferous about our dietary sins claim that about 50 percent of heart disease and stroke and 35 percent of cancers are caused by bad eating habits.[2] One might ask, why did 65 percent *not* get cancer from these foods? Wouldn't it be instructive to know something about how some people resist disease, as well as how others succumb? The emotional truth that lies behind these statistics is that death has an innate randomness, that it steals away some of our control no matter how we plan to fight it. That is clearly not an idea that sits well in 1990s America.

But if the dread of this randomness is one of the wellsprings of our current food paranoia, there is, at the same time, one thing that the paranoids have indisputably gotten right: We do, as a nation, eat badly. And not just badly in terms of high fat and low fiber. We have created a vast infrastructure to support a culinary style that features overeating, eating too quickly, eating too much of processed foods and pseudo-foods and too little of things fresh—all of which leads then to guilt, dieting, fear, and obsessiveness. Consider: McDonald's had sales of $13 billion in the United States in 1992. Fast foods in general account for 35 percent of the sales of food eaten away from home, up from 5 percent in the 1950s. Frozen, dried, and canned goods greatly outnumber fresh food items offered for sale in most grocery stores. Pizza restaurants guarantee lunch served within ten minutes or your money back. Speed, instant gratification, convenience, constant snacking, meat and potatoes usually in the form of burger and fries—these have been considered basic culinary rights in America.

One central, and rather ironic, problem with the food paranoids' answer to this bad eating is that it is often based on some of the very proclivities that have helped lead to an impoverished cuisine: a disregard for pleasure, and even more basically, a disrespect for the power and the symbolism of food. Even when we went about consciously changing something for the better, the underlying disrespect for food remained the same. For example, one of the replacements for the admittedly unhealthy American breakfast of eggs, bacon, sausage, and buttered toast has been Carnation Instant Breakfast drink, an early symbol of techno-foods, whose recent advertising tag line is: "Because life doesn't stop for breakfast." The question that is begged here is, Why not? Maybe it should. Certainly it should stop for dinner.

The Carnation breakfast philosophy is emblematic of another powerful element fueling our food distress and making any essential change difficult: consumer food marketing, the business that found its first audience in the anxious and alienated Victorians. The voraciousness and influence of the marketing machine was pointed up recently when the U.S. Health Service advised all women of childbearing age to take a daily folic acid supplement of .4 milligrams, based on research that showed such doses in the early stages of pregnancy might help prevent neural-tube defects. One consumer watchdog organization worried about the recommendation for this reason: Food manufacturers might be so eager to exploit this latest opening for health claims—"Contains your daily amount of folic acid in one serving!"—that women might inadvertently take in too much folic acid simply by eating fortified breakfast cereal and drinking fortified orange juice.[3] This fear is not farfetched: Marketers have an unlimited appetite for nutritional gimmicks in this age, based on repeated research that shows the public responding happily to most things "lite," "healthy," and "fortified."

The marketing forces realize that consumers straddle two opposing ideas: We know we eat badly, but in our hearts we don't want to change. Guilt and overcompensation follow naturally. At a recent meeting of the Food Marketing Institute (FMI), attended by food manufacturers, marketers, and grocers, the institute unveiled results of its consumer attitude surveys, one of which showed that only 10 percent of those questioned felt their diet was as healthy as it could be; 69 percent felt it could be healthier. Many respondents spoke of a concern about too much fat and cholesterol; 75 percent said nutrition was very important to them when they shop for food. Fat topped the list of nutritional elements they were most worried about (42 percent said it was their greatest concern, up from 8 percent in 1984), followed by cholesterol (37), salt (22), calories (12), and sugar content (12). But those worthy sentiments were at odds with some other realities, presented at the same meeting by an editor from *Prevention* magazine and based on that magazine's Louis Harris surveys. These showed that 64 percent of adults over twenty-five are above the recommended weight range for their age, sex, height, and body build, up from 58 percent in 1983—the same period of time during which Americans' concern about eating dietary fat went up 34 percent. The *Prevention* editor who presented these numbers summed them up this way: "People talk about good nutrition, but they're eating lots of junk."

The same schizophrenia was on display in abundance at the FMI convention, which sprawled over several floors of Chicago's huge McCormick Center. NutraSweet, the monolithic new artificial sweetener company, touted a list of the hundreds of products that are sweetened with NutraSweet, from hot cocoa mix to Fiber

One cereal to laxatives. The Kraft booth unveiled Velveeta Light (one-third less fat and less cholesterol than regular Velveeta) and Light n' Lively Free Nonfat Sour Cream Alternative, "the first fat free product in the sour cream category." General Mills contributed Basic 4, a new breakfast cereal that, with milk, provides "the key nutrients of the four food groups." Eskimo Pie brought out a fat-free version, "which consists of a vanilla nonfat frozen dairy dessert center sandwiched between two fat-free chocolate wafers." A supermarket consultant spoke to grocers about "the defatting of America," suggesting various promotions to draw new customers: "Look to the Label Week," "No-Fat/Low-Fat Fridays," "A No-Fat Festival," "Lean Days," "Low-Fat/High-Flavor Week," or even a "Low-Fat/No-Fat/Fake Fat Week," in which all items that apply are flagged for easier shopping. Or how about an international symbol for no-fat, similar to the no-smoking sign?

But a funny thing was happening on the convention floor. People were clustering, practically shoving, around the Tombstone's frozen pizza stand for free slices; lining up for chocolate bar handouts; popping cheese doodles and potato chips and chocolate-chip cookies. The Weight Watchers Pizza stand, not far from Tombstone's, attracted a few lonely takers. Mini-foods, or what marketers call "fractionables"—tiny Keebler's cookies, mini Oreos, mini Ritz crackers stuffed with peanut butter, pop-up Eggo Minis toaster waffles that break into round, stackable discs ("the bite size waffle with the great big taste!")—were flying out of the booths. A speaker from a consumer survey group whose talk was billed "Food Consumers in the Year 2000" predicted that with grazing taking over as a dominant eating style, snack foods would soon become the number-one grocery category.

Others at the convention spoke about the power of convenience, the necessity of quick meals. "Diversity in the freezer case allows consumers to plan an entire day's menu around frozen foods," proclaimed an article entitled "Shopping with the New American Family" in an issue of *Frozen Food Report* distributed at the convention. "Today's selections include products for breakfast, lunch, dinner, snacktime *and* dessert."[4] Anyone who has tasted the gummy cheeses that don't melt properly, the gelatinous sauces, the overcooked vegetables of even the pricier frozen foods, or who has read the paragraphs of ingredients that go into making a food that can be instantly prepared, knows that it's not hard to do better. But there is an ongoing allure to America's instant gourmet foods—vegetable lasagna, chicken à l'orange, beef oriental stir-fry, turkey scallopini, all in five minutes, all under 350 calories—that aces out the idea of the simplest home-cooked meal.

If we are to truly eat better, and we seem to want to do that despite the evidence of our Tombstone pizza feasts, we must first give up this predilection for utter convenience and scientific certainty when it comes to food. The microwave dinner that guarantees precisely 5 grams of fat may be easy, and may be reassuring in its exactness, but ultimately instead of satisfying it leaves us wanting more—so we snack. These behaviors are more than habits or simply practical choices about how we spend our days; they are stand-ins for our deepest feelings about food. When food is stripped of its dignity, its significance, and its power, it eventually fights back, demanding our attention and tempting our all-or-nothing resolves. We will not be healthier, both psychologically and physically, about our food until we learn to love it more, not less—not in the way a smoker loves his cigarettes or a chronic dieter loves her forbidden treats, but with a relaxed, generous, unashamed emotion. That will be the only way to free ourselves from our sad and fruitless struggle against its power. In the process, it may be that we will have to redefine fundamentally the concept of "eating well." The phrase now, in the hands of the food paranoids, is often used to convey the idea of following a diet scientifically programmed to prevent disease, balanced to the last ounce with beta-carotene and whatever other nutrients the latest studies tout, and almost religiously outlawing certain forbidden foods. Perhaps eating well instead ought to mean eating fresh, well-prepared foods that are varied and satisfying, served in an appealing way, eaten at leisure—a way of eating that, because nothing is completely ruled out, obviates the need for snacking, for "cheating," for obsessing and bingeing. That might also end the driving anxiety about our food—the idea that what we eat is killing us, and that we must do something drastic and painful to repair the damage.

The name for this philosophy might be Enlightened Hedonism: a balance between information and pleasure, an educated hedging of bets. One takes in as much of the volumes of health information that comes flooding toward us as is comfortable, and then weighs the logic and the possibilities. These days we know that a half-pound of butter is probably not only unnecessary but also not good for anyone, and especially for those who have reason—genetic or otherwise—to fear a predisposition to diseases like cancer and heart disease. But a dab of butter to sauté garlic or smooth a sauce—that's moderation (not to mention pleasure). The same sort of moderation dictates that if you don't eat a Burger King Whopper every day, you can without guilt enjoy a tender filet mignon on some festive occasion. It may also make sense to switch to skim milk for most uses, for instance on the morning bowl of cereal, while leaving open the option of the occasional teaspoon of whole milk or even cream in your coffee. Or you can decide that there is enough evidence in support of the anticancer sulforaphanes in broccoli to dictate including it in your diet a few times a week, without having to simultaneously swear that you will never ever again touch a pork chop.

The logic of Enlightened Hedonism might lead in another direction as well: We have made much in the last decade or two of the possible role of stress in promoting various diseases, perhaps through changes in the immune system. Might not effective relaxation, active enjoyment, pleasure, be a proactive factor in good health? Some researchers, pondering what has been called the "French Paradox"—the fact that the French eat a diet rich in cheese, foie gras, and other high-fat delicacies and yet have a lower rate of heart attack than Americans—have suggested that the answers to that discrepancy might be found in things like more relaxed meals and consumption of wines.[5]

This change—from the awkward combination of guilty gluttony and stringent self-denial to something like Enlightened Hedonism—is a big order, and perhaps unfeasible in a country whose culinary traditions have long been based on powerfully ambivalent emotions. If we are to attempt change, we may need to look beyond the conflicts of our own national way of eating to consider the ways some other countries think about their food, gathering instruction as much about an emotional approach to food as about what is put on the plate. The late Angelo Pellegrini, who emigrated from Italy as a child in the early part of this century and later wrote lovingly of the culinary traditions he grew up with, exclaimed in his 1948 memoir *The Unprejudiced Palate*, "Nothing is so effective in keeping one young and full of lust as a discriminating palate thoroughly satisfied at least once a day." He describes in his Italian upbringing a life in which food, whether the simplest broth with escarole and country bread or an elaborate rabbit stew with polenta, is celebrated on a daily basis—though not to the point of overkill. "The basic principle in the achievement of good living is a sane, wholesome attitude toward food and drink," Pellegrini wrote. "An accomplished cuisine is only one of the ingredients in the good life. It is perhaps the basic ingredient; but to look upon it as either more or less than that is to pervert its meaning. Man should enjoy his meals as much as he enjoys his work, his friends, his favorite recreation. And he *will* enjoy them once he discovers how pleasant the business of nourishing oneself can be. . . . One who approaches the dinner table glowing with the anticipation of good food—and ready to raise hell if it isn't—usually exhibits the same zest for other phases of life also."[6]

With the typical Italian philosophy toward food and living in mind, it's revealing to compare actual per capita consumption of various foods in Italy to consumption patterns in the United States. The Italian diet, for all of its unconsciousness of nutrition and its emphasis on pleasure, is in many ways a big step toward the diet most nutritionists would have us all follow: Italians eat more complex carbohydrates than we do (three times more pasta and bread), three times as much fresh fruit, one-third less beef, and almost twice as much fish. Although "apple pie" is a metaphor for old-fashioned American food and apples are produced in several parts of the country, the average American consumes a little more than 18 pounds of apples a year while the average Italian consumes 56 pounds annually. (It's not all quite as clear-cut, of course: they drink nine times as much wine, eat one-third more cheese, and an equal amount of butter.) According to figures compiled by the American Heart Association, death rates from cardiovascular disease in Italy remain substantially lower than those in the United States.

Once we decide to give food, its preparation and enjoyment, some time and what might even occasionally be called reverence, we may find that good food and good-for-you food is more likely to come from deep in the past—from ancient cultures and traditions that, much like those related by Angelo Pellegrini, found their inspiration close to the land—than from the future, in the form of plasticized fat-free cheeses and vegetable gums that glue together foods from which all natural moisture has been sucked out. (Even as recently as seventy-five years ago, the American diet derived 32 percent of its calories from fat, very close to the 30 percent now suggested by public health organizations.[7]) "The produce of the earth to me is sacred," wrote Pellegrini, "sacred in a sense completely outside a theological frame of reference. . . . Everything that man needs for the nourishment of his body and the elevation of his soul is as sacred as himself and should be so regarded."[8] In our concentration on shoring up the potential weaknesses of the body, we in this country have come far from the idea of food nourishing the soul. With the loss of that, we have lost also a sense of unashamed pleasure in that nourishing. Here is Pellegrini describing his everyday thoughts about his food: "I know that my butcher, who serves me so well, will have my favorite cut of meat when I shall call at his shop at the end of the day's work. What will it be? A roast? A steak? Sweetbreads? Lamb kidneys? Whatever the choice, it will be prepared with care and served with the appropriate vegetable from the garden. Before dinner there will be the customary descent down the cellar stairs . . . I will see there a sight familiar enough: shelves stocked with last year's produce from the garden; mushrooms from the meadows and the hills; sea food from the waters of Puget Sound; bottles of red and white wine of various ages; and the cradled oak barrels in which last year's vintage is 'breathing through the wood.' A sight familiar enough! But always evocative, pleasantly reassuring, and mildly exciting."[9]

To regain the species of delight that Pellegrini describes so eloquently, however, there is something we must surrender: that false sense of control that serves to compensate for our loss of pleasure. Statistics being what they are, it is up to the individual to plot exactly how much faith he or she will put in them, and eat accordingly. But a life lived by the numbers seeks to evade the most central of truths: Even the most religious of dieters cannot dictate the exact moment or nature of one's death. Perhaps the most disturbing, and disheartening, aspect of the current food paranoia is that it seems driven far more by a fear of death than by a love of life. It is possible to become so engaged in the business of fleeing illness and decay that one forgets how to truly and fully live—or forgets that one point of living is to enjoy.

Angelo Pellegrini, incidentally, lived to the age of eighty-eight and died in his bed, one week after observing the crush of the year's wine grapes for his cellar.

NOTES

Introduction
A PINCH OF ANXIETY, A DASH OF SIN

1. Hillel Schwartz, *Never Satisfied: A Cultural History of Diets, Fantasies, and Fat* (New York: Anchor/Doubleday, 1986), 25.

2. James C. Whorton, *Crusaders for Fitness: The History of American Health Reformers* (Princeton, NJ: Princeton University Press, 1984), 201–5.

3. Ibid.

4. Harvey Green, *The Light of the Home: An Intimate View of the Lives of Women in Victorian America* (New York: Pantheon, 1983), 135.

5. Schwartz, *Never Satisfied*, 186.

6. John Harvey Kellogg, *Rules for "Right Living"* (Battle Creek, Michigan: Health Extension Department, Battle Creek Sanitarium, 1935).

7. Harvey A. Levenstein, *Revolution at the Table: The Transformation of the American Diet* (New York: Oxford University Press, 1988), 33–34; Schwartz, *Never Satisfied*, 184.

8. Charles W. Purdy, "Popular Errors in Living and Their Influence Over the Public Health," *North American Review*, June 1897, 664.

9. Anastasia Toufexis, "Battle of the Food Blurbs," *Time*, 11 Sept. 1989, 66; Densie Webb, Eating Well, "A Study of the Effects of Beta Carotene," *New York Times*, 28 Nov. 1990, sec. C; Eben Shapiro, "Wary Public Gets a New Bran (Rice)," *New York Times*, 29 Mar. 1991, sec. D; Marian Burros, Eating Well, "Myth and Science Converge on the Virtues

of Garlic, and Business Takes an Interest," *New York Times*, 15 May 1991, sec. C.

10. Laura Shapiro with Fiona Gleizes, "Eat, Drink and Be Wary," *Newsweek*, 2 Mar. 1992, 68–9; "CBS and Your Health," *New York Times*, 29 Jan., 1992, sec. C.

11. "Just the Facts," *Nutrition Action Healthletter*, July/August 1992, 2.

12. Interview with Lynn Dornblaser, publisher, *Gorman's New Product News*, 18 June 1993.

13. Mary Roach, "Let It Be Light," *Vogue*, Oct. 1991, 369.

14. Marian Burros, Eating Well, "The Dream of Low-Fat Baking," *New York Times*, 20 May 1992, sec. C.

15. Burros, Eating Well, "Weaning Americans from the Meat Habit," *New York Times*, 24 Apr. 1991, sec. C; "Fat's in the Fire: A Guide for the Wary," *New York Times*, 27 Mar. 1991, sec. C; "You May Not Realize How Much Fat You Really Eat," *New York Times*, 8 Apr. 1992, sec. C.

16. Jane Brody, *Jane Brody's Nutrition Book* (New York: Norton, 1981), 6.

17. Roach, "Let It Be Light," 327.

18. Anastasia Toufexis, "The Latest Word on What to Eat," *Time*, 13 Mar. 1989, 51.

19. Densie Webb, Eating Well, "Are Official Diet Guidelines the Best?" *New York Times*, 4 Dec. 1991, sec. C.

20. Molly O'Neill, "New Rules on Labeling May Change Foods, Too," *New York Times*, 13 Nov. 1991, sec. C.

21. O'Neill, "The New Nutrition: Protein on the Side," *New York Times*, 28 Nov. 1990, sec. C.

22. Marian Burros, Eating Well, "Of French Fries, Ice Cream, and the Will to Change," *New York Times*, 29 Apr. 1992, sec. C.

23. Shapiro, "The Skinny on No-Fat Sweets," *Newsweek*, 30 Nov. 1992, 92.

24. Burros, "Dream of Low-Fat Baking," sec. C.

25. Janet Polivy and C. Peter Herman, "Dieting and Bingeing," *American Psychologist* 40: 193–210.

26. Samuel Eliot Morison, *The Puritan Pronaos: Studies in the Intellectual Life of New England in the Seventeenth Century* (New York: New York University Press, 1936), 7, 9–10.

27. Roberta Pollack Seid, *Never Too Thin: Why Women Are at War with Their Bodies* (New York: Prentice-Hall, 1989), 69–70.

28. Hillel Schwartz, "Fin-de-Siècle Fantasies," *New Republic*, 30 July and 6 Aug. 1990, 22.

Chapter One
SEEDS OF SELF-DENIAL

1. Levenstein, *Revolution at the Table*, 46.
2. Wilbur Olin Atwater, *U.S. Dept. of Agriculture Farmer's Bulletin No. 142: Principles of Nutrition and Nutritive Value of Food* (Washington, DC: Government Printing Office, 1902), 13.
3. Atwater, "What the Coming Man Will Eat," *Forum*, June 1892, 488–96.
4. Oliver Alabaster, Letters to the Editor, "New Diet Guide to Improve Shape You're In," *New York Times*, 26 May 1991, sec. 4.
5. Atwater, *Food and Diet* (Washington, DC: Government Printing Office, 1895), 368, 381.
6. Ibid., 360.
7. Molly O'Neill, "The 90's Woman: How Fat Is Fat?" *New York Times*, 2 Jan. 1991, sec. C.
8. Schwartz, *Never Satisfied*, 87.
9. Ibid., 25, 31.
10. Whorton, *Crusaders for Fitness*, 8–9.
11. Atwater, *Food and Diet*, 357.
12. Atwater, "What We Should Eat," *Century*, June 1888, 261.
13. Roach, "Let It Be Light," 369.
14. Ellen H. Richards, *Food Materials and Their Adulterations* (Boston: Home Science Publishing Co., 1st ed. 1885, rev. 1898), 7.
15. Susan Williams, *Savory Suppers and Fashionable Feasts: Dining in Victorian America* (New York: Pantheon, 1985), 94.
16. Richards, *Food Materials*, 13–15.
17. Laura Shapiro, *Perfection Salad: Women and Cooking at the Turn of the Century* (New York: Farrar, Straus & Giroux, 1986), 76–79.
18. M. A. Boland, "Scientific Cooking: A Plea for Education in Household Affairs," *Popular Science Monthly*, Sept. 1893, 653.
19. Molly O'Neill, "Riddle for Healthful Cooks: How to Leave Out the Fat?" *New York Times*, 9 Oct. 1991, sec. C.
20. Marian Burros, Eating Well, "Enough of This Third World Diet," *New York Times*, 1 May 1991, sec. C.
21. Pierre Franey, "60 Minute Gourmet," *New York Times*, 9 Dec. 1992, sec. C.
22. Schwartz, *Never Satisfied*, 44.
23. Levenstein, *Revolution at the Table*, 86–87.
24. Pan [pseud.], *Dinnerology: Our Experiments in Diet from Crankery to Common Sense* (Chicago: Belford, Clark & Co., 1889),

21–22, 72.

25. M. L. Holbrook, *Eating for Strength; or, Food and Diet in Their Relation to Health and Work* (New York: Fowler & Wells Co., 1888), Preface.

26. Laura Shapiro, "Feeding Frenzy," *Newsweek*, 27 May 1991, 46–53.

27. John Mariani, "Stuff Yourself and Be Happy," *New York Times*, 27 Nov. 1991, sec. A.

28. Burros, "Weaning Americans from the Meat Habit."

29. Alabaster, "New Diet Guide."

30. Densie Webb, Eating Well: "Two Cheers for Fiber—It's Healthy, and You Need a Lot," *New York Times*, 11 Dec. 1991, sec. C.

31. *Nutrition Action Healthletter* Direct Mail Package, Center for Science in the Public Interest (Washington, DC), n.d.

32. Richards, *Food Materials*, 18.

33. Ronald Gottesman, Introduction, *The Jungle* (New York: Viking Penguin, 1985), xxii–iv.

34. Boland, "Scientific Cooking," 654–55.

35. Levenstein, *Revolution at the Table*, 36–37; Williams, *Savory Suppers*, 46.

36. Levenstein, 33–37.

37. Susan Strasser, *Satisfaction Guaranteed: The Making of the American Mass Market* (New York: McGraw-Hill, 1989), 30–2; Williams, *Savory Suppers*, 102–3.

38. Levenstein, *Revolution at the Table*, 35–36.

39. Ibid., 42–43.

40. T. J. Jackson Lears, "From Salvation to Self-Realization: Advertising and the Therapeutic Roots of the Consumer Culture, 1880–1930," in *The Culture of Consumption*, ed. Richard Wrightman Fox and T. J. Jackson Lears (New York: Pantheon, 1983), 4–23.

41. Richards, *Food Materials*, 162–63.

42. Atwater, "What We Should Eat," 262.

43. Atwater, "What the Coming Man Will Eat," 496.

44. Ibid., 498.

45. Purdy, "Popular Errors in Living," 671–72.

46. Levenstein, *Revolution at the Table*, 87–95.

47. Schwartz, *Never Satisfied*, 88.

48. Ibid., 81.

49. Christine Gorman, "The Fight Over Food Labels," *Time*, 15 July 1991, 54.

50. Webb, "Two Cheers for Fiber."

51. "Protein: Exploding the Myths," *Guide to Healthy Eating*, Sept./Oct. 1990, 2.

52. O'Neill, "New Nutrition."

53. Neal D. Barnard, "Foods and Immunity," *Guide to Healthy Eating*, July/Aug. 1991, 3.

54. Gina Kolata, "Report Urges Low-Fat Diet for Everyone," *New York Times*, 28 Feb. 1990, sec. A.

55. Jeffrey Steingarten, "High Satiety," *Vogue* (Oct. 1991), 325.

56. O'Neill, "The 90's Woman."

57. Trish Hall, "Broccoli, Hated by a President, Is Capturing Popular Votes," *New York Times*, 25 Mar. 1992, sec. C.

58. Zachary Schiller, "The Great American Health Pitch," *Business Week*, 9 Oct. 1989, 115.

59. Holbrook, *Eating for Strength*, 134–35.

60. Boland, "Scientific Cooking," 658–59.

61. Levenstein, *Revolution at the Table*, 12.

62. Schiller, "Great American Health Pitch," 116.

63. "Did You Know That . . . ," *Tufts University Diet & Nutrition Letter*, Nov. 1992, 7.

64. Bryan Miller, "The Fifth Deadly Sin," *New York Times*, 12 July 1992, sec. 9.

65. Anthony Ramirez, "Fast Food Lightens Up but Sales Are Often Thin," *New York Times*, 19 Mar. 1991, sec. D.

66. Burros, "Of French Fries, Ice Cream."

67. Ramirez, "Fast Food Lightens Up."

68. Barry Feig, "In Marketing, Logic Ain't Logical," *Food & Beverage Marketing*, May 1991, 24.

69. "Just the Facts," *Nutrition Action Healthletter*, Apr. 1992, 2.

Chapter Two
FOODS FROM THE LAB

1. Alix M. Freedman and Richard Gibson, "Maker of Simplesse Discovers Its Fake Fat Elicits Thin Demand," *Wall Street Journal*, 31 Jul. 1991, sec. A; "F.D.A. Backs New Version of Simplesse," *New York Times*, 14 Aug. 1991, sec. D; Alix M. Freedman, "New Fake Fat to Be Marketed by NutraSweet," *Wall Street Journal*, 14 Aug. 1991, sec. B; Eben Shapiro, "The Long, Hard Quest for Foods That Fool the Palate," *New York Times*, 29 Sept. 1991, sec. 3.

2. Alecia Swasy, "Substitute for Fat Isn't Gaining Fast," *Wall Street Journal*, 5 Feb. 1990, sec. B; Shapiro, "Long, Hard Quest for Foods."

3. Freedman and Gibson, "Maker of Simplesse Discovers . . . Thin Demand."

Chapter Three
INSIDE THE HYPE MACHINE

1. Julie Liesse, "Oat Bran Popularity Hitting the Skids," *Advertising Age,* 21 May 1990, 3.
2. Annetta Miller, "Oat-Bran Heartburn," *Newsweek,* 29 Jan. 1990, 50.
3. David Stipp, "Negative Oat Bran Study May Crimp Marketing Efforts," *Wall Street Journal,* 18 Jan. 1990, sec. B.
4. Kathleen M. Berry, "The Snap Has Turned to Slog," *New York Times,* 18 Nov. 1990, sec. 3.
5. Jerry E. Bishop, "Quaker Gets Boost for Oat-Bran Lines as Study Shows Declines in Cholesterol," *Wall Street Journal,* 19 Apr. 1991, sec. B.
6. Miller, "Oat-Bran Heartburn," 51.

Chapter Four
EATING YOUR MEDICINE

1. Elizabeth Whelan et al., *Panic in the Pantry: Fads and Fallacies About the Food You Buy* (New York: Atheneum, 1975), 30.
2. Jean Carper, *The Food Pharmacy: Dramatic New Evidence That Food Is Your Best Medicine* (New York: Bantam, 1989), 198–99.
3. Ibid., 190–1, 207, 211, 310, 314.
4. William Kinnear, "How to Prolong Life," *North American Review,* Aug. 1896, 251.
5. James E. Tillotson, "The Controversy over Health Claims on Labels: Where Will It All End?" *Food Technology,* Dec. 1988, 106.
6. Alan S. Levy and Raymond C. Stokes, "Effects of a Health Promotion Advertising Campaign on Sales of Ready-to-Eat Cereals," *Public Health Reports,* July/Aug. 1987, 398–403.

Chapter Six
FEAR OF FATS

1. Kolata, "Report Urges Low-Fat Diet."
2. *Trends: Consumer Attitudes and the Supermarket 1991* (Washington, DC: Research Department, Food Marketing Institute, 1991), 52.
3. Densie Webb, Eating Well, "Gourmets and Nutritionists Join in a

Drive Against Fats," *New York Times*, 14 Nov. 1990, sec. C.

4. Shapiro, "The Skinny on No-Fat Sweets," 92.

5. O'Neill, "Riddle for Healthful Cooks."

6. Molly O'Neill, "Leaner Hamburger Undergoes Trial by Taste," *New York Times*, 21 Apr. 1991, sec. A.

7. Letters, "What If Americans Ate Less Fat?" *Journal of the American Medical Association*, 15 Jan. 1992, 361–64.

8. Kenneth K. Carroll, Martin Lipkin, and John H. Weisburger, "Diet's Key Role in Preventing Cancer," *Patient Care*, 15 May 1989, 54.

9. Dean Ornish, *Dr. Dean Ornish's Program for Reversing Heart Disease Without Drugs or Surgery* (New York: Random House, 1990), 18–25.

10. Ibid., 11–31.

11. Roberto Suro, "Hearts and Minds," *New York Times Magazine*, 29 Dec. 1991, 19; Clancy, "The Ten Percent Solution," 62.

12. Marilyn Elias, "Kids' Low-fat Diets May Hurt Nutrition," *USA Today*, 5 Feb. 1992, sec. A.

13. Gina Kolata, "Cholesterol's New Image: High Is Bad; So Is Low," *New York Times*, 11 Aug. 1992, sec. C.

14. Christopher J. Georges, "Studies Find a Link Between Aggressiveness and Cholesterol Levels," *New York Times*, 11 Sept. 1990, sec. C.

Chapter Seven
FOOD CONTROL

1. *American Psychiatric Association: Diagnostic and Statistical Manual of Mental Disorders, Third Edition, Revised* (Washington, DC: American Psychiatric Association, 1987), 65–69.

2. From an interview with Jean Rubel, president of Anorexia Nervosa and Related Eating Disorders, Eugene, Oregon, 14 Jan. 1991.

3. Ibid.

4. Janet Polivy and C. Peter Herman, "Diagnosis and Treatment of Normal Eating," *Journal of Consulting and Clinical Psychology*, 1987, no. 5:1.

5. "What to Do About a Child's Finicky Eating . . . Nothing," *Tufts University Diet & Nutrition Letter*, Apr. 1991, 2.

6. Elizabeth Gleick, "The Fat Mind," *New York Woman*, Apr. 1990, 76–79.

7. Joan Jacobs Brumberg, *Fasting Girls: The History of Anorexia Nervosa* (New York: Plume, 1989), 41–42.

8. Ibid., 136.

9. Ibid., 178.

10. Laura Shapiro, *Perfection Salad*, 101.

11. Brumberg, *Fasting Girls*, 182.

12. Ibid., 7.

Chapter Eight
PUBLIC EATING

1. "Consumer Commitment to Nutrition Increases," *Restaurants USA*, Mar. 1990, 36–38.

2. *Zagat Survey*, Dec. 1990, 4.

3. Dean Ornish, *Program for Reversing Heart Disease*, 297–98.

4. Regina Schrambling, "Chefs Bite Back," *Allure*, Dec. 1992, 56.

Conclusion
A NEW (AND OLD) WAY OF EATING

1. Robert Ornstein and David Sobel, *The Healing Brain: Breakthrough Medical Discoveries About How the Brain Keeps Us Healthy* (New York: Simon & Schuster, 1987), 31.

2. Alabaster, "New Diet Guide."

3. "Folic Acid for Fighting Birth Defects?" *Tufts University Diet & Nutrition Letter*, Nov. 1992, 1–2.

4. "Shopping with the New American Family," *Frozen Food Report*, May/June 1991, 11.

5. Marian Burros, Eating Well, "In France, Wine and Pâté Days Seem Numbered," *New York Times*, 4 Mar. 1992, sec. C; Shapiro, "Eat, Drink and Be Wary," 68–69.

6. Angelo Pellegrini, *The Unprejudiced Palate* (New York: Lyons & Burford), 1984, 14.

7. L. Brewster and M. Jacobson, *The Changing American Diet* (Washington, DC: Center for Science in the Public Interest, 1978).

8. Pellegrini, *The Unprejudiced Palate*, 43.

9. Ibid., 234–35.

ACKNOWLEDGMENTS

I owe thanks to the many people who generously shared their time, ideas, and knowledge—and in some cases let me watch over their shoulders: Norm Singer, Steven Ink, Stephen DeFelice, Paul and Barbara Stitt, Neal Barnard, and Eric Bromberg, and the whole staff at Blue Ribbon. I am also indebted to the work of certain scholars and researchers for their valuable historical insights: Hillel Schwartz, Harvey A. Levenstein, James C. Whorton, Harvey Green, Roberta Pollack Seid, Susan Strasser, and Joan Jacobs Brumberg.

I owe a debt as well to Robert Gottlieb, who provided guidance on and later published in *The New Yorker* the article on low-cholesterol eggs that first put me on the trail of American eating, and to Amy Levin Cooper, who published my piece on subclinical eating disorders in *Mademoiselle* and in so many ways has encouraged and supported my writing.

For listening, advising, and offering continuous insight over a series of sumptuous meals, thanks to Kathy Rich, Kathy Samon, and Cathy Cavender.

I am grateful also to Gail Winston, for having faith in my ideas from day one, and to Dominick Anfuso, for guiding my book through the final stages. Special thanks go to my agent, Elizabeth Kaplan, for her unending support and invaluable advice at every turning point.

To my parents, for their inexhaustible enthusiasm for my writing, and to my daughter, for setting before me daily an example of the most unfettered love of food, I feel a particularly personal gratitude. And finally, this book would not have been possible without the endless consultation and advice of my in-house editor: my husband, Dave.

INDEX

"Today," 88, 98, 99
"Today's Gourmet," 9
Toronto, University of, 140, 179
Tufts University, 108, 144–45
"20/20," 126

Unprejudiced Palate, The
  (Pellegrini), 215

vaccines, 116
vegetable oils, 78, 138, 152, 154,
  156
vegetarianism, 13, 14, 31, 36–38,
  106, 154, 156–58, 164,
  167–170, 191
Vegetarian Times, 126
Victorian society, 36, 42, 47, 55, 59,
  183, 187, 210
Vietnam War, 110
vitamins, 23
  A, 108, 109, 128
  B, 35, 139, 149, 168
  C, 35, 109, 128, 143
  E, 145
  supplementary, 54, 145

Vogue, 17, 32

Wall Street Journal, 88, 98, 127,
  135
Walter Reed Army Institute of
  Research, 110
Washington Post, 88
"Weaning Americans from the
  Meat Habit," 40
Weintraub, Linda, 53
Weisburger, John H., 161, 162, 167
Western Health Reform Institute,
  13
"What We Should Eat" (Atwater),
  31–32
Willard, Walter, 161
Windsor, Duchess of, 183
wine, 16, 51, 208, 216, 217
Wisconsin Natural Foods
  Association Conference, 135
World War II, 115

yogurt, 103, 115, 161, 163

Zagat survey, 197

About the Author

Michelle Stacey has written for *The New Yorker* and other national magazines. She was formerly managing editor of *Mademoiselle*, and an editor for *Savvy* and *Outside* magazines. She lives in Larchmont, New York, with her husband, daughter, and son.